# Awakening a Living World on a *Kūṭiyāṭṭam* Stage

SUNY series in Hindu Studies

---

Wendy Doniger, editor

# Awakening a Living World on a *Kūṭiyāṭṭam* Stage

EINAT BAR-ON COHEN

Cover Credit: Brothers Madhu and Sajeev Chakyar as Rāma and Lakṣmaṇa, in the *Agnipraveśāṅkam*, when the sky opens and they see their father. Photograph by the author.

Published by State University of New York Press, Albany



For information, contact State University of New York Press, Albany, NY
www.sunypress.edu

**Library of Congress Cataloging-in-Publication Data**

Name: Bar-On Cohen, Einat, author.
Title: Awakening a living world on a *Kūṭiyāṭṭam* stage / Einat Bar-On Cohen.
Description: Albany : State University of New York Press, [2024] | Series: SUNY series in Hindu Studies | Includes bibliographical references and index.
Identifiers: ISBN 9781438496924 (hardcover : alk. paper) | ISBN 9781438496931 (ebook)
Further information is available at the Library of Congress.

10 9 8 7 6 5 4 3 2 1

*To Erela and Morale Bar On*

*To Ella and Michael Cohen*

# Contents

# Illustrations

# Acknowledgments

I dedicate this book to my parents and to my grandchildren, who fashion time to render it malleable, flexible, multidirectional, and confusing.

This book was written over ten years, during which much has changed in my life. One constant has been Don Handelman, who has offered unwavering encouragement in my work. He is for me fresh water. His anthropology is a magic potion drawing from the well of anthropological scholarship, mingled with freedom of imagination, anchored in life as it emerges. Since my training is in anthropology and not Indian studies, I depended heavily on the kindness of others. In particular, I received a hefty amount of thoughtful help from David Shulman, whose curiosity about everything human, and about everything Indian, is pure inspiration.

Warm thanks to Wendy Doniger for her kind support. I also thank the readers of the manuscript for their insightful remarks.

And, of course, there's my Nepathya family: Madhu, Indu G., Rahul, Yadukrishna, Sreeharri, Anjana, Arathy, and Vishnu; the drummers Janish, Mani, Rajan, and Ashwin; as well as numerous friends from Moozhikkulam who shared their patience, hospitality and friendship. Thank you to all. And special thanks to Aparna Nangiar, who shared with me her knowledge and experience with grace and kindness.

# Introduction

Moozhikkulam[1]—a village in central Kerala—is a cultural center that comprises a *Kūttambalam,* which is *a Kūṭiyāṭṭam* theater house, and a school of *Kūṭiyāṭṭam* named Nepathya. At twilight, when the bats leave the big trees near the river to forage for fruit; the day's garbage is burned in front of the houses, filling the air with smells of decay and smoke; the shops at the crossroads are closing; while the neighbors, who have returned from the day's work, are now relaxing on their porches; and the evening worship at the great Lakṣmaṇa temple is on its way—at this time the lamps are lighted at the *Kūttambalam,* and a single drum beating can be heard.

*Kūṭiyāṭṭam,* the sole surviving Sanskrit theater form in India, is a sophisticated stage art that thrived in Kerala for many centuries, carried through the generations by particular temple-assistant families. So, too, it is performed until today at family events or as temple ritual and sacrifice when a patron pays for its performance to help fulfill a request. Since the middle of the twentieth century, it is also widely performed outside the temple and has seen some innovations without losing its intricacy. Over the centuries, *Kūṭiyāṭṭam* developed unique ways of performing acts taken from medieval Sanskrit dramas designed to entice the gods and other protagonists of the play to the *Kūttambalam,* and there, on-stage, to awaken a living world. *Kutiyattam*'s exceptional complexity, its delicate process of becoming, and its transformative capacity are the focus of this book.

Behind the stage, in the "green room," or *Nepathya*—the special room where the actors and actresses get ready—preparations start a few hours before the performance. A lamp is lit, and the actors tie a red band across their foreheads. Students of *Kutiyattam* are busy rolling many cotton balls, mixing rice paste to stick on the actor's legs, and preparing the costumes; the makeup artist cuts out pieces of white glossy paper for the beards, and then paint intricate masks on the actors' faces, gluing beards on those who play heroes, and cotton balls on those who are to be monkeys; the drummers check the brass *miḻāvu* drums, and two drummers carry each of these heavy drums to the stage, securing them on their stands. Finally, the lamps are filled with oil, and the chairs and mats for the audience are spread out in front of the stage. After two lamps—one at the entrance to the *Kūttambalam* and the other on stage—are lighted with a flame from the lamp in the "green room," a bare-chested young drummer mounts the drum stand and starts beating his enthralling rhythm, letting everyone know that the day's *Kūṭiyāṭṭam* performance is about to begin—and that all are welcome.

Then the gods are summoned via offerings, chanting, and dance (*kriyā*). The universe is now ready, nothing is inert, everything is sentient and active within the *Kūttambalam*. As the performance unfolds, going deeper into the night, deeper into the drama, changes occur that are inseparably cognitive, somatic, emotional, totalizing, irresistible, embodied, and personalized. Space is captured by movement as the human body and its senses are drowned in overwhelming stimuli that enable all at the *Kūttambalam* to enter the cosmos created on stage. Breaching the borders between humans and gods, between the sentient and the inert, between the stage and the audience, and also between the singular parts of the human body, so that seeing and hearing become muddled and we can see the drumbeat and listen to the mudrā words with our eyes. Movement and sound are continuously tying knots between personae and worlds, interconnecting in elaborate ways parts of a new and inescapable reality, one that is ready for a transformation. Through manifold repetitions of sound, sight, smell, and movement, hidden powers are awakened, activated by newly formed somatic, emotional, and cognitive combinations, which permit an entire new existence to appear.

As temple worship, *Kūṭiyāṭṭam* has been performed by members of two matrilineal temple assistant castes, and although today *Kūṭiyāṭṭam* performance outside the temple grounds includes trained actors and drummers from other castes, the performance is replete with elements of ritual such as invocations of the gods and offerings to them. Delivering the text in *Kūṭiyāṭṭam* is done mainly through elaborate mudrā gestures that include the grammatical parts of the sentence; the actors also communicate the text by moving their eyes in every direction and shaking their eyebrows and cheeks—their entire body is engaged in relating the story. Each of the drama's phrases is repeated many times in different forms: chanting, telling with mudrā gestures, playing out, or even "reciting" with the eyes alone. Because of these elaborations and repetitions, a few hours of each of many nights are necessary to complete a single act of a play.

Most of the classic Sanskrit dramas presented on the *Kūṭiyāṭṭam* stage tell stories taken from the great Indian epics. The protagonists often change roles to become other entities, gods, goddesses, demons, demonesses, men, women, animals, and even objects such as hair or feather, with no props or change of costume. This *kūttu* or play tradition comprises three forms: the *Naṅṅyārkūttu*—a single actress enacting the story of Kṛṣṇa; the *Cākyārkūttu*, in which a single actor orally recounts the stories of the *Rāmāyaṇa* in Malayalam; and *Kūṭiyāṭṭam*, in which both actors and actresses perform together in costume.

The actors do not simply imitate everyday behavior, since no one would ordinarily talk in mudrā gestures[2] or express emotion by shaking the cheeks; rather, mundane behavior on the *Kūṭiyāṭṭam* stage is purposely and systematically altered so that another mode of life may emerge. The actors do not stand in for the protagonists of the play, nor do they perform representation, "as if" they were those gods or demons; instead, they temporarily, albeit incompletely, become those protagonists. The stories unfolding on stage do not symbolize what occurred elsewhere in the playwright's imagination, or at some mythical time; rather, the dramas are vehicles that mix mundane life with the reality coming into being on stage.

This is why, although clearly a stage performance, *Kūṭiyāṭṭam* is not theater as we usually think of it. It sets into motion an actual alternative world that all at the *Kūttambalam*—including the audience—live in for the duration of the performance. The amalgamated reality generated in the *Kūttambalam*—mixing the mundane with the reality of the play—engages everyone, both when they are inside the *Kūttambalam* and when they are elsewhere. The drumbeat is overwhelming, seeping into one's living outside the *Kūttambalam* during waking hours and sleep alike. Thoughts, dreams, sensations, modes of consciousness, and somaticity are somewhat changed to usher all into a world made differently.

*Kūṭiyāṭṭam* is a specific way-of-doing, it is a practice, and its solutions to creating an alternative reality and to generating meaning are not abstract but practical ones. Analyzing it thus begins with practice itself: by noting the exact ways in which *Kūṭiyāṭṭam* is organized and performed in the small space of the stage, within the larger space of the *Kūttambalam*, in the village of Moozhikkulam, and in the world at large.

The bibliography concerning *Kūṭiyāṭṭam* is rich and varied. Some authors describe *Kūṭiyāṭṭam* in detail (Paniker 1992; Venu 2002; Gopalakrishnan 2011; Madhavan 2012; Oberlin and Shulman 2019; Narayanan 2022). Others concentrate on *Kūṭiyāṭṭam* as theater, and as part of the Indian theater heritage (Rajagopalan 1974a; Enros Pragna 1981; Richmond and Richmond 1985; Richmond 1990a, 1990b; Daugherty 2004; Johan 2014). Yet others focus on *Kūṭiyāṭṭam* as part of Indian folklore and, as such, designated as world heritage (Sullivan 2009; Lowthorp 2013a, 2013b, 2017, 2020). Some scholars also research *Kūṭiyāṭṭam* from a historical perspective (Rajagopalan 1987; Sullivan 1997; DuComb 2007; Rajendran 2012; Moser 2013, 2014).

Since *Kūṭiyāṭṭam* is the only surviving Sanskrit theater presenting classic Sanskrit text and stories, many scholars highlight the Sanskrit verses and drama (Unni 1990; Moser-Achuthath 1999–2000; Shulman 2022). *Kūṭiyāṭṭam* is also studied as a ritual (Narayanan 2006; Sullivan 2010, 2011; Johan 2017; Margi 2015; Shulman 2020). Moreover, some scholars give their attention to the unique features of *Kūṭiyāṭṭam*, such as *Kūṭiyāṭṭam* being a rare form of classic theater in which women act on stage (Paniker 1992; Daugherty 1996; Moser 2008, 2011; Johan 2011a; Lowthorp 2016); other singular features include drums, mudrā gestures, and facial expression (Rajagopalan 1968, 1974b; Jones 1984; Gopalakrishnan 2006; Pacciolla 2021). For a more comprehensive bibliography, see Moser (2011b).

I drew ample information as well as inspiration from all these publications. Yet since my perspective concerning *Kūṭiyāṭṭam* is markedly anthropological, my main source stems from fieldwork—

that is, encounters, interactions, and experiences in the field itself. Thus, many important aspects of *Kūṭiyāṭṭam* I will mention only in passing here, in particular the history of *Kūṭiyāṭṭam*, its poetry, and its temple performances.

Following in the footsteps of Don Handelman, I endeavor to drive symbolic anthropology beyond symbolism into the affects of practice in its own right and through this to explore the potentialities embedded in cultural events. Emphasizing, in the first instance, what is actually happening within the event itself—namely, the interactions among participants, and the setting within which this culturally informed entity unfolds. Through the practices adopted and those discarded, that also recursively organize the setting of an event, and through the degrees of its detachment from its social surrounding, an event, its intensity, and its affect are all formed.

Thus, too, through the meticulous ways in which *Kūṭiyāṭṭam* is put together, it develops the capacity to transport life away from the mundane.

I began exploring these kinds of transformative dynamics in Japanese martial art (Bar-On Cohen 2006, 2007, 2009, 2014) only to discover that *Kūṭiyāṭṭam* exploits them more grandly. *Kūṭiyāṭṭam* is a fantastically complex, sophisticated, layered, and traditionally informed way-of-doing—a way of toiling at amassing and perfecting ways of materializing a world where gods, demons, and mythical heroes live, while taking the audience into those other realities as they are emerging. Moreover, this feat is achieved without possession, indeed with only a slight change in modes of consciousness.

I conducted anthropological fieldwork on *Kūṭiyāṭṭam* on six occasions between 2012 and 2019 at several sites, mainly in Ernakulam, in central Kerala. I watched numerous hours of performance, over many days, and had the good fortune to live alongside and to befriend many actors and drummers, especially at Nepathya, sharing food and laughs with them, and testing their patience with my requests for information.

To introduce some of the basic features of *Kūṭiyāṭṭam*, I will describe a short scene, a story from the *Rāmāyaṇa* featuring Rāvaṇa, the mighty demon-king of Lanka. The scene, one that can be watched on YouTube, takes about fifteen minutes.

## A Scene from *Kailāsoddhāra*

The actor, Kalamandalam Sivan Namboodiri, in the costume of Rāvaṇa, is performing the Kailāsodhāraṇam.[3] Translations from Sanskrit are cited here as they appear in the captions of the recording: see www.indiavideo.org/kerala/arts/kutiyattam-part-1-3900.php#Desc.

The stage is empty apart from a stool and a three-wicked lamp, both in the middle of the stage in front of the actor. At the back of the stage, three bare-chested drummers are playing, and on the side of the stage sits the Naṅṅyār—the female actress—dressed in a white sari playing a small cymbal. The actor, dressed as Rāvaṇa—the demon-king of Lanka—sits on the stool holding a sword. Thoughtful, in his royal splendor, he is contemplating the curse cast upon him after he lifted mount Kailāsa, Śiva's abode. His face is entirely painted in vivid green, his eyes outlined in black; red patches mark out his forehead, nose, mouth, and neck; a white ball is attached to his nose; another white ball covers his "third eye" in the middle of his forehead; white paper is glued to his chin as a beard; and the whites of his eyes are dyed red. His face is mask-like, a living mask. Unlike a rigid mask, this makeup mask is capable of a multitude of expressions as the eyes, mouth, eyebrows, cheeks, and forehead are visibly moving and jumping.

Rāvaṇa sits there unmoving for a few seconds in a majestic pose, the gilded parts of his costume glittering in the flickering light of the lamp in front of him. The lamp focuses both the actor's and the audience's gaze.[4] He is a king. The drums keep their urgent rhythm. Now he slowly gets up to put the sword down in front of him and sits back on the stool. He fans himself with the edges of his shawl, performing wide, slow, circular movements with his right hand, with his left, and then with both hands. Now he is returning to his thoughts, the drums continuing their beat but quieting into the background of his musing. Rāvaṇa looks straight ahead, slowly rocking back and forth twice, and then moving his gaze downward, shaking his head in disbelief, or perhaps in regret. Every slight movement is clearly noticeable once the stable posture has been established.

Now he starts to talk, lifting both hands forward, his outward palms moving in a circle, and he throws his right hand backward, signaling the drummers to stop playing. Then he chants in Sanskrit. The artificial fangs in his mouth are showing as he accompanies his chanting with mudrā gestures, saying: "I have conquered in battle the three worlds inhabited by the Devas [gods] and the Asuras [demons], the same me, a man of great pride. Not only that, I have opposed Mount Kailāsa, the abode of Lord [Śiva] and his servant demons. I have shaken them and the Devi [Pārvatī]. I have received from him [Śiva] a boon as a token of his appreciation. Then Sri Pārvatī and Nandikēśvara [the bull Nandi] put curses on me for insulting them—two curses. In the deceitful guise of a monkey, have my curses come to claim me?" After the chanting, the drummers resume their playing, and Rāvaṇa recites the sentence again, now using only mudrā gestures, his hands traveling around his torso in different trajectories, his fingers folding and extending with great dexterity, changing positions and rhythm, while his gaze follows his hands. However, in the mudrā gesture rendition of the text, he adds: "How is that?," which is an invitation to retell the chain of events that resulted in the lifting of the mountain and the curses, expressed only in mudrā gestures with no chanting.

Rāvaṇa starts by describing his morning. His morning bath, prayer, and meal, and then, entering the ostentatious royal court in Lanka, he sits on his throne. Some of the words are rendered in acting. We can see Rāvaṇa shuddering in pleasure when the bathwater drips on his back, putting his hands together, moving to and fro in prayer, and eating out of the palm of his hand. The drums change their rhythm to accentuate the activities, imitating the sound of dripping water and that of the pleasurable shudder. Space is also delineated by the hands in movement—the court is drawn in the air as a square, while the throne is drawn in front of him, and parasols above his head are round; the white whisks fanned by demonesses are shown in wide waves of both hands. Once the court is established, all the court attendants perform obeisance to their king.

Then Rāvaṇa stops for a moment, leaning slightly to the side, listening—someone is coming. The god Vaiśrāvaṇa's messenger is approaching. Rāvaṇa hears the messenger bringing him presents of silk and weapons and delivering the god's request. His master Vaiśrāvaṇa asks Rāvaṇa to stop persecuting the Devas (the gods). Immediately, Rāvaṇa stands up, picks up his sword, cuts off the messenger's head, and swings it away with a great movement. Now Rāvaṇa and his army wage war against Vaiśrāvaṇa. He sees Vaiśrāvaṇa himself approaching, riding his chariot. Rāvaṇa gets angry, snatches the god from his vehicle, and is about to behead him as well, but then he thinks better of it and tosses him away. We see Rāvaṇa thinking and swinging Vaisrāvaṇa until he throws him into the distance.

I would like to point out a few of the remarkable traits of *Kūṭiyāṭṭam* that surface in this scene. Since the events in which Rāvaṇa takes part were dramatized from the great Indian epic the *Rāmāyaṇa,* the stories are well known to the audience, yet every phrase and every act is repeated many times. The chanting is doubled with the mudrā gestures, and the mudrā gestures, in turn, are repeated and accompanied by acting. Repetition is everywhere and pervasive. Rāvaṇa on the *Kūṭiyāṭṭam* stage creates a vital and vibrant world, replete with everything necessary for a world to function. Although objects (throne, fans, whisks), sentiments (thoughtfulness, regret, anger), personae (attendants, messenger, Vaishrāvaṇa), events, and space itself seem ephemeral—since they are made of body movements—they generate a concrete and dynamic actuality.

The single actor dressed as the mighty Rāvaṇa is alone on stage; he changes roles to embody his attendants and the messenger, alternating persona in the blink of an eye. Questions such as "How is that?" are crossroads that shift the course of the story, taking Rāvaṇa into another time and space. The objects, entities, and spaces become visible to the audience and exist on stage until the entire world is dismantled many days later. A densification of reality in the *Kūttambalam* occurs as a result of the constant repetitions, questions, and alterations in personae, as the actor dressed in the same costume changes roles and becomes one protagonist after another, also changing through time and in space over the scores of nights necessary to perform just one single act.

While sitting on his throne, Rāvaṇa is taken back and takes us with him to the memory of his encounter with Vaiśrāvaṇa, thus thickening time to what Shulman (2016a, 2022) calls "thick present," since the unfolding on stage "is almost always a series of past moments embedded as future from within a deeper past." We see Rāvaṇa musing on an event, the consequences of which have yet to unfold. He lifted Mount Kailāsa and was cursed for doing so; the consequences of that act and the curses that followed will concretize later, when his army will be defeated by an army of monkeys. In the *Rāmāyaṇa*, as well as in *Kūṭiyāṭṭam*, such connections between distant times and events defy linearity and generate multifaceted recursive relations between cause and effect, at times reversing their role and at others simply nullifying the effect of a cause altogether. Everything is added; nothing disappears. Events become nestled within other events, places within places, and times go back and forth, all enveloped in the subtle variations in drumbeat, acquiring depth.

Another feature of *Kūṭiyāṭṭam* that surfaces in this snippet is a moment of sudden reflexivity or realization. In this moment, the ruthless demon Rāvaṇa changes his mind about killing Vaiśrāvaṇa and tosses him away instead. Rāvaṇa recognizes himself, or parts of himself, in the god Vaiśrāvaṇa, since Vaiśrāvaṇa is an avatar of Rāvaṇa; here two avatars exist concomitantly, meeting and fighting. The gods, both in the *Rāmāyaṇa* and on the *Kūṭiyāṭṭam* stage, seem to be forgetful, and such moments of reflexivity—when they (Rāma, the hero of the *Rāmāyaṇa*, Hanūman the monkey-god) are made to recognize themselves, their past, and the extent of their power—become pivotal driving forces in *Kūṭiyāṭṭam*. Those powerful entities forget and must be reminded time and again who they are, what they are capable of, and what they must do to fulfill their cosmic role, and through these reminders they come into themselves.

## *Kūṭiyāṭṭam*—Anthropological Questions

Much of symbolic anthropology looks, first and foremost, for the congruences between social life and its representation in art or ritual, and the role those events may play within that sociality. For such an analysis, performance and ritual serve a purpose—they are often considered ways to alleviate tensions, to criticize social order, or simply to vent grievances. To show such links, symbolic anthropologists search for the beliefs that motivate behaviors, frequently looking for the binary oppositions at the root of such conflicts and motivations.

Ultimately, such attitudes explain cultural and religious phenomena through sociality alone without looking for the creative, generative force embedded in the events, as they are organized, in their own right. Moreover, they do not consider invisible forces such as gods, demons, or the outcome of sacrifice as having any kind of actual (real) existence. Naturally, too, such perspectives do not consider ways in which invisible forces are made to act. However, all of these suppositions—the role that cultural events necessarily play in sociality, symbolic reckoning, the requirement of belief itself, binary oppositions, the impossibility of (real) action by invisible forces—must be shown in the field and not assumed in advance.

Another scene that highlights well the consistency of the reality germinating on the *Kūṭiyāṭṭam* stage is Lakṣmaṇa building a hut for Rāma and his wife Sītā. This scene, which occurs often on the *Kūṭiyāṭṭam* stage, demands considerable effort and skill to perform. The royal human-cum-divine couple is living in exile, wandering the wilderness. Lakṣmaṇa, Rāma's loyal brother, who accompanies them, builds a hut—the *Parṇa-śālā*—to protect the couple. While carefully building the *Parṇa-śālā* on stage, Lakṣmaṇa is not using organic branches, twigs, leaves, and fragrant flowers; nonetheless, the hut he is building is real, made of branches, twigs, leaves, and fragrant flowers, which materialize through movement alone. He is digging holes to plant the poles that will hold up the hut; his digging is not symbolic, for he is not merely communicating "digging." He does not move on to something else once we, the audience, understand what he is doing; he meticulously digs one hole after another until all four are done; he is not concerned that the audience may find a quadruple repetition of the same movement tedious; this is because if he does not dig all four holes, and plant all four poles, the structure—a temple for divinities to live in—will not hold.

Symbols are quintessentially different in nature from true, real things. They stand instead of those real things to signify them; their working is based on an unbreachable, ontological gap between real reality and communicating its meaning. Moreover, symbols communicate meaning through reduction, foregoing differences. Thus, symbols can only represent a static, partial image of the cluttered, ever-evolving lived world, and, therefore, they cannot generate a living reality. As mentioned, much of the anthropology that analyzes symbols sees extensive efforts to tease meaning in ritual and art by analyzing the juxtapositions of symbols and the social reality represented by them. Yet symbols and representation are one culturally specific method among many of communicating meaning and making sense; they certainly do not trace the only way; the use of symbols is by no means universal (e.g., see Kapferer 2004, 2006, 2010; Handelman 2013). Defying symbols, causality and linearity are key to the workings of cultural dynamics embedded in *Kūṭiyāṭṭam,* and thus, too, to their anthropological analysis.

In *Kūṭiyāṭṭam,* acting in the world and producing meaning are achieved concomitantly, inseparably, and recursively, so that no ontological gap opens up between things in the world and their existence in the *Kūttambalam*. To accomplish this, *Kūṭiyāṭṭam* employs a wide array of cultural dynamics that can avoid generating a gap between the occurrences on stage and what they actually do. Specific methods are harnessed on stage to disrupt the mundane relations between things-in-the-world and rearranging them; new connections are then established and sent on their trajectories, taking on lives of their own.

This is why my main anthropological questions concern three elements: the search for the cultural dynamics that enable keeping the performance close to doing rather than to representing so that emergence can occur; the organizing properties embedded in practice (Venkatesan 2020); and the *modes d'emploi* that this practice carries within itself. Cultural dynamics are not abstract principles, nor are they theoretical guidelines; rather, they are revealed only by following practice itself, within unfolding processes. Through these processes, complex, flexible, adaptive connections are set into motion and transmitted, mainly from body to body. These connections are made of traditional knowledge, inculcated in the actors' bodies from childhood. Moreover, the actors use imaginative creativity to trigger connections capable of activating systems of know-how that awaken dynamics embedded in the world. These dynamics also generate that self-same world.

Observing *Kūṭiyāṭṭam* in the attempt to discern the cultural dynamics that operate this form of theater, "how" questions are central and critical. How does this new reality come to life and survive? Even scrutinizing the short scene from Kailāsodhāraṇam, and then Lakṣmaṇa's building of the *Parṇa-śālā,* already calls up a multitude of questions. How do the empty stage, the female Naṅṅyārs, the mudrā gestures, the drummers, the three-wicked lamp, and the living, expressive mask of Rāvaṇa shape *Kūṭiyāṭṭam*? How do they contribute to generating an alternative mode of life that can last days or even several weeks? What sort of reality comes into existence? How does it work and how is it kept alive? How are the body, its faculties and potentialities—the muscles, senses, modes of consciousness—engaged in creating such change? What happens to bodies and selves while living this extraordinary existence? Moreover, this tradition is no less a temple ritual and sacrifice in which the actors become the heroes of the great epic in an effort to entice the gods to join in at the *Kūttambalam* and grant a request. So, what can *Kūṭiyāṭṭam* do, and what transformation does it yield?

Furthermore, what do the frequent questions asked on stage contribute as they send the protagonists into other events, times, and places, into the very "thickening" of the present? What does the multitude of repetitions accomplish? What cultural, semiotic, somatic, and ritual dynamics are employed to yield the unobstructed flow between aspects of the world? How does *Kūṭiyāṭṭam* resonate with the audience, with the *Rāmāyaṇa* of the Sanskrit play, with past generations of actors, drummers, and actresses who performed *Kūṭiyāṭṭam* as a ritual in temples? On the other hand, how did *Kūṭiyāṭṭam* modernize, secularize, and globalize to the point that—like the scene described here—it can be watched worldwide on YouTube?

More generally, how can practice in its own right (Handelman 2004b) generate an alternative way of acting, one that concomitantly communicates meaning? How can this way of acting overcome what is usually considered the unbreachable semiotic gap, as Artaud (1964) famously put it, between reality and its double? What sort of connections can be established to avoid representation as well as their logical kin, such as linearity and causality? How does this elaborate way-of-doing challenge clear distinctions between imagination and reality, and more specifically, how can movement and imagination become materials for actual sophisticated practices employed to generate alternative lived-in-worlds?[5] All of this, as I would like to show, can be achieved through that which I term *inclusiveness*.

## Building an "Inclusive" World in *Kūṭiyāṭṭam*

To animate its reality, *Kūṭiyāṭṭam* actively, purposely, and consistently endeavors to unravel any gap that may arise between abstraction and concreteness, between reality and its representation, among the different faculties of the body, and between humans and non-humans.[6] It sets into motion a complex endeavor that can bring forth a visceral and savory world, one that disseminates freshness and animation.

To bring to life a real reality through movement, albeit an ephemeral one, *Kūṭiyāṭṭam* creates an "inclusive" world. Inclusive cultural dynamics are often called non-dual, and indeed they shun duality. However, negating the dual by calling it "non-dual" not only declares the dual as the standard but, more importantly, does not indicate what inclusion and non-duality, or rather a-duality, are capable of in a positive, constructive way.[7]

We are accustomed to worlds that promote exclusivity rather than inclusivity, worlds that seek stability to enable abstraction as a higher or meta level, one deemed of greater complexity and value than is materiality—moreover, worlds that sustain a clear gap between representations and the real world. Yet the dynamics that generate exclusivity, that enable these neat organizations, must constantly compile any emerging differences into neat, stable, understandable, abstract terms. To fix them into place, to keep them from moving—as time and life constantly do—differences must be subdued, subjected to the generalizations of identity, and piled into agglomerations.[8] Thus, repetitions, slight modifications, and accidental processes are excluded and collapsed into clear-cut categories and codes. Relying solely on linearity, the cultural dynamics of exclusivity treat iterations as redundancies, tedious noise, decoration, or as straightforward detritus. Such traditions employ only one semiotic tool, that of representation, and reject—even patronize—all other options (see also Deleuze 1994[9]; Xin 2012).

Inclusive cosmologies combat exclusions by vigorously working to retain as many iterations and potentialities as possible. They largely depend on practice, on actual movement, vigorously toiling to control and collect as many potential repetitions of that practice as possible, and, thus, to avoid the crystallization of gaps. Yet as a consequence, an inclusive world is vulnerable, unsteady, and susceptible to erosion. Whereas an exclusive system may crumble due to variations generated through the movement of life, the erosion of an inclusive system arises from inertia, from the very obstruction of movement. Inclusive worlds abhor stasis, which yields chaos (Handelman and Lindquist 2011: 25–26; Handelman and Shulman 1997, 2004). Therefore, a constant effort is required to build and sustain a world of movement.

Nevertheless, inclusivity is not the simple contrary of exclusivity. Whereas exclusivity employs just one way-of-doing, that of linearity, inclusive cosmologies do not exclude any way-of-doing. Despite the aversion toward compilations and approximations, inclusive worlds may also include snippets of linearity, causality, and representation, which are no more than an option within a myriad of perspectives, without awarding them precedence over other ways of communicating and world-building.

While systems based on exclusion refer to something outside themselves, perhaps a "meta-level," that encompasses them, inclusive worlds refer to nothing outside themselves. They grow out of their own material, expanding and shrinking, intensifying and rarifying. Handelman calls such a world intra-grated (in my terms, inclusive), as opposed to integrated (in my terms, exclusive). While integrated worlds are held together by an external carapace, a "meta-level," (often a single god) closing off a series of well-partitioned hierarchical levels, an intra-grated world is held together from its interiority through synergetic relations between the parts within the whole (Handelman 2014a: 96; Handelman and Lindquist 2011).

In *Kūṭiyāṭṭam,* the multiplicity of vantage points does not include any "meta" position. Nothing encompasses the *Kūttambalam* from outside itself; the gods are within, and nothing is more abstract than the performance itself—it is self-referential, referring to nothing outside itself (Handelman 2014: 98). *Kūṭiyāṭṭam* is inclusive in all domains: cosmological, social, and somatic. Storytelling in *Kūṭiyāṭṭam* meanders the world to supply more and more events, embracing countless repetitions that lead to no particular end or climax but instead create whirls within whirls, establishing the story on multiple levels of existence. Such practice depends on complex traditions developed over centuries.

To construct, sustain, and operate a world of inclusion, a relatively enclosed bubble or life-pocket must be created—a nearly secluded chamber including everything necessary for it to function continuously within itself. Namely, an inclusive practice must concentrate on one aspect of life and burrow into it to include as many iterations as possible to near-perfection while concomitantly distancing itself from life outside its confines. Moreover, only separation from mundane living can ensure its capacity to include everything within that life-pocket. This is why inclusive worlds are always busy severing ties, disregarding everything not included in the practice at hand, to exploit to the fullest the potentialities of inclusion, delving into every aspect of a certain domain or activity.

When the *Kūṭiyāṭṭam* actors tie on their headbands at the beginning of preparations for the performance, this act renders them immune to ritual pollution. The headband covers the *ucci* (understood as the highest orifice in the cranium) and is an act of separation, one severing social, familial, and religious ties and obligations. While gently separating from mundane living, by entering the secluded life-pocket of *Kūṭiyāṭṭam,* the actors and actresses ensure protection against human fragility stemming from sociality that may result in disruption and ritual pollution.[10]

Many Indian worlds are inclusive life-pockets (Handelman and Shulman 2004); thus, *Kūṭiyāṭṭam* is part of a widespread tradition, one that relies more heavily on what Ramanujan (1989) calls unique context-sensitive relational understandings rather than context-free generalization or universals.

In a world made of actual, physical material, maintaining the endless versions, iterations, and repetitions will engender such density and clutter that it will soon become impossible to contain; too many objects cannot fit into a three-dimensional space and into linear time. Yet since the entities and events on the *Kūttambalam* stage are made of *movement,* they can fill space and time, without overflowing them, into borderless depth. *Kūṭiyāṭṭam* preserves everything that is created on stage for the duration of the performance; whatever is meandering within the *Kūttambalam* is carefully collected. The innumerable repetitions deepen the world as it comes to be—open-ended, never complete.

## How Body Generates a World

The world of *Kūṭiyāṭṭam* depends for its existence on a myriad of both large and minute body movements. The potentialities of the human body center both the training of the actors and the performances themselves.

When I started thinking in anthropological terms, my main question quickly became the following: how are worlds of meaning formed through culturally informed somatic practices, those centered on the living, moving, perceiving, thinking, and feeling human body?[11] I looked at delineated life-pockets such as martial arts—karate, aikidō, kyūdo (Japanese archery), sumo, and Israeli close combat—and the different ways in which each shapes a world of meaning. Although they are all concerned with embodied fighting, each may generate a radically different way-of-doing, ways based on alternative cosmologies actually formed through practice (e.g., Bar-On Cohen 2006, 2012, 2014, 2021).

These practices determine the body's faculties and potentialities and how they interrelate. Thus, through the specific ways of organizing space and time and through the choice of exercises, while forgoing alternative options, these worlds also recursively form the actual living body of the participants. As a result of long years of training, the body itself becomes stronger, more sensitive and mindful, and more adept in using those faculties and potentialities. Body practice thus shapes a world, not as part of our consciousness alone, but also by becoming integral to the world's materiality, just as cooking, eating, procreating, and making tools are all shaped by the body and recursively shape capacities, forms, and the environment itself.

## India, Practice, and Body

To analyze *Kūṭiyāṭṭam,* I firmly stand on the broad shoulders of two thinkers: Anthropologist Don Handelman and Indologist David Shulman.

In his work (specifically on *Kūṭiyāṭṭam*), Shulman (2022) allows the reader to savor the lush and formidable potentialities embedded in South Indian creativity—in stories, poetry, drama, language, and thought—to reveal the animated character of Indian cosmology. Masks, dreams, games, words, and even grammar all come alive to become active and transformative. Meanwhile, the clear distinctions between real reality and the affects of culture become blurred. And, the world reveals unexpected facets flowing from human creativity, and since imagination becomes sentient, it enables challenging the directionality of causality, linearity, and time.

Handelman suggests that diverse modes of framing are culturally employed to determine the potentialities embedded in the interface between parts of a world, and, thus too, its cosmology. In other words, a particular cosmos comes to be through modes of fashioning frames and the interactions among its parts, and that same cosmos is constructed through those same formations. Thus, there is no delay or separation between an abstract blueprint or intention and its emergence in practice; both come to be together and nourish one another.

By suggesting to carefully observe ritual, art, and other cultural events, in their own right, Handelman opens a way of following the making of a cosmology not out of principles or discourse but as emerging out of the way it is put together. Such an approach favors "how" questions over "why" questions. Looking closely in the first instance at practice as it is done permits to glimpse the emic point of view—without prior premises, whether theoretical or concerning the social context in which a practice thrives. And so, too, to keep a distance from the assumptions that the anthropologist brings to her analysis from her own cultural restraints and biases. That is why Handelman's suggestion to look at practice in its own right is not simply a methodological one (Shapiro 2015); it is a basis for analysis, and for anthropology itself.

In my research of martial arts, as well as *Kūṭiyāṭṭam*, I engaged with Handelman and Shulman to see how the most intricate tool available to us—the human body—in all of its potentialities and aspects is used to generate and sustain different realities. In this respect, I am also following in the footsteps of some of the anthropologists who consider the centrality of the body itself as actively promoting certain cosmologies. One such anthropologist is Joseph Alter, who shows that in India the body is porous vis-à-vis its environment, and that body practice and body images play a central role within Indian social orderings, culture, and politics

(Alter 1992, 2000). Faculties of the body often considered distinct from each other are inseparably linked. Thus, wrestlers in northern India keep themselves strong and pure; they control their food intake, their semen, and other bodily functions. They avoid street food, which might pollute their bodies because it could contain bad emotions. Alter (1994, 1996) stresses the importance of sexual restraint and the upkeep of the body in Gandhi's thought and its profound influence on modernized India and its politics, as well as the importance of yoga and the yogic body in the Indian political arena (2004).

Ethnomusicologist Steven Friedson looks into how drumming and music in African ritual can generate an alternative reality and bring the gods into the world (Friedson 1996, 2009). He shows that one prevalent African rhythm among the Tumbuka in Northern Malawi is a mix of a beat of three and a beat of four, creating a confusing and hypnotic rhythm—a "gestalt"-switch similar to the optical illusion of an old woman who is also a young woman, depending on how you concentrate your gaze on the drawing. This chimera can reveal the gods to the ritualists. Another ethnomusicologist, Steven Feld (1996, 2012), introduces "the anthropology of sound" (2012: xxvii). Feld shows how body potentialities shape the environment. The Kaluli people of Papua New Guinea have developed intimate relations with sounds from their environment and culture, such as water, birdsong, and women weeping, going beyond sung songs that convey emotion to encompass geographical soundscapes, particularly by discerning different sounds of water as they navigate the land.

These anthropologists do not relate to the body as a metaphor or as a source of symbols, but to the amazing potentialities that the body can create when painstakingly formed to become a cosmogenic tool.

## Structure of the Book

The first chapter presents both the traditional organization of *Kūṭiyāṭṭam* and the challenges it faces in today's social reality. Modernization has dramatically altered lifestyles in Kerala, and in order to allow its preservation under new conditions, *Kūṭiyāṭṭam* too needed to change and adapt. Nevertheless, despite efforts to perform *Kūṭiyāṭṭam* out of the temple, to open its ranks to new castes, to add female roles, to update costumes, and more, the survival of *Kūṭiyāṭṭam* is still threatened. In particular, the performances extending over many nights, both within and outside the temple, became rare and far apart (Johan 2011b.). Because of its unique features, *Kūṭiyāṭṭam* no longer draws new audiences. The ranks of those who appreciate the slow pace of the performances, and those who can even understand the mudrā words, are dwindling. These changes in social ordering present challenges to Nepathya as a family-centered school, as well as to other schools, especially since the prolonged and intense training for the actors over many years does not promise a potential livelihood. This chapter also introduces the difficulties of understanding and analyzing *Kūṭiyāṭṭam,* since it cannot be analyzed solely as theater.

The second chapter delves deeper into the performance itself. It describes in detail an extraordinary performance of the *Aṅgulīyāṅkam,* the sixth act of the play "the Wondrous Head-Jewel," featuring the heroes of the *Rāmāyaṇa.* In the *Aṅgulīyāṅkam,* for twenty-eight straight nights a single actor performs in the costume of the monkey-god and messenger Hanūman. This performance embodies many of the potentialities of *Kūṭiyāṭṭam,* with its somatic and sensual diversity. The royal couple-cum-deities Sītā and Rāma are living in exile in the forest when Sītā—tricked through *māyā* (magical illusion) by Rāvaṇa the demon king of Lanka—is abducted. The act unfolds while Hanūman the monkey messenger is hiding inside a tree in Rāvaṇa's *aśōka* garden, where Sītā is imprisoned. Hanūman is carrying a message to Sītā from her husband Rāma in the form of a magic ring (the *Aṅgulīyāṅkam*). While Sītā is contemplating ending her life, Hanūman is waiting for an opportunity to give her the ring, a ring that allows *māyā* to be discerned from "real" reality. As Hanūman takes on a myriad of roles, the performance allows the forming of a rich reality existing alongside the mundane one.

The third chapter makes use of the features revealed mainly through the Aṅgulīyāṅkam to suggest theoretical tools for understanding *Kūṭiyāṭṭam.* The chapter relates to the cultural dynamics of storytelling in *Kūṭiyāṭṭam* and how they push toward creating and shaping an inclusive world. The stories told on stage are famous and well known to the audience, so revealing the plot is not the goal of their telling. The more profound accomplishment of *Kūṭiyāṭṭam* is generating a smooth, unobstructed world through particular cultural dynamics that are employed to accomplish this feat. Among the dynamics generated on stage, some especially stand out: the *negative* that creates space, the *interrogative* that fills that space, and *repetition* that brings the events to life and unleashes a world of intensities comprised of emotional tenors.

The fourth chapter engages with energizing the world through *Kūṭiyāṭṭam* through two cases of female power injecting into the world. The first is the aftermath of the mutilation of the mighty female demon Śūrpaṇākhā. During a battle in the sky, Lakṣmaṇa, Rāma's loyal brother, cuts off Śūrpaṇākhā's breasts and nose. Shamed, hurt and vengeful, she appears in the *Kūttambalam,* spewing her blood in every direction, rendering the entire world red. In the second case of female energy, its dissemination pours out of the ordeal of fire undergone by the lovely goddess-cum-woman Sītā. She walks into a funeral pyre as if it were refreshing water, thereby casting a golden hue throughout the world and opening both the domain of the gods and the dead to humans. Both the urgent energizing and dangerousness of female energy unleashed by the demoness's mutilation and the serene and harmonious energy released by Sītā's ordeal of fire are necessary for the well-being of the world.

The fifth chapter addresses an ancient ritual recently revived after a hiatus of 150 years—the *Cūṭala-k-kūttu*. The ritual is performed by an actress, a Naṅṅyār performing *Naṅṅyārkūttu,* at the cremation ground on the property of a Brahmin (Nampūdiri) family, for a deceased Brahmin. Many conditions must be met for the ritual to be called forth, particularly that the deceased must have performed the grand fire ritual, the *Agnicayana,* during his lifetime. The event is thus a convergence of two rituals—the *Cūṭala-k-kūttu* and the *Agnicayana*—that took place years earlier. Through the performance of *Naṅṅyārkūttu* and other funerary rituals, the deceased may depart for his new, liberated, and eternal existence. While telling the story of the frivolous, ludic Kṛṣṇa, the Naṅṅyār helps to "separate" and release the Nampūdiri's widow from her dead husband, and thus to help usher him into his new existence.

The sixth chapter is dedicated to a playful character, the Vidūṣaka, who introduces constant movement and a flow of talk in Malayalam, teasing the audience, interpreting the words of the play in an unabashedly gluttonous and sensuous manner. Vidūṣaka is consistent in his humanity, bringing to the stage the messiness, silliness, and fate (karma) of mundane human life; he embodies the essence of humanness and its potentiality to become more than human.

The last chapter ties together, albeit loosely, some of the strands developed in the book by looking at the most concentrated space on stage: the scintillating focal point between the three wicks of the lamp and the actor's two eyes. This intense site of movement and reverberation coaxes to life, nurtures, radiates and collects back the entire *Kūṭiyāṭṭam* cosmos shared by humans and gods.

~

Movement is a condition for life, yet both hyper-movement and stasis are dangerous and may lead to extinction. Śiva's visit to the mythological Forest of Pines (in its South Indian recension) relates the hazards of movement both in its scarcity and in its excess. The stoppage of movement generates a brittle and congealed world, yet extreme movement can destroy the world. Thus, in the Forest of Pines, the sages who dwell there have forgotten Śiva and have frozen him out of their rituals. Consequently, parts of himself coagulate and break away, diminishing his being. Śiva visits the forest to stop his self-coagulation, and there he becomes Naṭarāja, the dancer, the melting flow of extreme movement. When the "continuous internal movement" within the god, "his flowing interconnectedness or self-interiorization," is disturbed, he dances, and "the whole world shudders, and the great mass of living beings tremble in fear" (Handelman and Shulman 2004: 15, 14). Within his dance, the world becomes overly fluid and diluted, unable to hold together, so drunk to be in danger of destruction: "he threatens to suck the entire cosmos into himself. Drawn into the vortex opening to infinity, the cosmos and perhaps the God himself will cease to exist" (2004: 24).

Movement and life are intricately interconnected so that the constant movement on stage is the reason *Kūṭiyāṭṭam* is always auspicious; its constant dynamism nourishes the world while expanding it from within. Gods can disseminate auspiciousness writ large, throughout the cosmos; for humans to do so, however, an inclusive ritual enclave—delineated and protected—must be secured. *Kūṭiyāṭṭam* follows complex ways to meet this challenge. Thus, Hanūman in the *Aṅgulīyāṅkam* shapes a world, delineating space where none existed, and filling it with a dense myriad of questions and repetitions until he himself, together with the cosmos he awakens over many nights, comes to realize who he is and what extraordinary feats he can and must perform. Female energy is necessary for movement and reproduction, and through performance the two goddesses disseminate both hyper-energetic and docile energy onto the world. In the *Cūṭala-k-kūttu*, Agni, the god of fire, mediates between people and the gods, while Kṛṣṇa brings joy and mischief; and through the female performance, both gods propel the dead Nampūdiri to complete the transformation he began years before with the *Agnicayana*. And the all-too-human Vidūṣaka reveals the divine potentialities embedded in the human body, desire, and messiness. Excess of movement is as dangerous as is its cessation, which is why *Kūṭiyāṭṭam* must be carefully protected from interruption and ritual pollution. Śūrpaṇakhā's blood pouring from the sky might drown the world, and the war that resulted in Rāvaṇa's death disperses havoc; yet, if controlled, even these violent unsettling and unbalancing occurrences energize the world and enable renewal.

# Chapter 1

# *Kūṭiyāṭṭam*

When Sreehari was ten years old in the summer of 2012, on many of the twenty-eight nights of the *Aṅgulīyāṅkam,* while waiting for the performance to begin he would sit on the stairs, silently telling himself the stories of the *Rāmāyaṇa* and accompanying them with the facial movements of a *Kūṭiyāṭṭam* actor while counting his own rhythm. He was trying on the roles that would be played later that evening by the solo actor at the *Kūttambalam.* Sitting there, the young boy grimaced to himself with exaggerated eye movements, whirling his fingers from time to time into the mudrā gestures, imitating his parents, the students at their Nepathya school, and the other guest actors. Sreehari had been trained from a very early age in the traditional ways, within his family, to become an actor. The world of *Kūṭiyāṭṭam* was also his private world. Its imagination was his imagination, and growing up he discovered his own life within the art. He was born into the cosmos created on stage, which spills over to fill the entire world. *Kūṭiyāṭṭam* is both his interior and his exterior reality.

Sreehari's parents, Madhu and Indu G., showed me family videos of little Sreehari at three years of age already performing to the beat of drums at a family gathering; in the film, he demands that his uncle Sajeev continue his drumming so that he can continue his energetic drama-dance. When he was six, his mother would take him to school on her motorcycle; he was still sleepy in the early morning hours, and as he was behind her, she was afraid he would fall asleep, loosen his grip on her, and fall off the motorcycle. To keep him entertained, she played games, teaching him Sanskrit while chanting *ślokas* (poetry lines) from classical drama. The boy was fascinated. At the same age, he also demonstrated the *Kūṭiyāṭṭam* mudrā on film for Farley Richmond.[1] When he was ten, sitting on the steps and performing for himself, Sreehari was small in stature but already an accomplished actor. When asked what he wanted to be when he grew up, his answer was immediate: "*Kūṭiyāṭṭam*," he said. "*Kūṭiyāṭṭam!*"[2]

On my first evening at the theater, I too was fascinated, although I could not understand what was going on. Yadukrishna, one of the students, whispered in my ear with his heavy Malayalam accent: "Now he is the storyteller, saying 'and then'? 'And then?' and going backward in time. And now he is the king, and now he is back to being Hanūman." All I could see was an actor on stage whirling his hands and following them with his eyes, his hands becoming little animals rushing around, followed closely by his eyes. I could not make sense of it. And indeed, *Kūṭiyāṭṭam* is very complex, a mind-boggling practice.

The world of *Kūṭiyāṭṭam*—Sreehari's world, his imagination, games, pastimes, and aspirations—brings to life realities long gone, yet eternal. The performance engages the deepest and most complex capacities of the human body to perceive, react emotionally, move to the rhythm, gaze at the flame of a lamp for hours, and imagine; it even engages with the potentialities brought about by the drowsiness induced by a long night's performance as the actors go forward and backward in time, traveling great distances in an instant. Meanwhile, borders are eroded—and made to collapse and disappear.

## Nepathya

Nepathya is a small and active private school of *Kūṭiyāṭṭam* in the village of Moozhikkulam, about twenty kilometers from Kochi. Founded in 2004, it operates in the traditional *Kūṭiyāṭṭam* way to train artists, within a family setting. Nepathya was founded by Madhu and his wife Indu G. Madhu was born into a Cākyār family and thus belongs to the community that has carried the tradition through generations and still holds the exclusive right to perform *Kūṭiyāṭṭam* at temples; he was trained by his father and uncle. Indu

G. studied *Kūṭiyāṭṭam* in the Kalamandalam School for Kerala Arts but stems from an aristocratic matrilineal Nayar community.

The emblem of the Nepathya school is a stylized depiction of legs in the basic stance of *Kūṭiyāṭṭam*: bent with feet pointing outward. The name "Nepathya" means "green room," the dressing room in which the actors and actresses undergo a transformation, becoming the protagonists they soon will play on stage. The choice of both the emblem and the name of the school matches its straightforward aims, tenaciously upheld at the school—the preservation of *Kūṭiyāṭṭam* in its traditional form.

There is no difference between the training of male and female actors,[3] and there are no examinations; the guru decides when a pupil is ready to move on to the next level of training and performance. The daily training is free of charge, and no tickets are sold for the performances at the *Kūttambalam*. Everyone is welcome. And indeed, it is not unusual for neighbors, with their children and babies, to wander in during a performance and leave after a while.

Despite the intimate, traditional mode, like other schools, Nepathya welcomes students and artists who do not belong to the "correct" communities, who are not members of the families that carried this tradition through the generations, the matrilineal temple assistants (*ampalavāsi*), the Cākyārs and the Nambyārs and their womenfolk, the Naṅṅyārs.

The Nepathya school organizes multi-day performances of different acts every year, which is why, during my fieldwork visits to Kerala, I spent most of my time in Moozhikkulam and developed close ties with the family. The school also includes several drummers, other female actresses who play the cymbals (*tāḷam*) and chant sitting at the side of the stage, a make-up artist, and three student-actors, including Rahul, Madhu's nephew, the son of his sister, and hence also a Cākyār according to the traditional matrilineal lineage, who can thus perform *Kūṭiyāṭṭam* as a ritual at temples. Vishu and Yadukrishna, the other two students, belong to the matrilineal temple assistants' community, but not the Cākyārs, and thus can perform only outside temples. When I first met the three students in 2012, they were in their late teens. The youngest member of the troupe, Shreehari, had been performing various tasks and was responsible for blowing the conch. However, a few years after our first meeting, he integrated into the troupe as a full-fledged actor.

Figure 1.1. Indu G. and Arathy playing *tāḷam*. Author photo.

On a performance day, the members of the permanent cast work from afternoon until late at night. The young actors double as stage assistants, helping with the make-up and costumes and tending to the lamps. The stone lamp on which the school emblem is engraved is situated outside the theater, and the three-wicked brass lamp is on stage. The gods reside in the stage brass lamp when lit; prayers are directed at the lamp and offerings laid at its feet. It is said that if one of the wicks dies out during a performance, one of the actors' parents may die. In the olden days, the brass lamp was the only source of light in the *Kūttambalam*. Now too it plays a decisive role in the changes in perception that occur during the performance, since the actors concentrate their gaze at the lamp in front of them while performing. The audience too constantly sees the lamp, as they watch the actors performing behind it. The lamp is the focal point of the *Kūttambalam,* at times illuminating the actors and at times obstructing them from the audience's view. The three-wicked stage lamp must be tended with great care; indeed, during a performance, one of the students may cross the front of the stage, between actor and audience, to replenish the oil and arrange the wicks.

Unlike his son, Sreehari, whose future as an actor looks more promising, and despite Madhu's extraordinary talent, some forty years ago, it looked as if this art form would not support an actor economically, and Madhu himself was unsure he would be able to follow his calling. In 1981, when he was fifteen years old, Madhu moved to Trivandrum with his father Kochukuttan and his brother Sajeev; his mother and his sister Sailaja remained in Moozhikkulam. There they trained in *Kūṭiyāṭṭam*, learned Sanskrit, received monthly instructions from the great guru Ammanur, the boy's uncle,[4] and opened the *Kūṭiyāṭṭam* department in the Margi school, where Sajeev still teaches. The young Madhu, however, could not expect to make a livelihood as an actor, which is why he also studied shorthand in the hope of becoming a clerk, perhaps at the post office.

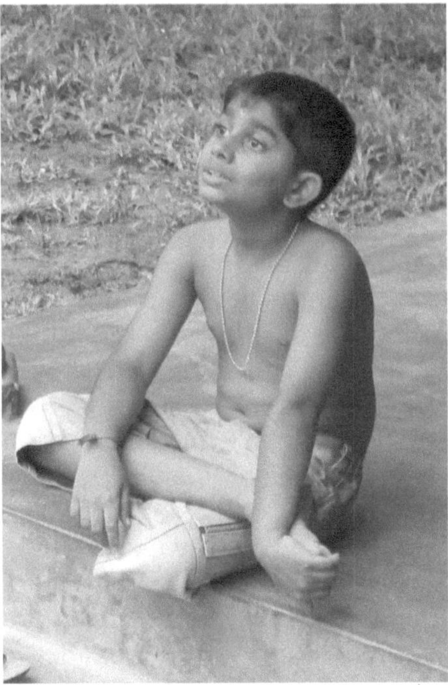

Figure 1.2. Shreehari as a child acting on the stairs. Author photo.

Madhu and Indu G. are highly trained and experienced actors, but despite their outstanding skills and talents, and although their lives and that of their only son, Sreehari, as well as their home—the top floor of which is another *Kūttambalam*—are all devoted to *Kūṭiyāṭṭam* and its preservation, they do not come close to earning a livelihood from *Kūṭiyāṭṭam*. Because *Kūṭiyāṭṭam* cannot support the family, Madhu teaches theater at the Sankaracharya Sanskrit University in Kaladi, and Indu G., who wrote her PhD on *Kūṭiyāṭṭam,* is a teacher at a government high school.[5]

Indu G. has often told me that she would gladly give up her teaching job if she could consecrate her life to *Kūṭiyāṭṭam,* but not only are the actors rarely paid for their performances, but maintenance of the school and organizing the performances—paying the drummers, make-up artist, and guest actors—is a heavy financial burden. Paid performances, she adds, occur perhaps three times a year. Occasionally, the troupe or individual actors are invited to entertain guests at local family celebrations, for instance, on the day before a wedding. At times they are asked to perform for tourists as a presentation of the Kerala theatrical traditions, together with other Kerala stage arts, mainly *Kathakaḷi* and *Teyyam*.

Indeed, the connection between Nepathya and David Shulman of the Hebrew University, which resulted in a long-term documentation project of the *Kūṭiyāṭṭam* repertoire, began when Indu G. performed at the hotel in the nearby town of Angamaly during an academic conference. Despite the financial hardship, the troupe does not perform under all circumstances; for instance, they refuse to perform while tourists are having a meal. In any event, all of the paid performances are relatively short, and the traditional long performances of a full act, which take place over many days, are rare. In recent years, because of its connections with universities, Nepathya has been invited to tour Europe and North America, and these tours have become a major financial resource that allows the school to be maintained.[6]

A temple performance is always paid since for it to become the sacrifice on behalf of a patron, it must be bought from the performer, who then stands in for the patron. But such payment is often only symbolic. The financial difficulties of the performers are not new—Madhu recounts that when his father was young, he often performed for a handful of bananas.

Figure 1.3. Indu G. performing Naṅṅyārkūttu. *Source*: Nepathya Centre for Excellence.

Since the Nepathya performances are not a temple ritual, they define their *Kūṭiyāṭṭam* as theater. However, the performance is not a mere cultural event or just entertainment; it is solemn and serious, and intimately connected with the gods and with ritual practice. The gods are invoked and remain present at the theater throughout the performances. This is why every performance requires pure and respectful conditions. Ritualistic practices are part of the artists' private lives—the Cākyārs traditionally perform a special daily Cākyār pūjā at home or a nearby temple and take ritual baths before performances. The performance in Moozhikkulam is strongly linked to the large, active Moozhikulam temple dedicated to Lakṣmaṇa, serving local villagers and pilgrims alike.[7] To the left of the temple's main entrance, inside the courtyard, stands a *Kūttambalam*, which hosts temple performances. Also, many ritualistic gestures and laws of purity are kept at the Nepathya *Kūttambalam*, which was built with great care in accordance with the ritual requirements. Its measurements are identical to the *Kūttambalam* inside the temple court, and the stage is oriented toward Lakṣmaṇa in the inner sanctum of the temple.

Nepathya's *Kūttambalam* is a beautiful structure, made in the Kerala style of dark wood lattice, open to the elements with a big square, an overhanging slanted tiled roof protecting from the harsh monsoon rain. Under the exterior roof hangs another roof that covers the stage alone. Since there are no walls, not only can the air circulate and relieve the heat inside, but also the large fruit bats—who live in the tall trees near the river and who search for food at night—can zoom into the theater during the performance to eat the banana offerings, which ripen over the days of the performance, as they hang from the poles holding up the interior roof.[8]

*Kūṭiyāṭṭam* refers directly to Indian religions, as it enacts plays based on the stories of the great epics, the *Rāmāyaṇa* or the *Mahābhārata*, in Sanskrit, the language of rites and scriptures, while using the mudrā gestures that are a ritualistic means to invoke the deities.[9] The performers touch the instrument of their craft, whether the drums, the cymbals, the stage, the actor's hat, or the stool; they cross their arms and touch their ears several times in a gesture of separation between their roles on- and off-stage, called "touching of the earrings." Prayers are recited several times, notably during the preparations, again when they come on stage, and again when they leave.

On ordinary nights, the flame for the three-wicked lamp is brought from the dressing room where it was lit, but on special occasions, such as an actor's first performance (*araṅṅēṯṯam*), the flame is carried from the Lakṣmaṇa temple sanctum. An image of Hanūman is affixed to the wall of the dressing room, and the actor faces the image while putting on his make-up. Madhu prays to Hanūman when he goes off-stage in the middle of a performance for a drink of tea; this, he says, summons his late gurus, his father, and uncle, who then accompany him during the performance and provide him with much-needed stamina to continue his strenuous acting.

The very first action the actors undertake is to tie on a red headband that covers the *ucci*, thus rendering the actor safe from ritual pollution (Richmond 1971). Within the temple, this is done before the sanctum is closed so that tying the headband creates a connection between the actor and the god in the sanctum (Johan 2017: 64). With this action, the actors leave their everyday life outside the *Kūttambalam*, including their connections to others, their caste, and family obligations, and even if a close family member dies—which would otherwise render the actors impure and unfit for performance—they are safe from pollution until the headband is removed.

Parts of the *Kūttambalam* and the objects used in the performance are ritually pure and are imbued with the deities' powers. The "green room"—*Nepathya*—contains features of a temple, including a lamp that, when lit, men who enter the room must remove their shirts. The large *miḻāvu* drums are temple instruments that should not be touched by anyone but the drummers and that may be played only during the performance—thus, students can train only on small wooden drums (Rajagopalan 1974b). The *miḻāvu* drum is treated as a Brahmin boy, and the little hole drilled into it to improve its sound is thus tantamount to the orifice of the Brahmin boy's ear; for this reason, the drums undergo the Brahmin rite of passage, the *Upanayanam* (the sacred thread ceremony), as well as Brahmin funeral rites when they cannot be used anymore. The drums are said to be self-generating, so that the sound of the *miḻāvu* is the first source, the sound-born world-seed of the universe. The *miḻāvu* (like the actors and drummers) undergoes

Figure 1.4. *Miḻāvu* drums. Author photo.

a first performance ritual, *araṅṅēṯṯam,* to infuse them with the consciousness of the god. The different rhythms, too, are sacred since they correspond to mantras as well as to Malayalam letters (Rajagopalan 1974b: 114–115; Pacciolla 2021).

## The Structure of a Performance

Every performance comprises three separate parts: *Puṟappāḍu, Nirvahaṇam,* and *Kūṭiyāṭṭam*. During the *Purappāḍu,* or presentation of the new protagonist, the actor asks, "Who am I? What am I doing here?" After presenting his questions, he chants part of the first *śloka* of the play and performs the dance steps that invoke the gods, the *kriyā*. The second part of the performance, which typically extends over many days, is the *Nirvahaṇam,* in which the actor tells the story backward, from the point at which the act begins toward the beginning of the story, answering the questions he posed in the *Puṟappāḍu*. Any *śloka* that is not in the original play—and many are added for the *Nirvahanam*—is chanted not by the actor but by the Naṅṅyār. The *Nirvahaṇam* continues with the actor performing the *Rāmāyaṇa Saṃkṣepam* (an abbreviated version of the *Rāmāyaṇa*), this time starting from the beginning of the story and going forward in time to the point at which the act starts. Finally, he explains the first *śloka* of the act. Only then may the *Kūṭiyāṭṭam* begin—namely, the playing of the original act, often by several actors (see Margi 2015: 6–7).

Both the *Purappāḍu* and the *Nirvahaṇam* are not part of the original play; they follow the *Kūṭiyāṭṭam* manuals, the *āṭṭa-prakāram,* that indicates which elaborations are to be enacted, and the *kramadīpikā,* which provides stage directions—namely, specific instructions for the actors, drummers, and Naṅṅyārs. Both the *āṭṭa-prakāram* and the *kramadīpikā* were passed down from one generation to the next within the actors' families. Generations of *Kūṭiyāṭṭam* actors replenished and refurbished the play to yield the *āṭṭa-prakāram,* and thus the text of the drama becomes overshadowed by the interpretation and annotation of even the smallest detail (Rajagopalan 1974a: 93).

Moreover, the *āṭṭa-prakāram* is a living thing; it includes traces of past actors, and still leaves space for the current actors' additions. Although it is very detailed and rich, it is said to be only the basis for the actual performance. The actor can interpret it and supplement it, following his own design; he can decide to elaborate on a certain passage while passing quickly through another. In fact, since the world on stage is made of the actors' movement as they bring to life objects and entities with their hands, eyes, and bodies, this world depends to a great extent on the way the actor, and previous generations of actors, imagined the stories, creating realities through the mind by the vehicle of the body, or through the body by the vehicle of the mind. Just as Rāvaṇa creates Sītā in his mind as a result of his sister's description, and falls desperately in love with her, which in *Kūṭiyāṭṭam* may take several nights to perform; just as *māyā* creates alternative realities that cannot be discerned as illusions from the viewpoints of other realities that we usually call "real" realities—so, too, the imagination of the artists, anchored in their bodies, generates a living cosmos. Moreover, to achieve such multiplicity and continuous movement, imagination must always be open and uninterrupted.

One night of the *Aṅgulīyāṅkam*, Madhu elaborated on a scene of merriment from the lives of soldiers during a war on Ayodhya, the capital of Rāma's family kingdom. He was preparing and distributing betel leaves to everyone, and then constructed an entire orchestra with drums, trumpets, and conch, with the drumming recreating the sounds of the instruments. In this respect, *Kūṭiyāṭṭam* differs from the more famous form of traditional Kerala theater, the *Kathakaḷi*. The *Kathakaḷi* actor can act only for four series of drumbeats because after the fourth beat the singer accompanying him moves on to the next phrase. *Kūṭiyāṭṭam* is not bound by such limitations; the actor may play out a longer scene or shorten it to only mudrā gestures, while the drummers lead him or respond to his cue. Like life itself, the performance is prone to surprises and changes.

The actor takes different perspectives. When Lakṣmaṇa is constructing a hut to protect Rāma and Sītā in the forest, he gathers branches and plants them into the ground as pillars; then he gathers twigs and leaves, plucking them from the air to cover the ground and make a bed for the couple with a fragrant leaf and flower canopy. Once the hut is built, both actor and audience can enter and observe the finished work with satisfaction. This multiplicity of observations and viewpoints occurs many times in *Kūṭiyāṭṭam*. The actor will depict a river, a fire, or bees with mudrā gestures, increasing his movements while the river flows, the fire roars, or the bees buzz all around, then shifting his gaze to look far away at the water flowing, showing his dread or heat from the fire burning, or enjoying the bees drinking nectar from the flowers. After creating these realities, he experiences them as an observer, and we in the audience can see them continuing their movement even after the actor has stopped exhibiting them through his acting and mudrā gestures. First, the actor is the river, the fire, or the bees, and then the object acquires its own autonomous life, and the actor, as a protagonist, can observe it.

Though while building the hut the actor's movements are simple and mundane, applying force when a twig resists and gently preparing a mattress of leaves and flowers, there is nothing simple about the mechanism set into motion, because as the actor transforms himself to become Hanūman, and then alters himself—but not his costume—to become Lakṣmaṇa, he is all of these layers together and more; nothing is excluded, only added. Then the actor becomes the storyteller, dressed as Hanūman. He *is* Hanūman, enacting the battle between mighty Rāvaṇa and Indra's white elephant Airāvata, the elephant scarring Rāvaṇa's hands and eventually dying in the fierce battle—all this in front of our eyes, inside our eyelids. Yet these are not distinct frames presenting Hanūman, Lakṣmaṇa, the storyteller, Rāvaṇa, the elephant, the actor, or us, the audience. Within this living, organic cosmos, all of these are enmeshed, to pierce one another with no obstruction, concomitantly maintaining their own distinct existence. The actor is on the stage looking at the flames of the lamp, yet he is in the forest working and sweating, on the battlefield between the two giants once he is many-headed Rāvaṇa, then Airāvata, then the storyteller looking at this battle, and all the while also with us, the audience, subject to the cooling affect of the Sanskrit chanting when the actor stops toiling for a brief moment and the Naṅṅyār's clear voice fills the *Kūttambalam* (on Rāvaṇa's power and access of the virile combative *Tejas* energy, see Whitaker 2002).

During the *Nirvahaṇam*, the main character becomes the storyteller; while telling the story, he assumes the roles of the other protagonists of the story. In the *Aṅgulīyāṅkam, pakarnnāṭṭam* ("exchanging roles") is constantly performed, continuing with many additions and elaborations during which the actor becomes the other protagonists, both male and female. Then he tells the story of the *Rāmāyaṇa* in the abbreviated *Saṃkṣepam* up to the point at which he arrives at Rāvaṇa's Aśōka garden to find the imprisoned Sītā. On one of the nights, the actor told the entire *Rāmāyaṇa samkṣepam* twice. The carrier of the news from the gods tells the story to an eagle who lost its wings, and then that eagle tells Hanūman the story to remind him of who he is, and the eagle's wings grow back. The performance is not meant for the audience alone, as while the audience already saw the *samkṣepam* that same evening, Hanūman (who is telling the story) has not at that time and must be informed by the retelling of the Rāmāyaṇa.

On the opening night, the gods are praised, described, and summoned through invocative steps, *kriyā,* as the actor builds a world in which the play will take place, and in which we will all live for the duration of the performance. *Kriyā* is comprised of stylized steps and mudrā gestures, yet unlike the mudrā gestures that tell the story, the *kriyā* mudrā are not words but rather tokens of respect and veneration toward the gods to please them and coax them onto the *Kūttambalam*. The *kriyās* are oriented toward all eight directions and the deities that reside there. Some *kriyās* are accompanied by chants of praise sung by the Naṅṅyārs. Then the actor performing the *kriyā* goes on to describe Śiva from head to toe in an enthralling rhythm of three steps forward, three steps back. After he has described the great god, he describes Pārvatī his wife as she is imagined by the actor in his meditations. Then, through mudrā gestures, the actor exteriorizes everything that fills the three worlds—heaven, earth, and the abyss—from the gods and demons, through humans and animals, to the tiniest insects and blades of grass. Finally, he plucks flowers from the cosmos he has just put in place and offers them to the gods. This world is tied into place after the evening's performance.[10] On the last night, the actor removes his hat, offers to the gods water and fire from the lamp, and takes this world apart, returning it to the gods—or perhaps sending it back to its permanent abode.

Many of the cultural tools and somatic dynamics employed on stage are drawn from temple rituals, using long-established means that permit the invocation of worlds. The ability to build a real animate world on stage and to live within it for several days, for the duration of the act, demands complex skills that draw heavily on religious traditions. A performance outside the temple still summons realities that are not available in mundane life to gradually yield cosmological shifts.

## *Kūṭiyāṭṭam* as an Endangered Art Form

Becoming a *Kūṭiyāṭṭam* actor is a long and strenuous process; it demands talent, discipline, perseverance, and intelligence as well as physical stamina. The students must learn Sanskrit and memorize all the necessary movements, mudrā gestures, and texts, as well as strengthen their legs, train their eyes and cheeks to move freely in all directions, and more. The three young actors of Nepathya, who as mere children began consecrating all their free time to *Kūṭiyāṭṭam*, training every day, have over the years attained a level sufficient for each of them to carry the weight of a performance alone on stage, over several hours. These gifted young men are also good students in their academic schools. As such, the talented students at the *Kūṭiyāṭṭam* have grown up to become engineers. Since acting cannot provide them with a livelihood, Indu G. dreads the day when the three boys, when entering the professional world, despite the prolonged investment in their vigorous training, may no longer have the leisure to dedicate themselves to *Kūṭiyāṭṭam*.

Even within the small world of Nepathya, the future is uncertain; and indeed, *Kūṭiyāṭṭam* as a tradition is endangered: the traditional audiences and patrons of *Kūṭiyāṭṭam* were comprised of the old elites, namely, Brahmins, aristocrats, and members of the royal family (Rajagopalan 1974a: 102; Rajagopalan 1987; Gopalakrishnan 2011: 17), but that audience has been dwindling and has by now all but disappeared. Times have changed, and the old audiences have lost much of their standing in society, and concomitantly, have adopted very different lifestyles and rhythms, no longer adhering to their former ways of life. For the most part, they are not as tightly connected to temple life as their ancestors once were and are not trained to understand Sanskrit or mudrā gestures. They have less leisure time at their disposal and prefer modern entertainment such as watching TV at home and thus have little patience for long performances that stretch over many nights. Even within the communities that have maintained these traditions over the centuries—the Cākyār male actors, the Nambyār drummers and makeup artists, and the Naṅṅyārs, the actresses, as well as the Nampūdiri Brahmin patrons—most no longer understand the mudrā gestures that would allow them to follow and enjoy the plays, let alone perform *Kūṭiyāṭṭam*.[11]

Given these obstacles hindering *Kūṭiyāṭṭam's* survival, since the middle of the twentieth century attempts have been made to adapt *Kūṭiyāṭṭam* to modern conditions. The most dramatic change was opening both drumming and acting to all communities, to non-Cākyār and non-Nambyār or Naṅṅyārs students, and even to foreigners. Since *Kūṭiyāṭṭam* is also an eye sacrifice (*darshan*), a temple ritual that requires aspects of ritual purity for the performance—and in particular the strict matrilineal lineage of the performers—the attempts to adapt *Kūṭiyāṭṭam* to change by opening it to members of other communities initially encountered considerable objections from some of the artist families.[12] However, by the 1970s, nearly all acting families became part of the change in one way or another.[13]

Kerala was a very traditional society regulated by the Nampūdiri landowners but experienced thoroughgoing changes. It was governed by the communist party throughout most of the second half of the twentieth century, when radical reforms were introduced. Its society thus incorporates both traditional practices, mainly within the private family and community sphere, and bold egalitarian values in the public sphere. A first step toward change in *Kūṭiyāṭṭam* was taken by the Kalamandalam Kerala school of arts and its *Kūṭiyāṭṭam* department, founded in 1965 (Gopalakrishnan 2011: 9; Moser 2014). It extracted *Kūṭiyāṭṭam* from the relatively secluded private domain and placed it in a more public sphere, separating the art from the cycle of rites in the temples to encourage performances on public stages, while maintaining the performance in its traditional forms.

Another major change concerns the actresses. While at the beginning of the twentieth century, the traditional Naṅṅyārs could chant the *śloka* and knew that text by heart as no one else did, many of them were not trained in acting; they neither danced, nor performed mudrā gestures, nor moved their facial muscles. So, when the Kalamandalam School welcomed female students, they were trained in acting skills. The Kalamandalam School also established a new costume for women that enables broader movements. Moreover, the teachers at the Kalamandalam School introduced more female roles to the *Kūṭiyāṭṭam* repertoire, thus radically changing the standard of female acting.[14]

As part of the attempt to reenergize *Kūṭiyāṭṭam*, present it to new publics, and expose its cultural value, since the late 1970s, performances have been organized in Europe. Interestingly, the move toward international exposure was also initiated and led by the traditional patrons of the art, namely, the Nampūtiri Brahmins, such as Sudha Gopalakrishnan and Kunju Vasudevan of Killimangalam, whose family has been closely connected to the Kalamandalam School ever since the opening of the *Kūṭiyāṭṭam* department. As a result of such efforts, in 2008, UNESCO declared *Kūṭiyāṭṭam* a "Masterpiece of the Oral and Intangible Heritage of Humanity" (see Sullivan 2009, 2011; Lowthorp 2020).[15]

Despite the efforts of enthusiastic youngsters graduating from the Kalamandalam and other schools, such as the Margi School in Trivandrum founded in 1970 (Gopalakrishnan 2011: 9); and despite the efforts to introduce *Kūṭiyāṭṭam* to new venues and audiences, and fresh financial sources—that resulted in featuring *Kūṭiyāṭṭam* in festivals both within India and overseas—*Kūṭiyāṭṭam* remains in peril.[16] The long performances are very demanding on the artists, and the audience, and they are expensive. For these reasons, for nearly a decade a massive documentation effort has been undertaken at the initiative of David Shulman. Harnessing the financial support of the Hebrew University of Jerusalem and the Yad Hanadiv Rothschild Foundation, working through the Humanities Fund of the Israeli Higher Education Authority and the University of Tübingen in Germany led by Heike Moser, the entire *Kūṭiyāṭṭam* repertoire is being filmed. Even the construction of the Nepathya *Kūttambalam* in Moozhikkulam on land that belongs to the Cākyār family was facilitated by funds from Jerusalem. In addition, those connections also led to extensive tours at European festivals and in North American universities.

My own fieldwork was conducted during the performances organized from 2012 to 2019 in the framework of this academic initiative. And this is also why the audience at the performances that I attended comprised the artists' families and a few Kerala enthusiasts, together with many Israelis, German, American, Italian, and Indian students and professors who came to Kerala for the duration of the performances.

This in turn touches upon the question of authenticity. Are the performances that I saw—which were financed by foreign academic initiatives and attended mainly by foreigners—and the social dynamics around them an authentic form of *Kūṭiyāṭṭam*, or are they contrived because of the intervention of foreign patrons? *Kūṭiyāṭṭam* has always depended on patrons for its existence, and the circumstances of the play were not altered to accommodate the universities but followed the precise family tradition as inscribed in the *āṭṭa-prakāram* and the *kramadīpikā* manuals that give instructions as to how to perform, yet the patrons and the audience certainly differed. Some foreign students who come back to watch *Kūṭiyāṭṭam* year after year already understand mudrā gestures better than many members of the local audience and can therefore follow the performance in detail. It is impossible, of course, to assess what would have changed without foreign audiences and support, especially because prolonged performances are few and far between.[17] This is why the extended performances funded through the academic initiative may be one of the only authentic forms of the long *Kūṭiyāṭṭam* performance existent today.

When Bateson and Mead (1942) filmed dance and trance in Bali, they paid the actors. Moreover, their equipment was not capable of night filming, so they had to organize a nontraditional day performance. Nevertheless, members of the audience did enter a trance, and the "contrived" performance still followed the same lines as the original one and yielded the same ritualistic consequence. The circumstances generated by modern conditions, which limited some possibilities, at the same time also created new opportunities, and through international connections, the protracted performances can be maintained, at least for now.

## Performance and Ritual

When the death of Rāvaṇa, the fierce demon king of Lanka, was performed in the seventh and last act of the *Āścaryacūḍāmaṇi*—"The Wondrous Head-Jewel," a retelling of the *Rāmāyaṇa*—we felt neither happiness nor relief at the god's triumph over the demon. Instead, we all felt a great loss as the world became flattened, colorless, soundless, and devoid of something important. After watching many performances of this play over many years, with different acts performed each time, and each act including the entire course of events up to the starting point of that particular act, we seem to have gotten attached to the ten-headed demon-king, raptly watching his extraordinary feats of power; lifting Mount Kailāsa, defeating Indra's giant white elephant Airāvata. Moreover, Rāvaṇa is also a master of *māyā* (disguise; illusion), and with great emotional scope, when he falls desperately in love with Sītā and abducts her. All of us, and particularly the widows among us, cried with Mandodarī, Rāvaṇa's bereaved wife, who tearfully lamented the great demon-king. Of course, we all knew what was coming—we all expected his death, as well as the ensuing ordeal of fire that Sītā would endure. But with this death, the entire cosmos created by the actors and drummers began to wane. We felt no sense of satisfaction or achievement, or of having reached the goal of this cosmic epic. No, not at all, because Rāvaṇa is an important part of the world we lived in within the *Āścaryacūḍāmaṇi*, and when he was gone, an organ within this world was severed.[18]

Art in non-Western societies, claims Gell, has agency (Gell 1998). It is not simply an object of aesthetic value but can act in the world, induce transformation such as taking a person's place in ritual. In *Kūṭiyāṭṭam,* indeed, both objects and actors in costume are imbued with what Gell calls a "magical" sort of agency, namely, an agency to transform that involves entities other than humans. The actors put on the costumes of certain protagonists (*veṣam*), becoming a certain hero, god, or demon, and immediately begin changing personas. Even a lighted lamp can become Sītā receiving amorous gifts from Rāvaṇa, as the Naṅṅyār sitting at the side of the stage, wearing a red sash, chants Sītā's lines.

*Kūṭiyāṭṭam* is world-generating and, concomitantly, the expression of that world, and thus cannot be described and analyzed in terms of theater or performance alone.[19] And, thus too, anthropology of performance cannot contribute much to the understanding of *Kūṭiyāṭṭam*; rather, *Kūṭiyāṭṭam* is a ritual performance, as Kapferer understands it: a structure of practice. Although the ancient text and epic are central, *Kūṭiyāṭṭam* is "not simply the vehicle of a 'text,' or a means for expressing cultural and social meaning, or a way of communicating information which somehow lies outside of it"; ritual performance is itself constitutive of that which it intends, expresses, or communicates (Kapferer 1991: 10). Rāvaṇa, who has died countless times over the centuries in different renditions of the *Rāmāyaṇa*, has actually and visibly died again at the end of the *Āścaryacūḍāmaṇi*.

The main thrust of "anthropology of performance" is to see performance itself as an epitome of the cultural form of communication, which is understood as key to all human behavior. Drama, according to this viewpoint, reflects and represents the tensions created by social order: political, economic, kinship, generational, and gender relations. A performance, therefore, is the structural and institutionalized communicative way of drawing from, and it informs how we all symbolize our messages even in everyday life (Beeman 1993; on the relations between ritual and theater in anthropology, see Ganser 2017). It provides an opportunity to deal with social tensions in a liminal stylized space, and in turn educates us on how to express ourselves and how to communicate in everyday life—how I learn to play the role of "me." Moreover, according to the "anthropology of performance," theater can act as a sort of sublimation and social healing. The transformative power of performance to overcome social tensions stems precisely from its positioning of communication in a liminal space; by trying out solutions under controlled conditions, the often devastating consequences that real disorder may bring in its wake are avoided. The transformative power of theater resides in the "as if" quality of acting; the actor behaves "as if" she were the real protagonist of the play, thus reflecting the social behavior of that protagonist in a situation adapted from the natural way of communicating in a mundane reality (e.g., see Avorgbedor's succinct description of the Turner-Schechner paradigm 1999; see also Palmer and Jankowiak 1996; Lewis 2008; Wilkinson-Weber 2012).[20]

The transformative power of this ritual theater evidently does not emanate from its mimetic trait. The *Kūṭiyāṭṭam* actors are covered in thick mask-like makeup and speak through mudrā gestures, changing roles, which immediately distances them from any mundane social behavior.

In *Kūṭiyāṭṭam*, *māyā*, often glossed as "illusion," brings us closer to an understanding of how this ritual performance works. *Māyā* is not make-believe; it is not "as if," but a much more profound experiential and transformative power, as *māyā* also implies "deception," "a mysterious power of will," "energy," and a "mental power" (Shāstrī 1911: 8–11). The presence of *māyā* makes it very difficult to discern the constant mirroring of reality, its reflection, and reflection of reflection on stage.

A brief comparison of the way Sax (1990) describes the Rāmlīlā in Ramnagar in northern India, and Schechner and Hess's (1977) remarks on the same event may clarify the difference in the perspectives of *theater* and that of *ritual performance*. Rāmlīlā tells the *Rāmāyaṇa*, and in Ramnagar (near Varanasi) it is performed in a grandiose way, spread out over more than twenty-five square kilometers and lasting thirty-one days. The grand event that draws hundreds of thousands of pilgrims each year, in which the local maharaja holds a central role, also includes spectacular visual artifacts, large effigies, actors, and storytellers (for a detailed description, see Kapur 2006; Lutgendorf 1991).

Schechner and Hess (1977; Schechner 2017) see the Rāmlīlā of Ramnagar as a linear story, from the incarnation of Viṣṇu in Rāma to his coronation as king, all in a straight line, passing through the time spent in the wilderness to the victory in the war against Rāvaṇa. They delineate binary differentiations: sacred and profane, pilgrimage and storytelling, performers and audience, entertainment and ritual, actors and gods, background and foreground, the "real" world, and *līlā*, which they understand as performance. They differentiate between Rāma breaking Siva's bow to earn Sītā's hand in marriage, which is ritual action, and the political action of winning the war against Rāvaṇa, with the result that "Rama absorbs his adversary into himself (cosmic ritual action), affirming the essential indivisibility of existence that is the kernel of Hindu thought" (Schechner and Hess 1977: 54). They remark on standards of good acting, emotionally convincing, well-articulated words, and "flat" acting (1977: 78). Clearly, they do not consider the Rāmlīlā "real" but an "as if" world.

*Līlā*, however, is not equivalent to performance; it "means no 'ordinary' play, no 'ordinary' theater, but communicates the fact of the gods and the divine becoming *activated and manifest in the world*, and thus stands for the intensified *experience* of the divine," perhaps the play of the cosmos (Tambiah 1996: 496, original emphasis;) in other words, "a self-staged divine 'sport' " (Lutgendorf 1991: 5). In contrast to Schechner and Hess, Sax (1990) thinks that the dualism between sacred and profane "is inapplicable to the Rāmlīlā, because in it, boundaries between gods and humans, and between the geographies of text and performance, are blurred or nonexistent. Brahmin boys are transformed into Hindu deities, and so is the maharaja of Banaras, chief patron of the drama" (Sax 1990: 133). Further, the distinctions between the "sacred" and the "profane" realms, and those between "actors" and "audience," are made to collapse by practice. The chief patron and main spectator of the *līlā*, often identified by audience members as an incarnation of the god Śiva, has here become a performer in his own right. Throughout the month-long performance, participants' lives came to be inexorably centered on the *līlā*, and the normal world fades into the background. In the Rāmlīlā of Ramnagar, according to Sax, the *Rāmāyaṇa* is the conquest and cleansing of the entire world, in all directions, through pilgrimage (Sax 1990: 142, 150). For Sax, then, the Rāmlīlā is not built on binary opposition or linearity. It is a transformative living space.

As Grimes (2006) states, theorizing on performance in the framework of ritual: "Any label—'ritual,' 'liturgy,' 'art,' 'dance,' 'music,' 'religion,' or 'drama'—used without qualification to describe a traditional activity would likely be misleading, since the term would segregate a phenomenon that was intended to be deliberately integrative. So, if we are to talk religious activities as rites or performances, our definitions must be broad and provisional rather than restricted to what we in the West usually label 'religion' or 'theater'" (Grimes R. 2006: 379–380). *Kūṭiyāṭṭam* is not theater; it is not ritual, not a mere art form, not "a happening," where the audience is engaged and lives around the artist in temporary settings. It is, however, all these and more. Like the world we live in, *Kūṭiyāṭṭam* opens its own space and then ties its own connections, a bottomless space, that can keep on growing, expanding, falling apart, and then solidifying until it is dismantled.

## The Indian-*Kūṭiyāṭṭam* Body

The potentialities of the human body are at the center of training the actors, the performances, and the world of *Kūṭiyāṭṭam* at large. Sanskrit sources, as well as other Indian practices involving the body such as yoga, dance, and medicine, point to trajectories and cultural dynamics that are at work in *Kūṭiyāṭṭam* as well. Nevertheless, here I take the liberty of extracting the sources from their precise historical, geographical and philosophical context, although they show no direct influence on *Kūṭiyāṭṭam*. My only claim here is that the same dynamics of the body are found both in *Kūṭiyāṭṭam* and in other Indian traditions and, thus, looking at them helps to discern the particular body as nurtured and used in *Kūṭiyāṭṭam* (see also Colas 2003; Coorlawala 2004; Mitra 2006; Alter 2004; van der Veer 2014; Das 2014).

Clearly, there is no quintessential nature of "the Indian body," whether it is understood to be made of different substances from birth depending on caste, according to Dumont, or nurtured through interaction, according to Marriot (Bouillier and Tarabout 2003). Exactly as "Hinduism" is not one unified tradition but is worshiped mainly as different temple traditions, so too the "Indian body" is diverse. Nevertheless, Dumont's and Marriot's contentions, together with Indian scriptures and traditions dealing with the body, enable its potentialities to be discerned, revealing how it is made, what it can do, and what it cannot do.

The human body is at the source of Indian cosmology, and the relations between the human body and the universe depend on the materiality of somaticity itself. Through homology and resonance, the universe is created out of the sacrificed human body, while the body is recursively shaped by the universe. The human body resembles the universe—they are congruent, and the two resonate with each other (Tarabout 2003). According to the Upaniṣad, the world was born out of the sacrifice of the original man, Puruṣa, and everything, including humans and their bodies, sprouted from the parts of his dismembered body.

"He (Ātman) thought to himself, 'Here then are the worlds. Let me now bring forth the guardians of the worlds.' From those very waters, he drew forth and shaped a Man (Puruṣa). He brooded upon him. From him who was thus brooded upon a mouth was separated out, like an egg; from the mouth, speech; from speech, Agni, fire. Nostrils were separated out; from the nostrils, breath; from breath, Vāyu, wind. Eyes were separated out; from the eyes, sight; from sight, Āditya, the sun. Ears were separated out; from the ears, hearing; from hearing, the cardinal directions. Skin was separated out; from the skin, body hair; from body hair, plants and trees. A heart was separated out; from the heart, mind; from the mind, the moon. A navel was separated out; from the navel, the downward breath; from the downward breath, death. A generative organ was separated out; from the generative organ, semen; from semen, the waters" (Aitareya Upaniṣad 1.1.14, in Holdrege 1998: 359).

Puruṣa's sacrifice and dismemberment created things of different orders, large and small, visible and invisible, sentient and inanimate. Skin, hair, and vegetation; eyes, sight, and sun; mouth, speech, and fire; genitalia, semen, waters—all these are connected through reflection, hierarchy, and homology. The body is a multilevel construction, a composite of hierarchically arranged parts that establish homologies among the various types of existence: worlds, gods, time and space, natural elements and forces, animals, plants, psychophysical components, social classes, ritual elements—everything in the world. The body of Puruṣa is an egg, an embryonic potential that includes and interconnects the hierarchically differentiated parts of the body of the cosmos, the human body, and the social body. The three bodies are integral in that each is a complex whole that is inherent in the structure of reality. A system of homologies is thus established among the macrocosmos, which includes both the divine body and the body of the cosmos; the microcosmos, which is the private human body; and the mesocosmos, which is the social body that is the intermediate structure (Holdrege 1998: 355).[21]

Wagner (1991) proposes another way of describing such a complex body. He shows the relations between individual and group in some Melanesian societies to be fractal. The individual is not part, and the group, family, or society are not wholes; rather, a system of the same pattern forms all relations, which operates among persons, groups, and things in the world, and varies in scale alone. According to the Upaniṣad above, relations among things, bodies, and the social also follow a fractal pattern. The egg generates the body, while the body, concomitantly, generates the egg, and these relations are repeated on all levels of the cosmos. The sacrifice of Puruṣa leads to a cosmos that like an egg is inclusive of all potentialities, self-poietic, created by itself.

The human body assumes various modalities to mediate transactions among the divine body, the body of the cosmos, and the social body. The hierarchical relation between those bodies varies in the Indian scriptures, depending on the source and its prime concern, but the principle that Puruṣa's body is differentiated, and that the different parts of the divine *Anthropos* are generative of the world, is maintained. The divine body of Puruṣa is thus celebrated as the paradigmatic ritual body, the body of the sacrifice itself (Holdrege 1998: 348–352; for an overview of the philosophical attitude toward the body in India, see the introduction to Bouillier and Tarabout [2003] in Halliburton 2002).

Thus, the system of relations between the body and the exterior world is organized according to this central notion of sacrifice as well. The parts of the body are not enumerated in correspondence to their anatomical organization but in relation to their dismemberment: a division of a whole that is said to be preliminary. Hence, calling something a "body" means that it is at the same time "one" and "multiple," and that the relations between this oneness and multiplicity are organic (Angot 2003). Such a relation between oneness and multiplicity is repeated on the social plane. Marriot called the South Indian person "dividual" because such a person is inextricably intertwined with others, exchanging both substance and influence with them and with the world (Marriot 1976: 111; see also Babb 1990; Daniel 1984; Ishii 2015a.). The dividual is "one" and "multiple," its sacrificed members being the separate persons who can exist only together in complex interconnectedness.

The main principles at work in the creation, maintenance, and operation of the body in Sanskrit sources are also at work in *Kūṭiyāṭṭam*: reflection, homology, and an inclusive hierarchy.[22]

The principle of reflection is the simple mirror-like reflection of the gods' world in the human world, the body and things-in-the-world, and so on. In other words, the things-in-the-world and their reflection seem the same, and indeed are the same, yet a profound difference is set between them because one is the "real" thing and the other a mere reflection. This distinction, however, is complicated by the constant hesitation as to which is real and which is a chimera. Reflection is also a connection between the spheres of the world. When Puruṣa's body was separated into organs to create the world, each body part fashioned elements within different orders. They generated body organs, castes, materiality, the divine universe, and more, all mirroring each other.

The microcosmos of the body, mesocosmos of the social, and macrocosmos itself are thus linked through reflection and homology. This reflection of the somatic, social, and physical orders of one another is not passive but acts in the world since they are interconnected in a practical way. Moreover, they are homological with one another. Homology is more than just resemblance or congruity; it also entails that since two things share some of their traits, manipulating one may influence another. So, homology can practically be used to encourage a certain result. This is also why manipulating the human body through movement in *Kūṭiyāṭṭam* can, in this fashion, influence the world of the gods (on homology, see Bar-On Cohen 2012).

Inclusive hierarchy assumes that the somatic, social, and material worlds are organized in levels and that each is not only exclusive of the other but also inclusive of the one beneath it—like the laws of purity in the Indian caste system. The laws of purity for Brahmins set the organization of the laws of purity and subsume all other castes beneath it, and the laws of purity for the caste directly beneath the Brahmins subsume those for the caste directly below it, and so on. This is a principle that operates equally in the somatic, social, physical, and divine worlds.

Logically, of course, these two principles are mutually exclusive. Anything can be reflective and have homological traits in common with anything else and can, therefore, create connections and infuse influences between one another, rather like wild weeds (or rhizome in Deleuzian terms). Inclusive hierarchy, on the other hand, stipulates a hard-and-fast order of things that can make connections only according to a certain order. In an exclusive world, the mixing of these two principles would create a paradox, but in this inclusive Indian world, the two live in peace and help each other in creating this complex world, maintaining it and operating within it.

However, the body in Indian thought and practice is not only the noble material of life but also perishable, revolting, and polluting. "In this foul-smelling, unsubstantial body, which is an aggregate of bone, skin, muscle, marrow, flesh, semen, blood, mucus, tears, rheuṃ, feces, urine, wind, bile, and phlegm, what good is the enjoyment of desires? In this body, which is afflicted with desire, anger, greed, delusion, fear, despondency, envy, separation from what is desired, union with what is not desired, hunger, thirst, old age, death, disease, sorrow, and so on, what good is the enjoyment of desires?" (Maitri Upaniṣad 1.3, cf. 3.4 cited in Holdrege 1998: 361).

In *Kūṭiyāṭṭam*, great efforts are invested to keep ritual pollution at bay. Nevertheless, the Vidūṣaka, who brings humanity and "the enjoyment of desires" to a cosmic level, makes use of these foul somatic attributes as a generative force.[23]

The Naṅṅyār actress's body can accompany the dead Agnihotri to his liberation.[24] But it needs to be both of a certain substance and have a particular skill. Only a woman, the daughter of a daughter of a daughter of a Naṅṅyār, whose male ancestors are of the same or a higher group, can perform this feat, provided she has been trained as an actress, has undergone an initiation ceremony, and has married correctly. Thus, both correct birth and interactions are central to what she can do. The *ucci*, the uppermost aperture of the body, homological to Śiva's third eye, is not visible; nevertheless, its use for protection against ritual pollution in *Kūṭiyāṭṭam*—when the actors tie on their headband—does not depend on belief; rather, its efficacy is part of a complex Indian tradition of understanding and healing the body.

Like the living body, the Hindu cosmos, claims Eck, is organic, governed by an organic ontology: It is "by its very nature, living, growing, and divine . . . not an act of fashioning by a creator, but literally a 'pouring forth' from the creator." Growing out of the stuff of itself with no input from its exterior, like a spider spewing threads (Eck 1981: 161), it engenders a whole that is larger than the sum of its components.

## How to Become a *Kūṭiyāṭṭam* Actor

Training as a *Kūṭiyāṭṭam* actor includes physical exercise of the leg and facial muscles, memorizing Sanskrit text, dance steps, chanting intonations, and mudrā gestures. But it does not include teaching the student how to express the moods (*bhāva*), how to act out complex scenes such as battles, how to lift mountains (as Rāvaṇa does), or how to play the chatty and comic Vidūṣaka; this is learned only by imitation, by observing the guru at a performance, so that these essential acting skills stem from the actor's life, mind, and imagination, as it is formed through the physical aspects of training. From work that seems purely technical and somatic, the profound capacities of the actors emerge.

Traditional training, which extends through the entire day, begins by assuming the basic position of *Kūṭiyāṭṭam* for ninety minutes—that is, standing with feet and knees pointing outward, legs bent low, lower back tucked in forcefully, spine aligned, elbows sticking out, and wrists turning round and round, all while chanting *ślokas*. This basic position enables the shoulders to slope, while holding the neck and head straight up without strain, and thus permits great flexibility of the wrists, which can move in any direction. It is a strenuous exercise that combines movement with the Sanskrit text, and with the twenty-four ways of chanting them, according to the emotional tenor of the *ślokas*.

A session in a special Japanese karate training camp is particularly dreaded: maintaining, as a group, a crouching position for an hour and a half. Through this painful exercise, the distinctions between mindful and physical capacities of the body are annihilated to draw mindful or mental power for the physical endeavor; at the same time, boundaries among the participants are undone to allow energy to pass among them and reinforce each other (Bar-On Cohen 2009). At this first *Kūṭiyāṭṭam* training session of the day, a similar process is set into motion, facilitating more than just a strengthening of the body and preparing it for the performance. The discipline and challenge presented by the painful body position help overcome boundaries both within one person and among people and yield more than just physical stamina.

During the evening session of a traditional training day, the trainees learn to recite the *Rāmāyaṇa saṃkṣepam*, an abbreviated version of the *Rāmāyaṇa*, which includes mudrā gestures followed by eye movement, and thus learn all the words necessary for *Kūṭiyāṭṭam*. The *Rāmāyaṇa saṃkṣepam* is repeated day after day for years, becoming so natural and familiar to the actor that it is part of their body, like standing or eating—part of who they are. Watching experienced actors like Madhu repeat it is hypnotic; something embedded deep within them surfaces and allows us to see it.

The mudrā gestures, learned by repeating the *Rāmāyaṇa saṃkṣepam*, can be performed in different intonations and accentuations, exactly like vocalizing words; they can be performed in a calm and leisurely manner, in an abrupt commanding or angry one, or they can become limp and express soft and erotic emotions.[25] Moreover, mudrā can express the hierarchical relations between the protagonists: the character to the actor's right is always his senior, so he or she will express more submissively than when addressing a character to his left. The mudrā gestures are connected to one another the way spoken words are, including grammar. Each movement is articulated distinctly, so that the hands reach their destination perfectly, accentuated by eye movement, yet flowing into one another without stops or disjunction. Thus, the mudrā words have a large repertoire of meaning, emotional timbre, rhythm, and expressivity.

Some words in mudrās gestures are reminiscent of the object they bring to life; these gestures are imitative, directly illustrating their meaning. The mudrā gesture for a deer, for instance, is the lifting of the index finger and pinkie to depict the horns, while the two other fingers curve toward the thumb to create a head. The mudrā gestures for fish swimming, birds pecking, humans drinking, and other mundane actions are all stylistically imitated by the hands. Other mudrās have lost their association with the things they denote. The difference between a mudrā word and a spoken one resembles the difference between phonetic letters and ideograms. While the phonetic letter is utterly abstract and devoid of intrinsic meaning, an ideogram such as the Sino-Japanese ideogram includes layers of meaning that are combinations of stylized depictions of objects. A multifaceted relation is woven between form, function, and meaning, between idea and picture, and due to the complexity, which has built up over generations, the meaning can no longer be intuited and must be painstakingly memorized. Mudrā words have also gathered a complexity that distances them from an intuitive understanding of their meaning and must be learned; they are not, however, abstractions, as they always maintain their connectivity to things in the world. Mudrā gestures are not sounds to be interpreted but rather are acts in the world.[26] Through the mudrās, *Kūṭiyāṭṭam* indulges in a myriad of details, yielding a rich, livable world. The mudrā can generate anything at all—no props are needed.

## A *Kūṭiyāṭṭam* Performance

My experience of observing and analyzing body practices in Japanese martial arts contributed to the understanding of the somatic workings of *Kūṭiyāṭṭam*, both the practical ways of using the body to achieve certain qualities of movement and the choice of cultural tools that generate a fluid reality. However, there are profound differences between the two bodies.[27] The main difference concerns sparseness, which is the mark of mastery in many traditional Japanese cultural events where redundancy is avoided. In Kerala, on the other hand, the potentialities of redundancy are exploited to the fullest. The Japanese movements, both in martial arts, in Noh theater, and more, are strict and aim at the most economical movement; no emotional expression is allowed, and any excess, any ornamentation, or futile movement is discarded, generating a very different attitude toward beauty, emotion, and mastery. In Japanese traditions, Occam's razor is a highly valued mark of elegance. Consider a Haiku: such rigid formal limitations enable a world to be encompassed in 11 syllables, generating a dynamic of intensity.

In *Kūṭiyāṭṭam*, movement is intensely abundant, a rounded flow of smooth gestures lush with embellishments, facial expressions, and endless imaginative supplements, as an overload of presence is the generative force of this world. This is why the movements of the actor did not seem sharp enough to me at first; he seemed to be strolling along from one mudrā to the next, without accentuation, using the body in a soft flow, in a consistency of movement that mirrors the undulations of speech where the flow itself is expressive.

In writing about Amerindian shamans, Viveiros de Castro said that the animal skins they use "to travel the cosmos, not as fantasies but instruments . . . are akin to diving equipment, or space suits, and not to carnival masks" (1998: 482). In the same way, the costume make-up and mudrā gestures of the *Kūṭiyāṭṭam* actors are instruments of the journey, of the potentiality of becoming the protagonists they are playing, and also of the potentiality of exchanging roles.

The actors begin preparations for a performance by putting on a red headband while saying a short prayer, then applying a foundation color, spreading it from five starting points. For most roles, the actor is completely covered with make-up during a performance, even the palms of his hands. The foundation color on the face depends on the role they are to play; heroes are green, monkeys are pink, while demons are red or black.[28] On top of the foundation color, black lines are added. The actor's eyes and lips are covered with thick black lines, and lines are also painted across the forehead and nose. Then the make-up artist affixes approximately one hundred tiny balls of cotton to the black lines on the face of the actor, embodying monkeys, or carefully glues white paper cuttings to the actor's face as a stylized beard. Nothing is ever affixed to an actress's face; hers is always an elegant make-up with a pink foundation color, red lips, and delicate black-and-white decorations. It takes over an hour to apply make-up to yield a mask-like face.

Once the make-up is ready, the actor twists his dhoti into pants and, with the help of others, puts on the rest of his heavy and cumbersome costume, which is uncomfortably hot in the Kerala weather, and then secures his hat and crown. Last, to redden his eyes, the actor puts flower seeds in them after they have been softened by wetting them and rubbing them between the fingers. Make-up and costume are worn only during the performance itself, so that the actor dons them for the first time at his or her *araṅṅēṟṟam* initiation performance. The main color on stage is white. The shirtless drummers wear white dhotis, the Naṅṅyār wears a white Kerala sari with colored borders, and the actors' costume is white with gilded ornaments and two stripes, black and red, at the bottom of his skirt. In the light of the flickering lamp, the white and gold colors stand out.

One morning, before class began, Madhu was coaching Misha, a New York playwright and actor. Misha wanted to insert *Kūṭiyāṭṭam*-style movements in his own plays and was showing Madhu what he intended to do. While Misha's difficulty and stress were evident, and he clearly seemed to be suffering, Madhu entreated him to "enjoy." One of the secrets of *Kūṭiyāṭṭam* is that the actor "enjoys." The actor in *Kūṭiyāṭṭam* always enters the stage in a good mood (Enros Pragna 1981: 279). He comes on stage with a slight smile, because if the hardships of acting were visible, it would be a barrier to imagination, the body would assert itself over the story, poking holes in the world pouring from the stage, interfering with the flow.

The drumming is not fixed but recursive—it adapts to the actor, just as the actor adapts to its sound; the abstract beat, and especially the mix of beats created by the three drums, opens space and duration. The stage is empty, to be filled with the objects and entities created in mudrā gestures; there is only a stool for the actor to sit or stand on, which can be moved aside to create empty space for the actor to move and jump in.

Only twice did I see an actor seriously distracted and his movements interrupted, generating an obstruction to the smooth flow. Actors who play demons often have fangs in their mouths, which they display when the demon becomes fierce. On one occasion, the fangs disturbed the actor, and he repeatedly moved them around in his mouth. On another night, an actor injured his leg while jumping, became confused, and lost concentration, his mouth going limp and his distress clearly showing. Although he went through the entire text with the mudrā gestures, he did so quickly, with no elaboration, and without fully enacting the scenes. These instances only accentuated the immense achievement of each night's performance when the actor has a slight smile on his face and appears to be enjoying his strenuous activity.

As the story unfolds, the actors' hands move up and down, whirling round and round in front of their bodies while their accentuated eyes either follow the hand movements or go off on their own trajectory to comment on what the hands are saying. The story unfolds carried by the drumbeat that fills the air, the lungs, rerouting the heartbeat, ushering all into a place where nothing is devoid of rhythm and the drum's intensity guides the emotional tone of the performance while recursively following the actors' lead. All tell the story through movement while enacting it, agitating it into life, until it is fully present.

## *Kūṭiyāṭṭam,* Ritual, and the Force of Vision

Continuous, organic, unbounded, inclusive, and based on movement are "central to Hindu cosmology" (Sax 1990: 136–138), in which the gods are coaxed into many manifestations at one and the same time. They can be embodied in solid objects, such as rocks or figures that serve as *mūrti* (a venerated image); a mound of kitchen turmeric can be a goddess (Burkhalter Flueckiger 2013); on Fridays, the goddess Lakṣmi inhabits a Tulsi plant (a sort of basil); and humans can become the gods, as do the *svarūpas* for the Rāmlīlā of Banares (Schechner and Hess 1977; Sax 1990; Kapur 2006). Access to these deities as living, seen entities is often embodied, intimate, and unmediated (on the various manifestations of the gods and goddesses in India, see McDaniel 2004; Tarabout 2011).[29]

In *Kūṭiyāṭṭam,* too, the gods manifest in various forms at once. Lakṣmaṇa, Rāma's loyal brother, is the main god in the Moozhikkulam temple, where he is the *mūrti* in the temple sanctum; and when Lakṣmaṇa cuts off the demoness Śūrpaṇākhā's breasts and nose,[30] the god can mutilate the demoness by the hands of his temple priest. The actor performing is also Lakṣmaṇa, and the stage itself is a god; the gods are also the wicks of the three-wicked lamp; and the actors invoke the gods through *kriyā* (invocative steps), chanting, and drumming. The *Kūttambalam* is a god, and, like a temple, is constructed to strict specifications; on the first night of the performance, an overloaded bale of rice, banana, and coconut branches are positioned at the front and sides of the stage as offerings.

*Kūṭiyāṭṭam* developed to a great extent within temple grounds (see Margi 2015; on the history of *Kūṭiyāṭṭam,* see Rajendran 2012),[31] and by the beginning of the twentieth century, it was performed exclusively at temples, after the daily duties in honor of the temple's chief deity were completed and in the god's presence.

In the past, temple performances would last until dawn; today they last only a few hours. Moreover, a temple performance takes fewer days to enact than the same performance outside the temple and thus includes fewer elaborations. There are three types of temple performances: "Performances that are part of a temple festival, performances that are made as votive offerings, and performances that were designed to entertain the public" (Margi 2015: 3). Temple *Kūṭiyāṭṭam* could be part of the yearly calendar of worship—such as the Naṅṅyār actress telling Kṛṣṇa's story at a Kṛṣṇa temple on the god's birthday—or commissioned as a private sacrifice, when a family, usually a Nampūdiri Brahmin, pays for a particular request. Certain *Kūṭiyāṭṭam* plays are more propitious for certain requests from the gods, such as the birth of a male child, success in a lawsuit, prosperity, retrieving of a lost object, or more generally removing obstacles. In addition, a performance may be commissioned as part of the initiation of a Nampūdiri boy presented to the gods for the first time. Since the uninitiated young boy is not yet a Nampūdiri before his initiation, he is brought to the temple by a Cākyār and not by his own father (Richmond and Richmond 1985: 51; Sullivan 1997: 100–101).[32]

A *Kūṭiyāṭṭam* performance is a sacrifice ritual, a cycle of construction and destruction, since the world of the play is formed and set into motion in great detail on the first night, tied together between the evenings,[33] ultimately dismantled at the end of the last evening and offered as a sacrifice. When performed at temples, *Kūṭiyāṭṭam* is *darśan* (Eck 1989), "eye sacrifice" or "visual sacrifice"; (*cākṣuṣayajña*) seeing the gods is central to Indian temple rituals, as the gods must see the worshipers and the devotees must see the deities. Thus, temple *Kūṭiyāṭṭam* is not meant solely for the audience to observe but also to please and entertain the gods, and since the stories tell of the gods' lives, they also remind the gods of their own biographies, powers, and trajectories.[34]

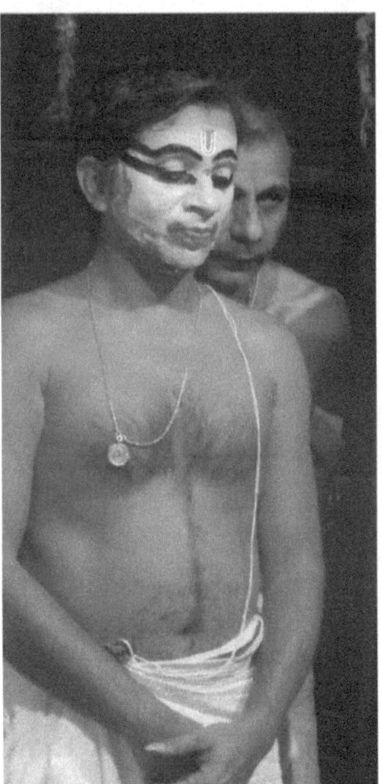

Figure 1.5. Maduh Chakyar after the last day of performance taking his head-gear off. Author photo.

The performance is also a "fire sacrifice," and that is why part of the costume is burned at the end of the performance, and all elements of the costume made for a specific performance are burned at the end of the final night. At the conclusion of the *Cūṭala-k-kūttu*, the Naṅṅyār actress's entire costume is burned.[35]

The *Kūṭiyāṭṭam* performance within temple grounds has remained essentially unchanged by modern conditions. *Kūṭiyāṭṭam* is still part of the yearly cycle of rituals in some temples, where only the matrilinear Cākyārs and Nambyārs may perform;[36] moreover, only members of a certain lineage within these families hold the right to perform at certain temples.[37] The performers as well as the spectators at the temple are expected to take a ritual bath before coming to the temple (Richmond 1990). Other restrictions that must be observed apply to the artists as well as to anyone else—for example, menstruating women and persons in mourning are forbidden from entering the temple or performing there (on menstruation and temples in Kerala, see Dinesan 2019).

Some taboos that apply to performances at the temple are also observed at the Nepathya performance outside the temple. As noted, the dressing room is treated like a temple; the *miḻāvu* drums, which only the drummers are allowed to touch, are not taken outside; and the *iṭakka,* the hour-glass drum that is hung on the drummer's side, must never touch the ground. Other temple-related taboos, however, are not observed. Some actors are not members of the traditional families, performances by menstruating women are permitted, and the requirement of a ritual purification bath is not followed in full.

During the building of the temple *Kūttambalam*, just as in the construction of the temple itself, a complex set of ritualistic processes must be followed. The positioning, construction, and consecration of the *Kūttambalam* are protracted and elaborate and must comply with multiple principles, dimensions, and directions, including the placement of seeds, precious metals, and stones at its foundation; purification is carried out with mustard seeds, cow dung water, incense, and other elements. Since the *Kūttambalam* itself is a god, part of the process of its construction consists of transforming it into a mirror, which is then immersed in water. This ritualistically destroys the *Kūttambalam* that was built by men, only to have it appear again, this time generated by the gods. The stage on which the dances are performed is considered to be the bull Nandi, the vehicle of Śiva since the god has danced on Nandi's back (Rajagopalan 1987). Also, defining the space of the temple, or *Kūttambalam*, corresponds to the reenactment of the original sacrifice of Puruṣa, the human creator of the world, which is at the same time both construction and destruction (Richmond and Richmond 1985: 52; Timalsina 2009; see also Michell 1988, especially 60–76; on Kerala Hindu temples, see Noble 1981). The presence of the gods is multiplied (on different aspects of a god's manifestations, see Tarabout 2011).

The meticulous ordering of space and the expulsion of any potential pollution permits the involuted, and at times subversive, world of the performance to come to life. Hence, great care must be taken to ensure that this space is protected since a space that lures and coaxes so much of the deities' manifestations is also highly susceptible to ritual pollution. Due to the proximity to divine forces, the stage becomes a site of lurking danger, and a slight mishap can have serious consequences. If the actor's crown falls, or if the actor removes his headdress in the middle of the play, the performance is immediately stopped, as the *Kūttambalam* has become impure. In some of the plays, if the actor makes so much as one mistake, a member of his family may die.

Both the Moozhikkulam temple and the Nepathya *Kūttambalam* down the street are of precisely the same measurements, form, and orientation; in the temple, however, the stage stands at the same level as the image of Lakṣmaṇa in the interior *sanctum*. When *Kūṭiyāṭṭam* is performed at the temple, the doors of the inner sanctum are opened so that the performance is held in the presence of the god. The drummers, in their roles as temple assistants, bring the fire from the sanctum, from the lamp of the god, to light the stage lamp. And on the last night of *Aṅgulīyāṅkam*,[38] when Hanūman has come fully into himself, the Cākyār, who is now the deity, is transported by several men into the sanctum where he is left with the god before returning to the *Kūttambalam* to dismantle the world that was created during the many consecutive nights of performance.

*Kūṭiyāṭṭam* is performed in the *Kūttambalam* for the audience, for the gods, and at times perhaps for the actor himself. When asked, Madhu often says he would perform *Kūṭiyāṭṭam* even without an audience. What does Madhu mean by that? I have no definite answer except to say that performing *Kūṭiyāṭṭam* is a personal pleasure, a fulfillment, a devotional act. More than that, making a world and sustaining it is a feat not easily accomplished; and once an actor has done so, perhaps he is drawn to the feeling of participation in the world's creation and mastery.

On the last night of the *Aṅgulīyāṅkam*, Madhu did just that. He performed for eight hours without an audience. Although most members of the audience were already asleep in the chairs and on the floor, he completed everything he needed to accomplish that night, without speeding up or omitting elaborations.

To actualize its world (both in the temple and outside of it), *Kūṭiyāṭṭam* employs cultural dynamics common to the performance and temple ritual. Narayanan (2006, 2022) warns against the tendency to see *Kūṭiyāṭṭam* merely in ritualistic terms, neglecting the aesthetic aspects.[39] But there is no contradiction between ritual and aesthetic, and it is precisely the ritual aesthetic that permits the smooth world of *Kūṭiyāṭṭam* to function. That same aesthetic—namely, the correct manner by which to attain sensation, emotion, and affect—is followed by *Kūṭiyāṭṭam* both in the temple and outside. More specifically, *Kūṭiyāṭṭam* is akin to ritual in its transformative capacities, in its choice of practices and dynamics, creating a complex and multilayered continuous cosmos, one that comes into existence in intimate connectivity with the world we usually live in. *Kūṭiyāṭṭam* employs ritualistic practices of transformativeness to generate connectivities between domains and levels of the world while collapsing time, as past, present, and duration are compressed and torqued together.

The entire setting, including the layers of ritualized action that went into the building of the *Kūttambalam*, the god watching from his sanctum, the dances and gestures, the multiplicity of viewpoints of all the entities watching the play or participating in it, the enhanced potentiality of vision—all are tools of generating a world.

## Chapter 2

# The World of Hanūman

## Creating a Fluid Cosmos on a *Kūṭiyāṭṭam* Stage[1]

The *Aṅgulīyāṅkam* propels the affects of *Kūṭiyāṭṭam* to their utmost. With its long nights of endless iterations, role changing, and repetitions by only a single actor on stage for many hours and days, it germinates the *Rāmāyaṇa* itself. The *Aṅgulīyāṅkam* does not merely take us back to the mythical time in which the *Rāmāyaṇa* originally took place but actually makes it happen now. All Hanūman, the monkey messenger, needs to do is hand Sītā, imprisoned by Rāvaṇa, the wondrous jewel (the *Aṅgulīyāṅkam*) sent by her husband Rāma—a jewel that can reveal *māyā*, the ability to discern true reality from magical impersonation. But in order to perform this simple gesture, he seems to have to painstakingly recreate all the realities that must be told apart. He is toiling hard, retelling over and over again all the events in which Sītā and her family could not tell different realities apart and fell prey to *māyā*, the stories that brought the protagonists of the *Rāmāyaṇa* to the point where they are now. Hanūman tries to convince Sītā not to despair, that help is on the way, beating down resistances, tiring them out, eliminating old connections to allow new ones, while carrying along everyone in the *Kūttambalam* until a world is revealed that includes everything necessary to live in—only then can he deliver the jewel to Sītā. Meanwhile, the reality on stage settles alongside mundane reality, and the two are more and more difficult to tell apart.

In August 2012, in Moozhikkulam, the *Aṅgulīyāṅkam* was performed for twenty-eight nights by a single actor. Although the *Aṅgulīyāṅkam*—the sixth act of the play *Āścaryacūḍāmaṇi*, "The Wondrous Head-Jewel,"[2] by the ninth-century Sanskrit drāmatist Śaktibhadra—comprises only a few pages, it took three to four hours each of the twenty-eight consecutive nights to perform in its entirety. The actor is dressed as Hanūman in a white furry shirt with a tail sticking out at the back, white cotton balls are glued on his pink-colored cheeks and nose, his eyes are accentuated by the make-up and dyed red. He becomes one protagonist after another: storyteller, human women and men, animals, demons and gods, as well as a peacock feather, hair, and more. Everything on stage, including objects, becomes sentient. Following the *āṭṭa-prakāram*, the manual for this performance, the episodes of the great Sanskrit epic the *Rāmāyaṇa* unfold, infold, repeat themselves, skipping, moving forward and backward to intersect, elaborate, parallel, and traverse one another, picking up speed when the actor paces through the entire *Rāmāyaṇa* in forty minutes, then slowing down to a near halt, exposing a short moment of lust, for three nights in a row.

Figure 2.1. Madhu Chakyar as Hanūman. *Source*: photo by Sarah Zweig, Nepathya Centre for Excellence.

As the many hours of movement go by—leaping from one modality of expression to another, mudrā gestures, chanting by the Naṅṅyār, acting the scene—the single actor is transported, as well as the audience,. The mind, muscles, eyes, imagination, ears, and sensation lose their distinct functions, melting into one another. On- and off-stage can no longer be discerned. The Aśōka garden, where demon king Rāvaṇa keeps Sītā imprisoned, and where the entire act takes place, becomes intermingled with the monsoon rain beating hard on the theater's roof, with the bats zooming in to eat the bananas attached to the columns of the stage, thus adding to the movement on stage. As the many hours and nights go by, separations between distinct selves are eroded as well—between the actor, the deity Hanūman (see Lutgendorf 2007), the spectators, and the other protagonists; all separations are systematically disintegrated to allow an unobstructed flow of energies, powers, emotions, and events.

Only rarely is the *Aṅgulīyāṅkam* performed in full length on twenty-eight consecutive nights; it is more often presented in temples in a shorter, twelve-night version. Neither Madhu, who currently performs most evenings, nor his gurus—his late father and late uncle—performed the entire act on twenty-eight consecutive nights, nor did the generation before them. Although thoroughly documented, this twenty-eight-night version was not performed by this family for a least three generations. They did perform the entire long version of the seven-act *Āścaryacūḍāmaṇi* about ten years ago, once a week, over a two-year period, so the *Aṅgulīyāṅkam* alone took more than six months to perform. The full twenty-eight-night performance is very demanding for actors and audience alike, and naturally is expensive. The *Aṅgulīyāṅkam* is considered the most difficult role for an actor, as, alone on stage, he must remember many verses of text. Nevertheless, although rare, the full twenty-eight-night performance is not extinct; concomitantly with the performance documented here, another family of actors was performing the sixth act on twenty-eight nights privately in honor of their deceased father, although they performed it at a slightly quicker pace.

Since the *Aṅgulīyāṅkam* is performed by a single actor, Madhu invited other actors to share the load with him on alternate nights. The three young Nepathya students also played one night each, so that several different actors carried the burden, dividing the evenings among them. In this way, although Hanūman went on stage every night, wearing the same costume and make-up, it was not the same actor each time.

The audience consisted of professors and students from Germany and Israel as well as from India, some students of *Kūṭiyāṭṭam* from other parts of Kerala, families of the performers, and a few neighbors who would drop by for an hour or two. The foreign audience's understanding of the *Aṅgulīyāṅkam* was enhanced by morning classes taught by Madhu in the small *Kūttambalam* on the top floor of the family home. During the classes, Madhu—fresh from his morning ablutions, adorned with stripes of rice paste from the nearby Lakṣmaṇa temple on his arms, shoulders, and forehead—would read the text of that evening's performance in Malayalam, one of the participants would translate it into English, and then Madhu would perform the text in mudrā gestures. We could also follow a handout of the abbreviated text in English. The morning classes presented an occasion to encourage Madhu to share with us some of his extensive knowledge and experience.

## Hanūman on the Stage

A single actor, dressed and made-up as a monkey, dominates the center stage. In front of him stands an oil lamp with three wicks, and behind him, three bare-chested drummers. Two seated drummers play the large *miḻāvu* drums; another one stands and plays an *iṭakka*, an hour-glass drum. On the left of the stage sits the Naṅṅyār, the female actress, dressed in an off-white Kerala sari; she plays the cymbal and chants the *śloka* (the Sanskrit poetry lines) from time to time. On the first night, great care was taken to entice the gods to be present at the performance and to ensure its success with *kriyā* and setting into place all the creatures of the three worlds, and then offering the freshly created flowers to the gods. The gods are invited through Sanskrit chants of praise and by a careful description of the alluring and amazing physical features of Śiva and Pārvatī. Smiling, the actor takes three steps forward and three steps back, to the constant enthralling cadence of the drums, each time describing the gods' glorious body parts from head to feet. As he constructs—unveils, summons—this world immediately begins to vibrate. After each evening's performance, the world is tied into place to await its reawakening the following evening.[3] At the end of the entire act, on the twenty-eighth night, after taking off Hanūman's hat, the actor prostrates himself on stage in the direction of Lakṣmaṇa in the sanctum of the nearby temple, extinguishing the fire to take this world apart.

In the sixth act of *Āścaryacūḍāmaṇi,* the actor utters no words; in fact, he seldom emits a sound. In other plays and other acts of the *Āścaryacūḍāmaṇi,* the actor would chant the *śloka* in Sanskrit.[4] Here, however, when he does utter sounds or words, it comes as a surprise, since, except for a few *ślokas* and random fierce cries in battle scenes, he is always silent. The stories are rendered through the flow of mudrā hand gestures, elegant faces, and body movements: sitting on the stool, getting up, walking, standing on the stool, turning, jumping, dancing.

At times Hanūman stops, and with a slight smile, he nods, listening to someone else talking—another protagonist on stage, someone we, the audience, can neither see nor hear. Perhaps he is listening to himself as another entity talking to him while he listens, so that not only does the actor change persona but also splits into two or more entities and then fuses them all into one again. He is creating, grooming, materializing out of himself a world from a myriad of viewpoints and perspectives, each contributing their part to its vitality and elaboration. The drums' rhythm and timbre, the "vital force" or "intensity" (Groesbeck 2003: 41) of sound, follow the mood of the acting and concomitantly generate the emotional hue. A feedback loop is generated between the actor and the drums, sustaining one another. The drums are the first to assault, engulf, draw the audience in, leaving no place empty of rhythm. At times, the drum rolls are deafening and war-like; at other times, they are delicate, imitating water or a horse's gallop, and then they may become even softer, lyrical, with only a hint of rhythm—whining, whispering, screeching. The drums heat the atmosphere into a rush of blood, and when they stop, as the Naṅṅyār chants the *śloka,* the mood cools down to neutral.

After the twenty-second day's performance, I could not sleep, and when I did fall asleep, I was pestered by distressing dreams. Other members of the audience were also reliving traumatic life experiences during and after the performance, and then on the following nights, as the performance unfolded, amid the incessant, deafening beat of the drums, I began to feel irresistibly drowsy, as did others. The complex rhythms of the drums penetrate to become part of oneself. The actors themselves tell of changes in their mode of consciousness on-stage, and during the entire period of the play, which persists after the performance is over. It takes about twenty minutes, they say, to get deep into this special mode, to leave their ordinary selves outside the dressing room. Then they live within the cosmos that emerges from their own imagination, as well as from the work of imagination inherited from former generations of *Kūṭiyāṭṭam* performers. Fully within the play, they can perform ordinary tasks on-stage, such as chewing betel nuts, playing music, and sleeping, and also accomplish extraordinary feats. They can lift mountains, travel in celestial chariots, fight heroic battles, wear jewels that can reveal *māyā*, and become small enough to hide inside a tree, as does Hanūman during the entire act.

*Kūṭiyāṭṭam* arouses profound and unusual reactions from everybody; the incessant drum renders everything permeable. They blend stimuli that enter through the senses while these realities become more familiar as time goes by and settle themselves alongside mundane life off-stage, not quite replacing it, but asserting its presence nonetheless, until we live within that world, our everyday actuality becoming merely a fragment of the vast cosmos emerging on stage, night after night.

David Shulman testifies to the overpowering affect of *Kūṭiyāṭṭam*, saying, "I have found from my own experience that in the course of watching a play spread out over more than two weeks, some three to five hours each night, the intervening hours of daytime 'normalcy' seemed to exist only by virtue of the far more integral, intensified hours of performance. The latter was, to me, real in a sense quite different from that of my daytime reality" (2012: 17). Everyone present undergoes intense changes, yet they are not fully transformed nor entranced, all keeping their connectivity to everyday life.

The cosmos of the play is more homogeneous and concentrated; it gradually becomes more vivid and absorbing, less haphazard than the world we ordinarily live in. Further, there is no difference in kind between the two worlds—both are fully present, looping into one another. The actor "may describe events that peel back the physical veil to reveal another, more mystical reality that was always there but not recognized" (O'Flaherty 1984: 3).

This potentiality of *Kūṭiyāṭṭam* stems, first and foremost, from movement—the motility of every possible facial, hand, and body muscle, of the flame, and the calfskin tightened over the drums—motility overwhelms and overtakes everything. Words, especially, are communicated in movement and perceived through vision instead of sound, not uttered but delivered in hand gestures, via the finger arrangements of mudrās that are made around the center of the actor's body, always on their smooth way to the next mudrā, drawing circular hand motions around the body, looping in and out, flowing from exclamation to hesitation, from question to answer. Mudrā gestures take words out of the mere cerebral abstract into the actual; they remold time, as speaking through mudrā slows down utterance and becomes a duration of *doing* concomitant with the time of *expressing*. Embedded in movement instead of voice, words are disengaged from speech, and the power of words—their concise capacity to generate connections in a holistic, virtual way—is engaged in creating an actuality.

Within the special structure of the *Kūttambalam*, the events of *the Rāmāyaṇa* flow into and out of each other, the incessant movement as sight replaces sound—all these powerfully draw the actor and everyone else present into a different mode of consciousness absorbed in this emerging world, without drowning in it. The actor exteriorizes the world of the play from within himself, his body, and his trained imagination. He exteriorizes the footprints left by his ancestors, by past generations of actors, as noted in the *āṭṭa-prakāram* manual, but also as imprinted on his body since childhood through long, intense, and painful training. He inhales over time and then exhales on-stage the layers of the complex traditions embedded in *Kūṭiyāṭṭam,* and what is more, the actor also externalizes the audience as part of the emerging world. As he comes to include everything present, the actor is a dynamic conduit generating this rich, live world, the story, the monkey messenger—all are part of him, part of this interpenetrating whole.

## The Performance

The *Kūttambalam* is mostly open to the elements, the stage is slightly elevated, and the two pillars in front are decorated with offerings of banana leaves and fruit. Upon entering the *Kūttambalam,* the audience can clearly hear the frogs, night birds, monsoon rains, and large bats flying in and out. The small opening at the top of the brass *miḻāvu* drums is covered in calfskin or black monkey skin (Pacciolla 2022). Since they are large and round, and must not touch the ground, they need a wooden lattice structure to stabilize and hold them, and the drummer sits on a folding ledge attached to the wooden structure, the drum between his legs. If the calfskin loosens during a performance, two men replace the drum, and after the performance, three men are needed to tighten the slack skin on the original drum.

Each night at dusk, one of the boys lights the lamps, the conch is blown, and a single drummer plays for a few minutes, waiting for the actor to appear. Hanūman enters at a slow pace, his hands covering his face, the conch is blown a second time, and with his back to the audience the actor begins to perform *kriyā;* he then turns to reveal his face, rolling his eyes to the rhythm of the drums, lifting and lowering his eyebrows to introduce Hanūman. The actor then sits on the stool and delivers a synopsis, describing the events that happened over the previous five acts. He moves his hands slowly, each word clearly outlined, and pauses from time to time in the pose of the storyteller. Only after this long introduction can the story continue from whatever point it reached the night before.

*Kūṭiyāṭṭam* often involves more actors on the stage, including actresses, and the actors chant their parts in Sanskrit in dialogue. The sixth act of *Āścaryacūḍāmaṇi,* however, is more complex in its simplicity, since Hanūman is alone on stage, and nearly all the Sanskrit text is chanted by the Naṅṅyār. The changing characters depend entirely on the actor's skill rather than on costume or make-up. Indeed, Hanūman is appropriate for changing into others; he is a malleable character, hesitant, unaware of his strengths and capabilities. He can become very small and fit into a tree, or enormous enough to cross the waters to Lanka in one leap, and he goes through these changes in form and mood, forgetting who he is and what he is capable of, throughout the twenty-eight nights.

By opening the hand, folding the fingers, alternating between bent and flexed fingers, twenty-four distinct gestures are formed—the mudrās. The mudrās are used in rituals to concentrate the power of the gods so that the person performing the ritual can make contact with the divine (Michell 1988: 63). The twenty-four mudrā gestures can be combined to make any number of mudrā words. During a performance, both hands can assume the same mudrā, or each can fold into a different one to yield many combinations that include both words and grammatical indications such as plurals,[5] negatives, prepositions, and questions.

The actor's hands coil from one mudrā word to the next, taking different routes and forms, settling down on his lap for a leisurely instant, bending this finger and another, fluttering like butterflies, moving in unison, then parting each to its own meandering way, piercing the air with determination, as one hand carefully comes to embrace the other, followed by one hand traveling to a faraway place near the ears in a dismissive gesture of negation. The hands are two lively creatures, yet they always curve back to the center of the body, between the naval and the neck, coming home after their adventures, bringing their deeds back inside.

The mudrā words also differ from each other in the trajectories of the hand: from the palm or the back of the hand turned toward the audience, or palms held parallel to each other, pushing forward, rotating, shivering, or galloping in a smooth and elegant dance. Although demanding special agility to perform the mudrās, the hands are never forced into a stressed, unnatural position or extension, so that the small, perfectly accentuated positioning of the fingers whirl into the delicate hand movements. Mudrā words have a large repertoire of meaning, emotional timbre, rhythm, and expressivity. Each word can also absorb a different mood or intonations by being performed either softly or with a determined dynamic. The mudrā words are connected to one another the way spoken words are, each one articulated distinctly so that the hands reach their destination in a perfectly visible, accentuated, and lucid way, yet flowing into one another without stops or disjunction.

Meanwhile, the eyebrows jump nimbly up and down, the lips smile slightly with enjoyment, always controlled, always a little tightened. And the eyes closely follow the intricate dance of the hands. They are inquisitive, understanding, interpretative—moving to one side and then to the other, moving up and down, and in perfect circles; however, like a dancing partner, the eyes do not simply mimic the hands but also follow their own independent trajectory, associated with the hands but independent of them, discovering their own feelings. Accentuated by the red dye, shining, they go on their way, looking outward to the hands and inward to the world opening from within the actor onto the stage. The muscles around the eyes can make the eyeballs spin in the smallest of curves, in synchrony with the larger axis of the curve of the hands, the body, and the entire world, the circular movement maximizing the tininess of their curvatures.

Over the hours of the performance, night after night, all succumb to the performance until the movement on stage becomes internal. Everything is suddenly happening within oneself and, it seems, will continue to enter even if your eyes are closed. The movement of sound and body no longer penetrates through the eyes, ears, or even the vibration of the skin alone but becomes totally pervasive and internalized. As the nights unfold, the bodies of the artists and the spectators lose the distinctions between the separate ways of assembling information; the senses are blurred until the beating of the drums is seen, and the movement of the actor is felt as emanating from within one's own body.

## States of Consciousness

Trance and possession in the Tamil Nadu theater of *Kuṭṭaikkūttu* and *Teyyam* ritual performances of Northern Kerala are very different in nature to *Kūṭiyāṭṭam*. In *Teyyam*, the actor is possessed by a certain deity before the dancing starts (Freeman 2006; see also Dinesan 2009).[6] In the Tamil *Kuṭṭaikkūttu*, the actor is not always in a trance and will try to avoid possession but, while possessed because of overheating, the actor—or even a member of the audience—loses consciousness and may assault someone (De Bruin 2006; on possession in a ritual/performance in Orissa, see Emigh 1996: 35–60).

In Kerala, a person is possessed through the body's orifices, the higher deities entering through the higher orifices while the lower, more troublesome deities, demons, and spirits enter through the lower orifices. The highest orifice is the *ucci*, which is at the front of the cranium (where a baby's fontanel is situated). Members of higher castes, such as Brahmins and aristocratic Nayars, avoid possession; it is even deemed shameful for a Brahmin to be possessed (Osella and Osella 1999; see also Osella and Osella 1996, particularly note 38 on p. 205). *Kūṭiyāṭṭam* certainly pertains to the higher strata of Kerala traditional society, including the Brahmin Nampūdiris, who are the traditional patrons of this art; the twice-born Cākyārs; and the Nambyārs, who are part of the elite. Correspondingly, it is the *ucci* that plays a central role in *Kūṭiyāṭṭam*: the jewel transported by Hanūman in this play is a head ornament probably worn on the *ucci*. More generally, the actor is separated from his mundane existence to become impervious to ritual pollution, donning the headband that covers the *ucci*. In *Kūṭiyāṭṭam*, the actor is not in a trance but is in full control of his actions, yet he is performing somewhere else as someone other than himself. The difference between the two traditions stems from different relations created between realities. Whereas in the Tamil *Kuṭṭaikkūttu*, everyday reality is contrasted to the reality of the play, and the actor travels between the two and sometimes gets caught up in the reality of the play and loses his way back, in *Kūṭiyāṭṭam*, an entire world is built within the interior of the actor (Gopalakrishnan 2006: 140), and in this world the actor lives, entering and exiting unobstructed.

As the nights advance, the actor becomes emptier, replaced by Hanūman, who comes to fuller presence. Madhu told us that he felt emptier as the nights went by for a very prosaic reason—his tasks become lighter. He no longer had to remember the entire text of the previous nights, and felt gradual relief the further the endeavor proceeded. As the nights progressed, he could be more relaxed, could detach himself more easily from Madhu as a person with social obligations, while conceding more space to Hanūman and the changing roles assumed through *pakarnnāṭṭam*, until he *was* the monkey messenger in full, delivering Rāma's ring to Sītā on the last night. Over time, the world that flows from the actor's imagination, ramified by past generations of actors and by this elaborate tradition that renders the current actor an intricate vehicle, slowly takes on its own dynamics, and Hanūman, a drowsy being that must always be reminded of who he is and what he is capable of, Hanūman himself becomes more aware of his world which, concomitantly, comes into fuller existence as he inhabits space that is created inside space and spans of time within time.

## Hanūman Breaks Down Boundaries

The entire sixth act takes place in the powerful demon-king Rāvaṇa's Aśōka garden, where Sītā, captured and taken to Lanka by Rāvaṇa, resists his insistent advances and chooses to take her own life. First, she goes out to the garden to purify herself. There, inside a tree, Hanūman appears; he has been sent, charged by Rāma with the mission of giving Sītā Rāma's wondrous ring, and with it the hope that her husband is on his way to rescue her. Although the theme of the sixth act of the *Āścaryacūḍāmaṇi* is the delivery of the ring, when at last Hanūman took the ring out and handed it to Sītā, on the last night, this gesture was not accentuated or especially noted. The act does not arrive at a dramatic climax because the teleology of the play is not the advancement of the story. The story is a tool. The twenty-eight nights unfold during this time of recognition until Hanūman presents himself and his mission to Sītā. At several points during the performance, Sītā in the garden asks Hanūman, in the voice of the Naṅṅyār, what had happened, repeating the question, "and then?" But instead of telling her what happened next, Hanūman's story goes backward in time. Thus, things that happened before the meeting in the Aśōka garden follow one another, go backward, leap to other places and times, and then return on their paths, again and again, folding, chasing each other, and trailing side by side.

Although Hanūman is *enacting* events through his movements, the movement on stage is not a *representation*. Cultural know-how, and in particular rituals, have been devised so that they can accomplish continuity between aspects of reality and its double (Artaud 1964) through means other than representation. For the potentialities embedded in the continuous body-self to be activated in *Kūṭiyāṭṭam*, certain ways of doing are adopted, and others are purposely avoided. This is how gaps between laws of grammar and those of physics; among humans, demons, and gods; between the actor and the audience; among distinctive viewpoints and perspectives; and between sight and sound are attenuated and erased, to be replaced by a rich and overflowing world.

Chapter 3

# Storytelling in *Kūṭiyāṭṭam*

## How an Inclusive World Is Created

So long as it works, there are no free agents in this cosmology, only complex interdependencies.

—Handelman, *On God, Two Goddesses, Three Studies of South Indian Cosmology*[1]

Since the stories in *Kūṭiyāṭṭam* are taken mainly from the great epics the *Rāmāyaṇa* and the *Mahābhārata,* they are usually familiar to the members of the audience. The audience knows that Sītā will be saved and that Rāvaṇa will be killed since they have heard the stories told and retold in different versions on many occasions. The story does not end in a climax, and no catharsis is offered. Surely, therefore, the aim of the performance goes beyond the mere unveiling of a plot. The audience is waiting for the affects of the performance such as the multiplication of reality, and the emotional echo that ensues.

This chapter is a more theoretical one; it brings to the fore the dynamics of storytelling at work in *Kūṭiyāṭṭam,* dynamics that permit redundancy, the lack of clear climaxes, and the concomitant presence of multiple points of view, while the forms of interconnectedness between them all yield an inclusive cosmology.

The fourteenth- or fifteenth-century Sanskrit text known as *Naṭāṅkuśa* criticizes *Kūṭiyāṭṭam,* and in particular the great elaborations. There is no reason to add to the original play, claims the author. About the *Aṅgulīyāṅkam,* he asks: "How can Sītā, the most beautiful of women in the three worlds, be enacted with a tail?" (Rajagopalan 1974b: 104; Paulose 1993).[2] And, indeed, when he agreed to the performance of the *Aṅgulīyāṅkam*, even Madhu was worried that the twenty-eight nights of a single actor performing in the same costume might be a problem.

However, the actors can indeed become a very feminine and bejeweled Sītā, even while wearing a monkey's tail. *Kūṭiyāṭṭam* enables such a feat by ensuring that imagination is not obstructed. The actors are birthing a world that is not palpable, and like the mundane world we live in, this world too is not linear; rather, it continues into other realities, opening up a multiplicity of potentialities, which Shulman calls "deep seeing" (2016b): "Kūṭiyāṭṭam is an art of sculpting time in three or, better, four dimensions so that we can see time moving, momentarily focusing or crystallizing, in various forms and vectors before our eyes. In particular, futures and pasts have a baffling habit of turning into one another" (Shulman 2016b: 229).

Dynamics that cultivate multiplicity are set into motion. Time is multiplied; the actor himself is multiplied. He becomes the character yet is not entranced or possessed by the god. He toils to retain some separation between himself and the character, by exchanging roles; so, he is the other protagonists of the play but still himself—he is the god, yet not quite. The drums maintain this multiplicity through their hypnotic rhythms and, especially, through the two *miḻāvu* drums beating out different rhythms that blend into one. The god in the sanctum, the god who is the stage itself, the god of the play and the invocations, and the actor performing the god—they are the same, yet a distinction is maintained between the different avatars of the same gods, for they too are multiplied. Kūṭiyāṭṭam allows seeing and living within multiplicity and non-duality.

## *Kūṭiyāṭṭam* as a Non-Dual, Inclusive Event

Evens (2008: xx) summarily formulates the distinction between the dual and the nondual in his crisp clarity: "By dualism I intend

(Cartesian) relationship of mutual exclusion, such that things are differentiated one from another in absolute terms. By nondualism, however, I do not have in mind monism or oneness, a state of being that, logically, can issue only from the kind of boundaries that dualism defines—an immaculate boundary. Instead, I use the term to denote basic ambiguity or inbetween-ness, an ontologically dynamic state in which boundaries connect as they separate, and a thing is always other than what it is."

While the dual can be neatly defined by its immaculate boundaries, the non-dual is slippery by its own nature. Replacing the notion of "non-dual" with some of its characteristics such as "inclusive," "continuous" or "fluid" helps to avoid the negative in "non-dual," and points also to the need for an overarching definition of the shifty non-dual. The term "inclusive" is proposed here to replace the non-dual. The "inclusive" neither assumes nor negates either the opposition of mutually exclusive binarity, nor the impenetrable superposition of levels of abstraction—which are the hallmark of duality with its clear-cut inflexible exclusivity; rather, those are potentialities, that together with many others, are employed in a way that permits interpenetration and open-endedness.[3]

I would like to stress that my issue here is not the vast ontological question (which has kept many philosophers busy in India and elsewhere) concerning the nature of the world, whether it is dual or non-dual; here, I refer specifically to the cultural dynamics that entice into existence a continuous cosmos through performance and ritual. Whereas *dual* and *representation* have one mechanism of expression, *non*-dual and *non*-representation adopt a multitude of different strategies. The strategy of the dual is summative—reducing complexity into aggregative categories; the continuous and non-representation, on the other hand, emulate the making of the world itself through the proliferation of intricate connectivities. These are often more subtle and complicated than a summative representation. Moreover, "inclusive" cultural events tend to erode and fall apart. They thus depend on practice and motility, and are in constant need of sustaining action.

The gap posited at the very foundation of representation also determines an order, one that implicitly assumes that the object in the world came first and that culture—even if polysemic, complex, and versatile—merely codes it. The quintessential semiotic gap of representation determines a difference of sorts between a word, a symbol, or other representation, and the thing it represents. That is to say, in the world of representation, a word and a symbol are not *things* in their own right but rather stand in place of real things. It is exactly those premises that are tackled and eradicated on the *Kūṭiyāṭṭam* stage. Moreover, the extreme potency of *Kūṭiyāṭṭam* stems from actively and systematically driving away any supremacy of one world over another, between the "real" world and its double on the stage—or the other way around (Artaud 1964; Bar-On Cohen 2013).

Removing the semiotic gap results in the creation of an embodied world, one that does not code some world that exists elsewhere, in "real" reality, or perhaps in the imagination; instead, it forces that world into actual somatic existence, within the bodies of all present. In this embodied world, both the object and its cultural expression are always in a process of becoming, the fruit of connectedness, movement, and effort. However, firm borders are alluring. The summative power of borders, namely, eliminating details in search of aggregate and categories, permits more stability, whereas the quest to recreate a living world, with all its haphazard and detailed movement, tends to engage in a constant battle against erosion. Moreover, the "inclusive" does not shun from using any tool according to need, including those typically pertaining to the exclusive world, so that in a continuous world some segments may be linear, causal, summative, and encourage borders, yet all without positing an ontological gap.

Meaning within such a world is inseparable from doing; any hierarchy between sign and signified, and between a word and its meaning, is blurred while linearity and the directionality of cause and effect are challenged. It is often unclear as to which came first, the result or the cause[4] (Bar-On Cohen 2012: 443; see also Wagner 2019).

## Inclusive Dynamics

Binaries can be complexified and rendered more dynamic through such means as hierarchy, intersection, homology, repetition, and interconnectivity, to avoid firm mutual exclusivity, as I indicate below.[5]

Hierarchy can serve an *exclusive* (dual) worldview if considered as a set of frames encompassing one another, with unbridgeable gaps between the different levels of the world, and for example, the monotheistic God closing the series, as Handelman and Lindquist claim (2011; Bateson 2000; see also Espírito Santo 2016a, 2016b). However, within an *inclusive* world, hierarchy can generate infinite potentialities, such as inserting more and more intermediate rungs into a ladder, or through the use of intersections, homology, repetition, and interconnectedness.[6]

The intersection in an *exclusive* narration becomes the endpoint of a story, as all strands that have been developed separately intersect to generate a climax, while the story is made to lead up to this convergence of ways. In an *inclusive* world, on the other hand, intersections are generative because they are sites where potentialities are revealed. Homology is a dynamic that belongs only to the *inclusive*—it concerns the efficaciousness of similarity. If things are homological with one another, even if they emanate from different domains, they may be coaxed into exchanging places or acting on one another (Bar-On Cohen 2012); repetition (to which I will return below) facilitates change from within, without alteration of identities (which are a hallmark of the *exclusive*). Interconnectedness, for its part, permits seepage between entities and opposites, like the relations between *yin* and *yang*.

## Movement

Movement is a raw material of world-building because of its unique nature as simultaneous sense and action. Indeed, movement is primordial; a baby is either still-born or animated—animation being the condition of life. We are not surprised by our own movement; we do not plan it; we are not otherwise reflective about it; "we grow into distinctive ways of moving that come with our being the bodies we are" (Sheets-Johnstone 1999: 136; 2013, 2017).

Movement is both active and passive; as we move, we perceive and understand through our own practice, collecting information about the environment, experiencing it, and our bodies also change, developing power and dexterity, while at the same time acting and shaping that surrounding. No gap is formed between perception, cognition, somatic change, and action; together in movement, they are inseparable and indistinguishable from one another. While learning how to perform a movement, we gather cognitive and emotional information about the world, while also already grabbing, displacing, ordering, and messing up.

Unlike other senses, movement is inextricably intertwined with practice. Movement collects information from within the body and from the world outside about distance, topography, texture, and the capacities of our bodies themselves. Since movement is already action, the barrier between plan and execution is broken. As a plan is formed, it is already done, thus weaving connections between the imagination that gives birth to the plan, the intentionality embedded within the plan, the body that executes the intention, and the world outside. Moreover, concomitantly, movement is social and contagious: it assaults, cajoles, and speeds up blood flow even without touch. The person watching the movement is affected within their own body, so that following body movement is reflected in the observer's constitution.

Through movement, the division between without and within erodes until the movements are enticing all present to feel and use their own body-self in a different and new way. Hence the mind, the imagination of the actor, or the movement as such, fill up with decorated palaces, cities, forests, and seas, all embedded in this constant movement to become a penetrating, overpowering, and livable world, an inseparable hand-drum, imagination-sensation, a new reality in which life is happening now, for the duration of the drumbeat, and later, in the night's invading dreams.

In contrast to Merleau-Ponty (2002)—who thinks that first perception is experienced and only then can subjectivization/cognition occur (these being for him the primal embodied tools we own for making sense of the world)—philosopher Maxine Sheets-Johnstone convincingly shows the many aspects of the primacy of movement that point to Merleau-Ponty's biased view. In movement there is no order between perception and cognition; no hierarchy exists to place mind over body, to grant the "aha, got it!" more importance, complexity, or nobility than any "doing."[7] Perception, reflection, and action occur at once, and none can come to be without the others. The primary relation to reality is the un-reflexive reality of "can do," a kinesthetic reality, while the way of doing can be self-correcting without passage through cognitive consciousness.[8]

However, whereas Sheets-Johnstone's concern as a phenomenologist is consciousness and the ways in which we come to have a view of the world, my concern as an anthropologist is cosmological, namely, how cultural knowledge and tradition, passed down from one moving body to another to form a reality. The potentialities of movement practiced in *Kūṭiyāṭṭam* entice into existence an actual world, albeit an ephemeral one, that depends entirely on active, deliberate effort and movement for its survival. Our bodies move, and our emotions sway with the beating drums as we yield to the rhythms; for the duration of the performance, we are fashioned differently through the uncertainty created by imagination, *māyā*, emotion, and the multiplicity of perspectives.

## The Lives of Imagination, Words, and Grammar in Indian Traditions

Widespread Indian traditions promote the conditions for the inclusive world on stage since words and imagination are to be shown as no different in nature than other things in our mundane world. They may heal and destroy, and ritually connect humans with gods in their capacity as powerful life forces. Thus, *Kūṭiyāṭṭam* can harness the potentialities of the human body, as well as those embedded in imagination, grammar, and words (Skora 2007, 2009; Beck 1976: 217–219). Grammar, "the queen of sciences," is a system that engenders infinity and a reflexivity that recognizes the infinite combinations and potentialities embedded in ordering words correctly and in the realities that words may generate (Shulman 2005, 2001).

Words in this sense are practical objects; they are used to denote one and only one thing unequivocally, and once having filled their communicative function, they disappear. Yet words have another "poetic" dimension, which provides "resonance" (Gnoli 1968: xxvii–xxix), connecting personal experiences with those of others, resonating with ancestral memory, and with the cosmos. All words, even mundane ones, have a poetic aspect, and poetic words can produce a myriad of options. Words are at once unequivocal and multidimensional without creating tension between their two incompatible aspects of denotation and the poetic—and in enmeshing the two, they resonate.

In South Indian traditions, imagination (like grammar) holds the potentiality to infringe on borders, notably the border between perception and the world of objects, as well as between inner and outer realities and, thus, to become a powerful cosmogenic instrument. Imagination is a living thing, a "procedure that informs all of perception and is never purely or simply internal. As such, it does not belong solely, perhaps even primarily, to the mind. That imagination should impinge to dramatic effect on the natural world is thus a necessary corollary to a culture-specific notion of objectivity, one in which objects, like thoughts, grow and ripen both inside and outside any living person" (Shulman 2012b: 270). Embodied imagination, one that is nourished on the actor's body, as in *Kūṭiyāṭṭam,* is a way of breathing the world to the rhythm of the drums, inhaling and exhaling while generating strings of transformative reactions.

## *Kūṭiyāṭṭam* as *Māyā*

The world cannot exist without *māyā*; it is one of the tools that enables free movement from one reality to another, and thus is central to Indian philosophy and *Kūṭiyāṭṭam*. *Māyā* can be understood as "illusion," "deception," "a mysterious power of will," "energy," and a "mental power" (Shāstrī 1911: 8–11). But *māyā* as "illusion" and as "mental power" interpenetrate each other—a mental power that both creates and reveals. Moreover, *māyā* is the only way in which the world can be perceived, and concomitantly the only way we can know anything about it. The world thus depends on our imagination, which generates both the world and illusion, both deception and mental power, often without an accurate way of distinguishing between real reality and illusion. *Māyā* is intimately connected to the energizing and generative power of *śakti* and its vitality since it is said that "the womb of Sakti is maya," both "veiling and revealing" (Beane 1973: 62, 65).

*Māyā,* therefore, is the dream world, or the multiple worlds, in which we actually exist. This is also a central theme of the *Āścaryacūḍāmaṇi,* "The Wondrous Head-Jewel." Many events unfold because of *māyā,* and the "wondrous jewel" itself is intended to sort out real reality from illusion, to protect its wearer by revealing *māyā.* Yet even when Sītā has already received the jewel, has gone through the fire ordeal, and is about to mount the chariot that will take her and her husband back to their royal status, she remains hesitant. Perhaps it is not Rāma next to her on the chariot but a demon in *māyā* form, as has already happened when Rāvaṇa in the form of *māyā*-Rāma tricked and abducted her. Is Rāma now again a demon in disguise? She is reassured by Rāma, who reminds her of the jewel she is wearing, but it seems that nothing can guarantee that reality is in fact what it seems to be and not an illusion. Perhaps his cruelty in leading her to the ordeal of fire creates this hesitation, but it probably emanates from the inherent confusion between *māyā* and "real" reality.

*Māyā* is also the source of the transformation produced by *Kūṭiyāṭṭam*, a cosmos emanating from the imagination of the actor and his gurus from generations ago. Using storytelling dynamics that shake loose borders to allow multiplicity, *Kūṭiyāṭṭam* is *māyā*, in that it enables a leak in the cosmic fabric through which *māyā*'s presence is strengthened. *Kūṭiyāṭṭam* obstructs our capacity to differentiate among the various aspects or appearances of realities, and it is precisely that which results in a cosmological shift. Like an Indian myth that "may appear to take different forms; sometimes as illusions, sometimes as dreams, sometimes as temporary magic changes in the physical nature of the world, sometimes as the unveiling of another level of reality" (O'Flaherty 1984: 3), this other, more profound level of the cosmos was revealed rather than created, since it was there all along.

## Emotion

*Kūṭiyāṭṭam* is a feast of feeling—emotions are its driving force. While the plots of the stories are strings of knots leading the performance along diverse looping routes without clear stops, starts, or climaxes, *Kūṭiyāṭṭam* storytelling is abounding with emotional articulations and tenors. Some emotions are delicate, and others eruptive and virulent; they are highly complexified by our anticipation since we know what is unfolding; emotions constitute the main matter of both its vehicle delivering the story and its actual substance.

Emotion concerns the "relations between self and the world" (Lutz 1988: 223; Timm 1991). They are the "sensate qualities of relationship that rise to the surface of awareness as a reflexive component of interactive contexts entailing interpersonal repositioning" (Berthomé and Houseman 2010: 65). Thus, emotions are both a result of interaction, and a force that stimulates the repositioning of relations, constituting their active-reflexive quality, which entails concrete changes.

Further, in Indian understanding, emotions are somatic conditions that include states of well-being, as well as those of weakness and sickness. They have a thick existence closer to actual material. They can be extremely potent and dangerous, since they also pass from one person to another, unknowingly, through substance—because the human body is a "relatively porous container through which substances, experiences, and influences flow" (Menon 2002: 143).[9] Sentiments can be contracted between strangers through touch and the consumption of matter, such as foods (Alter 1992: 107).[10]

Within a ritual, that goes beyond human interaction, and the mere "self," to include more than our life experience alone, emotion is the "felt qualities of ritual relationships" (Berthomé and Houseman 2010: 69). Emotion is the feeling emanating from the skilled and purposeful repositioning of relations among humans, deities, and the materiality of the world, through ritual. The quality resulting from ritual cosmological tweaking depends on the active-reflexive capacity of the emotional substance.

In *Kūṭiyāṭṭam*, emotions may speed up action into hyper-drive, in particular through emotions that Ngai calls "ugly feelings" (2005: 1), such as envy, irritation, anxiety, and disgust, or they may engender serenity and slowing down and restricting it even into paralysis.[11] Emotions are, therefore, "ongoing contextual shifters" (Berthomé and Houseman, 2010: 62), and as such, they can be harnessed to become powerful transformers. Whereas emotions are usually understood as spontaneous reactions to an unfolding situation, molding emotion into shifters in *Kūṭiyāṭṭam* is not merely a passive outcome of the plot, nor is it impulsive; rather the experience of potential manifestations of emotions is cultivated, and distilled, and, since it is presented over and over again in different forms, it intensifies through repetition. Emotion becomes an aesthetic affect, refined to ensure the profound connectedness between the deities, the protagonist of the play, the actors, the drummers, and the audience, while heightening the story and the movement, ushering the ritual repositioning of relations through a palette of giddiness, love, desire, awe, wonderment, fierce anger, despair, and other elaborate combinations of emotional hues.

Eight distinct emotional facial expressions, or *bhāva,* are taught to students of *Kūṭiyāṭṭam;* these are: affectionate, happy, miserable, angry, radiant, afraid, disgusted, and smiling.[12] The affectionate expression, for example, involves enlarging pupils; expressing desire is performed with a fixed gaze, and so forth (Madhavan 2012: 160). The twenty-four ways of chanting the *śloka* also vary according to the emotion they deliver (e.g., see Madhavan 2010: 151–202). The combination of *bhāva* facial expressions, and chanting, added to the drumbeat, to mudrā words, to body postures, and to their dynamics serve to multiply the potential affects.

The palette of emotions in *Kūṭiyāṭṭam,* therefore, is much wider than the *bhāva* alone; emotional expressions also include discouragement, weakness, apprehension, envy, intoxication, weariness, indolence, depression, anxiety, distraction, recollection, contentment, shame, inconstancy, joy, agitation, stupor, arrogance, despair, impatience, sleep, epilepsy, dreaming, awakening, indignation, dissimulation, cruelty, assurance, sickness, insanity, death, fright, and deliberation (Higgins 2007: 45–46). Some emotional expressions are somatic states such as sleep, epilepsy, and sickness; some are faculties that we usually attribute to the cognitive, such as distraction and recollection; and others are modes of consciousness such as dreaming, awakening, and stupor.

Berthomé and Houseman (2010) distinguish between the emotional tenor that is part of the ritual's intended plan purposefully leading the participants into a certain mood on the one hand and spontaneous emotions incurred by the participants as a reaction to the events on the other. In *Kūṭiyāṭṭam,* however, such distinctions are not maintained because the emotional tenors are internal to the interrelations among everything in the *Kūttambalam.* As in mundane life, the planned and the emergent cannot be distinguished; moreover, those differences are deliberately erased. The emotional tenors of the drama travel internally from person to person, from entity to person, and back.

Marriott (1976: 111; 1989) claims that South Indians live in a world of dividuals (rather than individuals), in which a person is inextricably intertwined in complex interconnectedness with others, exchanging substance and influence with them. Each person exists within a web of relations, enabling such seepage as emotion to flow through the interiority of these relations and be passed among "selves" from inside to inside without ever emerging outside. Such interior passages become clearly visible when the king-demon Rāvaṇa falls desperately in love with the loyal goddess-cum-human Sītā. Several days of performance (as part of the *Aṅgulīyāṅkam*) are dedicated to Rāvaṇa's emotion; they fill three evenings in a row. First, the emotion arises within Rāvaṇa's imagination when he is told about her beauty; then, Rāvaṇa's eyes see her and again a renewed emotion erupts. This time the actor describes her body and his love through eye movements alone (without chanting, mudrā gestures or acting), and, finally, his love is performed through the vantage point of each of his ten heads who argue which one of them will appropriate her body. The heads resolve the quarrel by dividing her body parts amongst them. Rāvaṇa's emotion has a life of its own, moving from one part of himself to another, traveling from his imagination to his eyes, and to each of his heads. Meanwhile, we, the audience, know and apprehend what is coming, namely, the abduction of Sītā, and are filled with complex sentiments. We can feel his awesome love and his complex constitution. We spend three evenings feeling this great love, knowing that Rāvaṇa is a demon, and that demons are full of uncontrollable emotions, which are immediately turned into action.

Both the artist and the audience are active in training and awakening their capacity to feel. According to the classic Indian theory of emotional reaction to theater the *Nāṭya Śāstra,* in the commentary of Abhinavagupta, *rasa*—the emotion awakened by theater—is a mechanism meant to evoke a profound sensitivity in an audience that is "suitably cultivated" (Higgins 2007: 44). Moreover, according to that dominant Indian understanding of theater and its role, the experience of feeling through the poetic is a liberating mental repose which, according to Abhinavagupta, is the ultimate purpose of *rasa* (Higgins 2007: 49). The aesthetic of feeling, an emotional mode of consciousness, and the capacity for wonderment triggered by drama or poetic experience result from stylized emotional upheavals that may bring forth a powerful reaction, even a spiritual revelation. The liberating mental repose, which is the true personal devotion, achieving higher spiritual capacities, is the final goal of traditional Sanskrit theater according to the dominant Kashmiri poeticians (Sliwczynska 2003).[13]

Although in the circles of *Kūṭiyāṭṭam* the artists talk in terms of *rasa,* this theater does not involve a personal aim, such as spiritual liberation indicated by Abhinavagupta. Rather, in *Kūṭiyāṭṭam,* emotion is in itself central in birthing the cosmos. In other, Deleuzian terms, emotion is pure intensity. Sensation "is the affect, which is neither subjective nor objective; rather it is both at once: we become in sensation and at the same time something happens because of it" (Boundas 2005: 132). This is why sensation is a suitable material for generating this cosmos made of movement and intensities.

## Multiplicity and Perspectives

The world emanating from the stage offers a multitude of added perspectives, that of the embodied, conscious person being only one of them. Ishii (2013, 2015b.) shows how *Bhūta* possession in South Karnataka can be seen as adding perspectives to the mundane one. While possessed by a *Bhūta* spirit, the possession specialist is still partly himself and can see the world from two concomitant perspectives. This potentiality takes advantage of our basic psychological capacity—which ensures our sociality and sanity—to take on a multiplicity of perspectives of other people. And as Viveiros de Castro's anthropological perspectivism suggests, we are also capable of taking on the perspective of other things in the world, such as animals, ghosts, and insentient objects (much as they might take on ours as humans). Viveiros de Castro's perspectivism is an ontological proposition, claiming that "the universe is inhabited by different sorts of persons, human and non-human, which apprehend reality from distinct points of view" (Ishii 2012, Part 2: 1)—that is, these beings live in different actual worlds. Since their worlds are constructed differently, they each have their own ontology.

The concomitant existence of a multitude of viewpoints also permits seepage—the passage of substances and parts into and through one another. Thus, an autopoietic (self-generated) process—more accurately, a self-poietic process—is enabled, shaped by the coherent actions of bodies and things. Divine worlds can be created, vitalized, and lived in by people, operating through sentient and inanimate things. And, thus too, no exegesis is needed to create novel experiences of the world. Rather, as Ishii asserts, divine "worlds are created through concrete relations and actions among persons, things, spirits, and deities that take tangible as well as intangible forms." Further, the emergence and formation of divine worlds are not "the realization of one possible alternative world, but an actualization of virtual, vital relations between persons and things that emerge only through their contingent coactions" (Ishii 2012: 372–373);[14] hence, humans play a passive as well as an active role in these relations while living within the divine world.

Eliminating divisions becomes crucial in a world based on interaction and intermingling of multiple viewpoints. During a *Kūṭiyāṭṭam* performance, the world itself opens up to include more, to allow us to share life with the protagonists of the story, who are also integral to this reality—a different reality, because we share it with entities that remain invisible in everyday life, but also because it holds options, textures, and profundities that differ from the mundane.

We are not merely spectators within the *Kūttambalam*—we enter a domain of blurred boundaries between different sentient entities, and also within ourselves. By reversing how somatic faculties grasp the world, the light, the sound, and the movement pound everyone present into an intimate and unmediated change. The eyes replace hearing, hearing becomes filled with the inescapable drumbeat streaming with emotion directly into the flow of the blood, the beat of the heart. The performance causes a thickening of reality, a deepening of sensation: time is multiplied, and space is filled many times over with objects and entities, yet is nevertheless capable of containing even more.

## Tools of Storytelling: Negative, Interrogative, and Repetition

The *negative*, the *interrogative*, and *repetition* are central among the tools that generate the dynamics of storytelling in *Kūṭiyāṭṭam*. The *negative* is used to delineate a space in which something exists; through the negative, what is negated becomes present. The *inter-*

*rogative* furnishes that space while engendering multiplicity and depth; interrogations enable endless space within space, and time within time, that can accommodate a multiple and simultaneous existence. *Repetition* produces difference in and of itself, obliterating unwavering identity or strict definition, and replacing them with vibrant intensities. The iteration of the same that generates the change emanating from difference in its own right, which, in turn, ensures that all points of view, all rhythms, all emotional tenors can survive without exclusion. Repetition, negation, and interrogation bring to life a cosmos in which nothing is lost—all realities are present concomitantly.

## Negative

On the twenty-first night of the *Aṅgulīyāṅkam*, Śūrpaṇakhā, the fierce female demon, describes to her brother Rāvaṇa, the demon-king of Lanka, the marvelous beauty of Sītā. She says: "She is not Indrāṇī, neither Rohiṇī nor Varuṇani,[15] they are not equal to her"; and she continues: "She is not a goddess, not an enchantress, nor a witch, she is not a snake-woman" (from the *āṭṭa-prakāram*). Śūrpaṇakhā lists extraordinary women and classes of powerful women known to Rāvaṇa to situate Sītā as superior to them all. Instead of describing the beautiful woman, she excludes all other wondrous and beautiful women who Rāvaṇa knows, to allow his (and our) imagination space to roam. While filling the world with these other beautiful women only to empty it of them, she is clearing an empty space in Rāvaṇa's imagination, and at the center of that void, she places Sītā. Śūrpaṇakhā uses no adjectives or superlatives while describing the most beautiful women in the three worlds, since adjectives and superlatives are abstract summations and approximations, the building blocks of representation; rather, she uses real objects, real females who exist, and thereby constitutes a real Sītā. And, indeed, Rāvaṇa falls deeply in love with her.

The use of the negative—"it is not this nor is it the other"—a delineation of space-time through elimination, designates empty space-time, but its emptiness is not just vacant nothingness; it is empty of what it has negated. This space empty of beautiful women is not this nor that, but something else, unique and as yet unexperienced in the space-time of exceptional women. Earlier in the story, the widowed Śūrpaṇakhā is ordered by her brother to look for a husband; her search becomes cosmological, as she casts about, eliminating all the gods from her list of prospective husbands. She looks around, and the gods she considers are ordered in space in the eight directions. In fact, they are ordering space in the world by their very positioning; so, while eliminating prospective husbands for a variety of reasons, Śūrpaṇakhā delineates the space of the entire world, striking all the gods from her list, leaving only the empty center available, which is where men live, notably Rāma and Lakṣmaṇa—and they are her choice for a husband.

### Interrogative

A space emptied by negation can be filled with a multiplicity of other times and spaces moving freely into a variety of pasts. The interrogative fills this emptied space with multiplicity. The question frequently asked by the *Kūṭiyāṭṭam* actor, "how is that?" can elicit elaboration and insert new space-time where none existed, since when he asks, "how is that?" the actor does not respond with abstract adjectives, since "beauty," "power," and "love" are generalities that encompass very different things. To answer the question "how is that?," the actor leaves the story he is telling, and moves to another time and place, unveiling yet another story, an occasion in which "how that is" comes to life and becomes explicit.

The actor transports us to where something that has happened clearly answers the question and enacts how it came to be. When looking at Rāvaṇa, the actor asks, "how are his hands?," and the answer transports the world on stage to the time when Rāvaṇa's hands were scarred in a battle against Indra's mighty white elephant Airāvata. The answer to the question "how is Rāvaṇa?" takes us to the time when Rāvaṇa's way was blocked by Mount Kailāsa and therefore he lifted it, demonstrating his power by enacting the lifting this abode of Śiva and his consort Pārvatī. Moreover, within the space opened up by the telling of this extraordinary feat, another space appears, since when Rāvaṇa lifted the mountain, Śiva and Pārvatī were in the middle of a dispute about the goddess Gangā, who lives inside Śiva's hair. Pārvatī is so angry that she begins her journey back to her father but cannot proceed because the mountain is in the air, and she has no choice but to rejoin her husband. Moreover, while the mountain is in the air, we can see Rāvaṇa and his charioteer playing dice. The mountain was thrown so high that while waiting for it to drop back down, a game of dice can be played.

These questions are cross-roads, leading to a multiplicity of time-places, opening inside one another as a certain detail is enlarged, looked at, and enacted. The question "how is it?" is where the world of the story forks,[16] where the story loses its linearity to curve upon itself, intersects, and proliferates, while other potentialities—already embedded within it—emerge, to generate a multitude of densities and intensities, always in a process of becoming, in perpetual movement. The interrogative opens up space within space, time within time. It is, however, never entirely filled up because the emptiness generated by the negative and filled by the interrogative is open-ended and holds a never-ending potentiality of depth to be filled. This filling is accomplished through repetition.

## Repetition

Repetition, or recursivity, is a major tool in *Kūṭiyāṭṭam*. Each time a repetition occurs, it is notably different, leading through another path in a rounded trajectory back to its middle—the middle of the story, the middle of the actor's body, the middle of the cosmos. The text of the play itself is repeated; first, the storyteller tells it with his hands, then he enacts it, then the Naṅṅyār will repeat the same text by chanting it in Sanskrit (for a fuller description of storytelling in *Kūṭiyāṭṭam* as the standard *nirvahaṇam* pattern of enactment, see Moser-Achuthath 1999–2000). Each sentence may be repeated up to five times. Different versions of a story may be included without exclusivity. In one version, Śūrpaṇakhā loses her nose and ears in the battle with Lakṣmaṇa, while in another she loses her nose and breasts; both versions co-exist in the play.[17] Another form of recursivity occurs when the same moment is shown in different ways, from different angles.

Repetition is everywhere: the incessant beat of the drums and cymbals repeating the same rhythm, the endless flexing of the facial muscles, the rolling of the eyes, the hands moving in circles, repeating their trajectories, and then returning to the center of the actor's body. On the twenty-sixth evening of the *Aṅgulīyāṅkam*, Jaṭayu, the brave vulture, tries to release Sītā from Rāvaṇa; he cries: "I will peck your ten faces." Then this sentence is unfolded by repeating it in question form: "How are Rāvaṇa's ten faces"? The answer is enacted: "Bleeding and smeared with blood. Shaggy haired. Shining like a forest fire in the night over the peak of Anjanam mountain." Finally, it is chanted in Sanskrit. The next night, this sentence will be repeated once again in the preliminary synopsis given by the actor as a storyteller.

From time to time, the actor sits on the stool to tell the entire *Rāmāyaṇa Saṃkṣepam*, from the beginning up to that evening's story. It has even been repeated twice in the same evening because Hanūman needed to hear it, to discover his own origins, story, and power. Madhu says that repeating the story from the beginning through the *Rāmāyaṇa Saṃkṣepam* is intended for the actor. The actor, as well as Hanūman and the other protagonists, must be reminded of what has happened as part of what is happening now. The telling may take a minimum of forty minutes and may last as long as four hours. This repetition is not merely the reenactment of the same thing, for each repetition of the *Rāmāyaṇa Saṃkṣepam* is different, including within it everything that has occurred on stage, and everything meticulously built up to that point. Repetition recursively leads the circular movement of the world of *Kūṭiyāṭṭam* to traverse itself, emerging elsewhere and engendering intensity and density.

French philosopher Gilles Deleuze, who dedicated much of his thought to the potentialities of repetition, labels repetition a "terrible power" because it can become subversive, undoing identity as it is positioned under the forces of representation of the identical. Deleuzian notions, in his and Guattari's work, are rare (in Western philosophy) yet a tenacious attempt to describe the world in non-dual terms, and they pursue this mission from various angles and perspectives. For Deleuze, "repetition" is never repetition of the same; it always entails difference. But this difference is not a difference between two distinct things, but rather difference in itself—pure difference. He writes, "In the theater of repetition, we experience pure forces, dynamic lines in space which act without intermediary upon the spirit, and link it directly with nature and history, with language which speaks before words, with gestures which develop before organized bodies, with masks before faces, with specters and phantoms before character—the whole apparatus of repetition as a 'terrible power'" (Deleuze 1994: 10). Repetition immediately yields difference without passing through words, organized bodies, character or faces, "it is a question of producing [. . .] a movement capable of affecting the mind outside of all representation; [. . .] of inventing vibrations, rotations, whirlings, gravitations, dance or leap which directly touch the mind" (1994: 8). Repetition as a creator of difference is a dynamic form of "discovery and experimentation" (Parr 2005: 223).

Like many Deleuzian notions, difference emanating from repetition can best be described in the negative: not summative, not yielding identity, not representation, not symbolic, and so forth. It is more difficult to account for repetition in positive terms to describe what it is instead of what it is not; but Deleuze and Guattari do not award much attention to that because they are more interested in criticizing the world they live in than looking seriously into inclusive worlds such as *Kūṭiyāṭṭam* that, in fact, depend on repetition and work through shunning from symbolic representation.

Repetition is the substance of life, and in order to stop the proliferation of repetition into difference, to force it into identity, repetition must be forced into the identical by semiotics and other strict divisions of thought. Left to roam freely, repetition never renders the identical, since the conditions of repetition are never the same. The second time comes after the first, after the surprise of the first time has already been spent. The act of repetition therefore may alter the intensity of the first iteration to become more accentuated and authoritative, or, on the contrary, bracketed and mellowed, humorous, or even totally absurd. And then there comes the third repetition, and the fourth, and, although they may be the same, they never play the same role, always bringing something new—cruelty, or tenderness and sensuality, perhaps boredom. However, unlike Deleuze's theoretical formulation, in practice, in *Kūṭiyāṭṭam,* the affects of repetition come to the surface. While the philosopher may deliberate what repetition *is,* the anthropologist wonders what repetition *does.*

## Multiplicity

The *negative,* the *interrogative,* and *repetition* generate intersections that allow the proliferation of multiplicity. According to Deleuze, multiplicity is "a complex structure that does not refer to a prior unity" (Roffe 2005: 176) but rather stems from interaction and is therefore greatly susceptible to encounter. "Multiplicity" indicates the straightforward, multiple things that appear concomitantly, in multiple places and times, as well as in multiple manifestations of the same entity. The god who is in the sanctum is also on stage; the gods are the *Kūttambalam* itself. The actors also amass multiple layers. Sometimes the multiple worlds are layered, at other times interpenetrating; some constitute a swelling, an added hue, or a deepening, as multiplicity grows, flourishes, and wanes. The manifold multiplication on stage leads to "multiplicity" as a more general organizing trait, an operational principle, of this cosmos.

### Intensity

The affects of repetition and multiplicity are changes in intensity, namely, a quantitative difference that becomes qualitative.[18] Intensity does not represent; rather, it acts on the world. Water, frozen or boiling, is still water; yet heat changes what water can do, heat changes its intensity. Heat, pain, hunger, speed, swelling, topological alterations, bliss, and well-being are all intensities (Boundas 2005a). While fluctuations in intensity do not alter the nature or identity of things, they make an immense practical difference.[19] Deleuze denounces what he sees as the error of thinking exclusively in terms of things and their qualities, overlooking the relations between forces in their own right and the intensity of these relations.

Sensation depends directly on intensity, something that we can grasp through our senses, sensibilities, thoughts, all within the body itself. In *Kūṭiyāṭṭam*, changes in space, time, the body are all fluctuations in intensity. As Sītā enters the fire in the final act of the *Āścaryacūḍāmaṇi*, female power fills the world, and this power is pure intensity. Not only does this female power enhance the intensity of sensation, but also of the cosmos itself, as the cosmos changes and becomes made of a different intensity. The bees still buzz, drinking the nectar of flowers, but their drinking is intensified, as is all movement in the world. In the golden world that emerges from the fire ordeal, the bees are tranquil, as is everything else, and this intense quietness renders a world full of wonder. Deleuze and Guattari (1987: 164–165) distinguish between sorts of intensities that are situated on a scale. A zero intensity is like an egg, unstratified, a whole, an undifferentiated potential that can develop and stratify into functions and organs yet is still without movement, direction, or desire. At the other end of the stratum is the "too-violent destratification," the result of desire gone wild, of a rapid process of development and the uncontrollable specification of parts of a whole.

Whereas the intensity generated by Sītā's ordeal is close to zero intensity or to a momentary stoppage of movement, another event—the mutilation of Śūrpaṇakhā—accelerates the universe; and the female energy that she spills into the world through her severed organs and blood is closer to the "too-violent destratification" energizing the world, which may also be dangerous.[20]

## The Nonlinear and Noncausal in *Kūṭiyāṭṭam*

In nonlinear dynamics there is no ordering of activities or events into means and ends, nor are there any causal or teleologic relationships (Lee 1950: 91), and this is a key to the transformative potentialities embedded in *Kūṭiyāṭṭam*. Whereas linearity organizes events so that they maintain their identity along with their existence—that is, once they have been established, they are constant—nonlinearity or multiplicity, on the other hand, adopts the processual dynamic of becoming. Instead of stable identity, the generative nonlinearity is full of twists, recursive turns, and variability, never settling down into constant distinctiveness. And since within such a vortex nothing can be certain to keep its nature after it meanders, temporality as well becomes nonlinear, picking up speed and slowing down to a near halt, going into the present and back to a myriad of pasts. Nevertheless, linear segments can emerge within nonlinear and causal setups since linearity is merely one potentiality of nonlinearity.

In the *Rāmāyaṇa* itself, events yield ever more events, generating circularity as the protagonists forget their real strength and divinity; and, as the writer of the epic appears within it, the events of the *Rāmāyaṇa* follow one another and fold onto themselves. The way of telling the story in *Kūṭiyāṭṭam* yields nonlinearity when questions yield crossings in time. Thus, events become threads, lines in a multidimensional Mandala intended to trap the gods and unleash powers. These threads are tied into place to constitute a certain actuality, one in which each intersection presents points of vulnerability and of opportunity within a cosmos where intensities such as the demonic can become unleashed or female energy can overflow.

## A Cosmos within a Life-Pocket

Cosmology, as mentioned before, is central to my understanding of *Kūṭiyāṭṭam*, but this term also summons some pitfalls. "Cosmology" in anthropology has been criticized because it has often been used to denote a radically different way of making sense of the world, one supposedly prevalent in so-called simpler societies. Cosmology was deemed less complex and less sophisticated than the world in which the anthropologist herself lives—the world as it is discovered by hard science as opposed to the different cosmologies developed by groups around the world, generating a totally different perspective: "Cosmology as the exoticized effect of the hierarchy of 'modern us' over 'primitive them' " (Abramson and Holbraad 2015: 9); the world as we "really" know it was opposed to "fantasized" existences that some people believe in. Anthropology was busy explaining "how and why the primitive or traditional other was wrong," but then as the tides turned anthropologists went on to argue why Western civilization got it all wrong. And, finally, anthropology became committed to explaining why there is no real "us and them," primitive and enlightened, Western and Oriental: we are all the same (Viveiros de Castro 2012, Part 1: 7).

The anthropological turn to phenomenology claims that all perception of the world, including the scientific one, originates in consciousness. Thus, our "necessarily situated emplacement" produces an "ever-shifting horizon of our experience" (Desjarlais and Throop 2011: 90). This turn has introduced into anthropology some relativity, some reflexivity and perhaps even some humility. And in recent years, "cosmology" has been taken up again to account for the horizons of human worlds, and the ways in which they are imagined and engaged (e.g., see Abramson and Holbraad 2015).

Cosmology might be, as Viveiros de Castro claims, too static a notion; yet he adds that we can still ask of a certain form of life "what sort of virtual conceptuality pulsates" within that segment or society? (Viveiros de Castro 2012, Part 1: 9). The idea of a stable cosmos created once and for all belongs to the biblical or Western world. In non-dual societies, one should talk about "counter-cosmogony" which is an eternal, relational becoming, in which "counter" is an acronym for cosmogonic processes that are continuous, open, unoriginated, nonlinear, transformational, emergent, and relational (Scott 2015: 44, 48).

The *Kūṭiyāṭṭam* world is indeed not stable but an evolving world with multiple dynamic processes of becoming, and thus belongs to this "continuous, open, unoriginated, nonlinear, transformational, emergent, and relational" sort of cosmos.[21] Here, however, I am not seeking to unveil a "virtual conceptuality," since, as mentioned, concepts are not central to this world. Consequently, questions of "how" are more relevant than the questions of "what is" of ontology. This is because such a cosmology is intimately interconnected with practice. Such a cosmology is not a series of principles that are shared by some in their attempt to decipher the world, principles that the anthropologist may be able to discover; nor is such a cosmology a set of beliefs that generate a coherent and holistic world. Instead, such a cosmology is a way of doing that actively generates a world (see Venkatesan 2015).

Moreover, a radically different way of making a holistic world within a confined unit comes to be. It may include traits prevalent in segments of society at large or share a way of understanding the world with its social environment, but it is exclusive to the *Kūttambalam*. A complex and sophisticated cultural life-pocket is created and simultaneously set into motion, controlling the interactions both on stage and with the audience. It stops the mundane give-and-take between people and with the environment, imposing a new and irresistible existence.[22]

Borrowing from temple ritual, Sanskrit classics, and other social and cultural practices, it becomes a transformative hot spot that radiates its auspiciousness, a holistic unit that entertains relations with the environment through its own cultural dynamics.

## Practice in its Own Right

A specific mode of analysis is required to discern cosmological life-pockets such as *Kūṭiyāṭṭam*. Whereas much of the anthropological attitude toward understanding ritual and other public events consists of looking for the meaning and function of that event in its social and cultural context, Handelman (2004b) calls for analyzing ritual in its own right and, more generally, practice in its own right. This entails examining an event, not as a reflection of something else outside of itself—social, kinship, gender, religious, ethnic, economic, ideological—but rather, first and foremost, as creating reality through its own organization of space, time, relations among the entities involved, within its environment. Only after the exact form, which takes shape through that activity, is clarified, the anthropologist turns to whatever social and cultural context contributes to its understanding.

Shapiro (2015) calls this proposition a method of fieldwork and analysis, but it is more than that. This way of thinking privileges practice over the essence and, in so doing, enables overcoming a serious hurdle in anthropology—namely, perceiving a social or cultural event as it is experienced by the participants, with less of the anthropologist's world posited onto the one observed. And, more importantly, in many cases—particularly in inclusive worlds—the form that emerges is also its very content.

Holbraad and Pedersen (2017) list the conundrums that make anthropology queasy about itself and its ability to decipher what is "out there" within societies that generate a feeling of alterity for the anthropologist. They seek a method allowing anthropologists to "trick" themselves into seeing something alien while foregoing their own looking glasses. They ask "how to enable the ethnographic material to reveal itself to me by allowing it to dictate its own terms of engagement" (2017: 5). And they claim that "without the conceptual agility that ontological relativizing provides, we suggest, anthropology is resigned to misunderstanding, even misdescribing, the very ethnographic material it seeks to elucidate" (Holbraad and Pedersen 2017: 4; see also Pickering 2017). They, therefore, propose the "ontological turn" as a solution, revealing the abstract principles governing social ways of doing. The main thrust of anthropology, then, is formulating the concepts behind social arrangements, and conceptualizing them.[23] However, ontology for them is not the way the world is actually built but the way it is defined by various groups. So, the solution of conceptualization is in fact an ontological-epistemological one—that is, we should come up with different abstract formulations of "what is" according to a certain perspective.

But what if a certain group is not prone to abstraction, and certainly does not consider the abstract as superior to the concrete, as do many inclusive worlds? What if an event does everything possible to avoid second-degree abstraction and exegesis (as do Japanese martial arts for example)? Should the anthropologist still impose abstract conceptualization on such an event? What if there are actually different worlds and not only different ways of conceptualizing "what is" into one coherent reality? Observing practice in its own terms, as Handelman (2004b) suggests, becomes a possible peephole into these worlds, in which ways of doing are not only a means to fulfill a necessary function, but rather the essence as well. Inclusive worlds are often made differently. The objects are different, the bodies of both animals and humans are different, the deities and demons are different, and all intervene in the world in different combinations. By looking at the stitches, the connective tissue that holds them together, a different weave and fabric will reveal itself.

~

What, then, is the cosmos practiced in *Kūṭiyāṭṭam* like? Going back to the building of the *Parṇa-śālā*: Rāma and Sītā are living in exile wandering in the wilderness with Lakṣmaṇa, Rāma's loyal brother. To protect the couple, Lakṣmaṇa builds a hut—the *Parṇa-śālā*—on the *Kūṭiyāṭṭam* stage. He is using the materials available in the forest: first, he delineates a space and clears it, and then he digs holes in the ground at each of the four corners of that space. Next, he clears the foliage from four large branches, though some of them resist and he needs to exert effort to detach them from the main branch. Then he drives each of the branches into the holes he has prepared, and they become the poles of the hut—he moves patiently from one corner to the other. No words are uttered over long minutes, but the drums are following the movement and carrying it along, determining the concentrated and solemn mood of this endeavor. His movements are forceful and clear, although, of course, no props are used. Then he gathers branches, twigs, and leaves, for the canopy to shade the couple, and to protect them from wild animals and demons that roam the forest, plucking them from the air, and reshaping space in front of our eyes with his exact movements. Now that the structure is standing, the greatest delicacy is employed to prepare the soft bed with fragrant leaves and flowers. Once the *Parṇa-śālā* is ready, he steps into it and changes perspective to join us in the audience in our perspective so that both actor/Hanūman/Lakṣmaṇa and audience can observe the finished work with satisfaction.

Lakṣmaṇa is making the simplest of temples, a protected, fresh, fragrant, consecrated space; a cosmos within a cosmos fit for the royal/divine couple; a life-pocket in the wilderness that includes all that is needed for life, without excess. In more than one way, the world of *Kūṭiyāṭṭam* is akin to Lakṣmaṇa's *Parṇa-śālā*; it is a haven of well-being, yet flimsy, temporary, unstable, made of the simplest material, namely, of movement; a well-delineated world, clean, and pure with safeguards from danger and defilement, and with porous, leafy borders that let in the air and light. The world on stage posits a powerful existence that contains everything it needs to sustain itself, shutting out the chaos of everyday life, deferring human fragility to replace reality with an alternative dense existence.

Chapter 4

# White, Black, and Red Śūrpaṇakhā, Golden Sītā

## Cosmic Events of Female Intensities in *Kūṭiyāṭṭam*

I melt. I fray. But he does not care
if I live or die.
If that stealthy thief, that duplicitous Govardhana
should even glance at me
I shall pluck these useless breasts of mine
from their roots
I will fling them at his chest
and staunch the fire scorching me.

—Nācciyār Tirumŏḻi 13.81,
translated from Tamil by Archana Venkatesan[1]

## Two Cosmic Events

Two cosmic events performed on the *Kūṭiyāṭṭam* stage disseminate female energy into the world. When femaleness spills over it imbues the entire world with a particular hue—red or golden—thus soaking the cosmos with different manifestations of feminine lifeforce. The two events are performed as part of the play *Āścaryacūḍāmaṇi*, "The Wondrous Head-Jewel," by the ninth-century Sanskrit dramatist Śaktibhadra (Jones 1984). The downfall and transformation of the mighty demoness Śūrpaṇakhā—rendering the entire world red—is at the center of the second act, called *Śūrpaṇakhāṅkam*. In the seventh and last act of the play, named *Agnipraveśāṅkam*, after Agni the god of fire brings forth another transformation, the world turning golden following Sītā's fire ordeal.

The two cosmic events cause an overflow in the world that disseminates female energy as excess. This happens through complex weaves of form, color, illusion, world formation, and destruction, in ways that melt, fuse, explode and overflow, so that the colors bleed into each other, and the forms cannot sustain themselves and transform. All are enmeshed together to generate a fertile yet dangerous spillover.

When the widow demoness (*asura*) Śūrpaṇakhā is looking for a new husband, she concludes that none of the gods will be suitable and turns her attention to humans, to Rāma and his brother Lakṣmaṇa in their forest hermitage. Using *māyā*—magic, illusion, a change of course, or transformation (Shāstrī 1911)—she appears before the brothers in a guise of a beautiful, white, adorned woman, Lalitā, played on the *Kūṭiyāṭṭam* stage by an actress who speaks in elegant mudrā gestures. However, Lakṣmaṇa suspects Lalitā since she is out of place all alone in the forest and uncovers her ruse. Frustrated by the brothers' rejection, and by the revelation of her *māyā*, Lalitā goes into an enraged, entrancing dance that increases in speed and fierceness, and resumes her powerful demonic form; she reverts to her ugly, old, and malformed black body played by a male actor who speaks in a shrieking voice in a low caste, distorted Malayalam (the language of Kerala). In her rage she resolves to eat Lakṣmaṇa, so she lifts him to the sky, and in his attempt to escape the danger, Lakṣmaṇa mutilates her in midair. This aggression paints the cosmos red. Lakṣmaṇa's sword severs her breasts and nose, scattering blood and organs while smearing everything with a red downpour. Then Śūrpaṇakhā appears in the *Kūttambalam* as a shrieking mutilated dripping red creature. The entire world together with the *Kūttambalam* are imbued with the color and stickiness of blood.

As a result of her insatiable desire to mate and to eat, Śūrpaṇakhā, the demoness, is robbed of her female parts and sexual appeal; she loses her, albeit, fierce femininity, which is scattered throughout the world.

The second cosmic event is a result of Sītā's fire ordeal rendering the cosmos golden. Unlike the very graphic, terrorizing appearances of Śūrpaṇakhā, we, at the theater, do not see Sītā's ordeal but are present when Lakṣmaṇa, transformed by the event into "wondrous Lakṣmaṇa," tells his brother Rāma what has transpired. The cosmic event distributes a very different femininity into nature and the world, since when the chaste woman-cum-goddess Sītā steps into a cremation pyre to prove her innocence, she is not consumed but remains whole, both in her living and in her sexual body. Lifted out of the cremation fire by Agni, the god of fire, her sexual pureness and self-sacrifice enhance the beauty of the entire world, and nature itself is endowed with a wondrous golden hue.

Both cosmic transformations are a result of Rāma's sexual rejection; he rejects Śūrpaṇakhā, who appears as Lalitā and wants to marry him, and he rejects his own wife Sītā after her imprisonment. These events also cause a transformation in Lakṣmaṇa. In *Kūṭiyāṭṭam*, when a new character enters the stage for the first time, they cover their face, and then perform *kriyā*—dance steps that can invoke the gods—behind a curtain held by two stage assistants. The invocative steps are danced first facing the drummers, and then, turning around, facing the audience; and only then is the curtain removed so that the audience can see the actor's face. After both events, although Lakṣmaṇa had already appeared in the act, he is presented again behind a curtain as a new protagonist. In the first instance, it is because he had escaped death at the hands of Śūrpaṇakhā, and in the second he is transformed by attending the fire ordeal to become "wondrous Lakṣmaṇa," who appears on stage with red flowers decorating his face.

The correspondence between those two cosmic events is also causal, at least on the surface of things: the first cosmic event causes the unfolding that will result in the second since Śūrpaṇakhā's disfigurement is the beginning of a chain of events that will lead to Sītā's abduction by the demon-king Rāvaṇa, Śūrpaṇakhā's brother. A bloody war will ensue between Rāvaṇa and his army of demons and Rāma assisted by an army of monkeys. And finally, Sītā will be rescued only to be challenged once more by her husband Rāma, who accuses her of having been defiled while imprisoned by the mighty Rāvaṇa. Thus, she immediately needs to prove her sexual integrity by stepping onto a cremation pyre. The dismembered, scattered Śūrpaṇakhā will eventually lead to the indestructible Sītā.[2]

Although the mutilation of Śūrpaṇakhā ultimately leads to Sītā's ordeal, in *Kūṭiyāṭṭam* no causality is straightforward since a *Kūṭiyāṭṭam* performance does not follow a linear chain of events alone. Rather, the performance espouses the dynamics of waves, moving back and forth through time, repeating the same events and leaping to events that took place at other times and places, swallowing events to generate higher waves or mere ripples, a movement that never ceases. So, Lakṣmaṇa tells about the fire ordeal to Rāma, and the latter keeps asking him anxiously "and then?," "and then?"; the complex densification of time and the cosmos itself is an infinity of "and thens" jumping to pasts and the present of the story, folding into each other and on and on. Objects are sentient, colors become active forces, and the relations among them follow their own dynamics. The performance ushers into existence different forms of time and of causality that relate to one another in nonlinear ways.[3]

The sacrifice of those two females reenergizes the cosmos, projecting female energy, and, in doing so, densifies interconnectedness in two different ways. Whereas the red world resulting from Śūrpaṇakhā's mutilation is one of activation, energy, desire, violence, and the speeding-up of time and chaos, the golden world issuing from Sītā's ordeal slows down time, and is one of restraint, of serenity, interiority, and order. Both—like the heat and cold of temperature or like the bright and dark of light—are intensities of the same, oscillating between these indispensable facets of the female contribution to the workings of the world.

The performances that I documented were the following: the entire *Śūrpaṇakhāṅkam* was performed by the Nepathya school in December 2014; Lalitā was performed by Indu G.; black and red Śūrpaṇakhā were sequentially performed by Margi Madhu. I have also seen the last night called *niṇam*, meaning "coagulated blood," performed in the Killimangalam Śiva-Viṣṇu temple in September 2016. The actors were mainly graduates of the Kalamandalam school of Kerala arts; Lalitā was performed by Kalamandalam Krishnendu, while black and red Śūrpaṇakhā were performed by the veteran actor Rāman Chakiar.

The last act, I watched the *Agnipraveśāṅkam* in a two-night abbreviated form at the Margi school in Trivandrum in December 2014, and the entire act in Nepathya from December 2017 to January 2018.

## Colors, Matrilineality, and the Female Body

Colors can act in complex and versatile ways, and in many South Indian rituals, the potentialities embedded in colors emerge. The actors' costumes are white, red, black, and golden, the same colors that will paint the cosmos following the transformation of Śūrpaṇakhā and Sītā. In South Indian rituals, colors are practical devices, active in a variety of ways; they can intervene in the world and affect it. They are not merely paint over a surface, a thin sheen that disguises form or true nature (see Taussig 2006: 33); rather, colors are full of potentiality, they are substances in their own right. Colors are not symbols with constant meaning; rather, they can often exchange roles between them. They play a role of intensifying or rarifying; they hold the tendency that may concentrate affects and change rhythms. Turner (1967; see also Hiltebeitel 1976: 68–74), in his effort to unveil a universal meaning of colors in ritual, claims that since the human body produces white matter such as milk and semen, red blood, and dark excrements, then white, red, and black must have universal significance. White is associated with life; red is ambivalent, since it invokes childbirth as well as injury; and black, he claims, is very often neglected since it is "the hidden, the secret, the dark, the unknown—and perhaps also of the potentiality as opposed to actuality" (Turner 1967: 73).[4]

But bestowing a fixed meaning to each color (universal or not) is tantamount to classifying them as symbols that represent abstractions such as life, rejuvenation, danger, detritus, or secrets. But as already mentioned, the use of symbols as a sole mechanism that produces meaning is not often used in *Kūṭiyāṭṭam*. Here colors assume an active role—namely, the question is not what colors represent, but what they do, how they are used, how they interact with other colors and with other elements. Colors in the two cosmic events related here do not operate through representation, nor do they acquire one stable meaning; they are practical tools put to work in an effort to open up new options through their interaction with other elements of the performance, so that female energy can be thrust to permeate the entire cosmos.

Employing colors as tools is practical rather than abstract; it shows how colors actually participate in attaining the aims of a performance or a ritual. And again, just as linear segments can exist within nonlinear storytelling, so, too, colors used as straightforward signifiers are one of a myriad of options within a practical, world-generating, nonsymbolic ritualistic mechanism.

As Turner asserted, in the two cosmic events on the *Kūttambalam* stage and in Kerala rituals in general, color is indeed often associated with bodily fluids and especially those pertaining to the female sexual body. In Kerala, the auspicious nature of female body fluids, the use of colors, and the ideal woman are all related to specific kinship arrangements. The prominence of matrilineal castes in Kerala means that traditionally marriage is often a loose arrangement depending on the woman's choice, while the children belong to the mother's family. Thus, connections between husband and wife in matrilineal castes have a more informal character than in patrilineal families.

Since within the patrilineal Nampūdiri (the Kerala Brahmin) families only the first-born son could marry, the younger sons would create liaisons called *sambandham* with women of matrilineal castes. That also meant that those men, being of an easily polluted caste (see Holdrege 1998: 368), did not live in the multigenerational matrilineal home, the *taravad*, and could not eat with their wives or children (e.g., see Gough 1959; Mencher and Goldberg 1967; Dumont 1969; Ishii 2014). These arrangements also applied to the *ambalavasi*, the matrilineal families of the Cākyār and the Nambyār, the temple assistants who are the carriers of the *Kūṭiyāṭṭam* tradition. This kind of family associations between the matrilineal and patrilineal groups are also at the foundation of the close relations between the Nampūdiri patrons of *Kūṭiyāṭṭam*, and the artists, a tight connection that persists even today, after many of the matrilineal arrangements, and in particular the *taravad*, have all but disappeared.[5]

Because of the prevalence of this traditional kinship system, the modest wife, who is the ideal woman in Northern India, is replaced by a breastfeeding mother associated with the color white. The ideal auspicious woman in Kerala is "Cool, fertile and flowing with nutritious milk" (Caldwell 2001: 124; on body fluids elsewhere in India, see Alter 1992; Bhattacharya 2003; Darmon 2003). Both red and white are associated with fertility. Red is closest to a virgin, sexualized, fertile, yet without a man, and thus unfulfilled, her body associates sacrifice with the unfertilized menstrual blood. She is auspicious and powerful but uncontrolled, her femaleness is dangerous. A widow, on the other hand, while also sexualized and without a man, is inauspicious as well as dangerous (e.g., see Tapper 1979; Rāmaswamy 2009). Semen and blood are both intimately connected without the potentiality of fertility. Moreover, semen and menstrual blood have similar powers both in their generative and destructive potentialities such that "both sex and war rely on sacrifice of male blood-seed to regenerate life in the field of the female body" (Caldwell 2001: 133). While both white and red are associated with fertility in the female body, red is closer to the untamed potentiality of the fertile sexualized body, while white is closer to satisfied, actualized fertility.

Black is associated with the nonsexualized and nonfertile ascetic; black results from the storing of sexual energy and is associated with the lower castes. Men on pilgrimage to the famous Ayyappan temple in Kerala wear black clothes. Ayyappan is an avowed bachelor, and therefore resembles an ascetic in his nonsexualized existence.[6] Such dense storage of energy can suddenly be released. When black is concentrated, a kind of spontaneous combustion occurs; a sort of internal fire appears, one that can be both destructive and reproductive. Like fire, black is essential to human life, yet is highly dangerous if uncontrolled. Black is also an important color in repelling evil influences. This is why parents smear lamp soot around children's eyes, and for the same reason, black beads are popular as charms. For the pilgrims to the Aiyappan temple, black is worn not only in empathy with the ascetic god but also for its protective capacities, since "pilgrims have to pass through a dangerous jungle full of wild animals on their way to the shrine" (Beck 1969: 571n4). Volatile and changeable goddesses like Kālī and the South Indian Māriyamman are black or red, fierce, and dangerous, but these goddesses also possess a benevolent facet. Moreover, blackness also varies in its glow. Rāma himself is a black sun, a luminosity that comes out of blackness (David Shulman, personal communication).

Combinations of colors enable yet more potentialities to emerge; the combination of red, black, and white is capable of drawing female energy in Kerala. In the Pāmbin Tuḷḷal, a ritual intended to encourage fertility and prevent misfortune in the *taravad,* the multigenerational house, of the Nayars the matrilineal high caste, the serpent gods are invoked by the low-caste ritual specialists, the Pulluvar. A sacred drawing, a *kaḷam,* is drawn in white over a black background, and then a red cloth is spread to shade the *kaḷam*. This combination of white and black shaded by red is a way to draw the women's power, *śakti,* to the ritual. After the red drape has been fixed, the *kaḷam* is drawn more elaborately and other colors are added. Then two Nayar women sit on the *kaḷam* and after becoming possessed by the serpent gods, wipe the painting with their buttocks (Neff 1987: 65). The female fluid that flows from a vagina is saturated with *śakti*. In Orissa, men may roll on the earth after Deva Dāsīs—women consecrated to the god—have passed by, in order to appropriate that *śakti* (on rituals of Deva Dāsīs in Orissa, see Apffel-Marglin 2008: 83; see also Davesh 2012; Freeman 2016).[7]

In a ritual of divination performed in Tamil Nadu, white and red are complementary, depending on the question asked. White brings forth continuation and calm, while red encourages action and change. Flowers hidden in a leaf, red or white, are drawn out two or three times to answer binary questions. A white leaf "expresses well-being and is an appropriate color to indicate recovery and stability after some crisis has passed. A red one, by contrast, is the color of vitality because of its association with blood. It is appropriate where something important and life-giving is about to occur" (Beck 1969: 553–554). Correspondingly, the colors are interpreted in accordance with the questions asked: white is auspicious where stability, well-being, and the absence of evil are primary concerns. It is desirable when one wants to indicate the end of some climax or disturbance. Red, on the other hand, supersedes the ordinary and is desirable where innovation is sought. The combination or sequence of colors is always important; indeed, the three-part divinatory sequencing of white, red, and white flowers is the very sequencing of colors found in most South Indian life-cycle and temple rituals. Generally, a ceremony begins with a ritual that employs white, proceeds through a climax where red is central, and concludes with a second white event (Beck 1969: 556). The colors should be taken together in their sequencing as this creates a dynamic: red substance reveals "heated" states, and white substances "cooled" ones (Beck 1969: 553).

Gold is held as the most important metal in the Indian scriptures and possesses a life of its own (Mehrotra 2004: 27). Its yellow color stands for auspiciousness and is associated with luster and beauty. It is the color of Sūrya the sun god, and is also a sign of fertility (Beck 1969: 559). Gold, which is understood as the most fluid of metals, is thought to be the solid closest to liquid (Handelman 2014: 136). It is a substance tightly connected with women since they wear the family wealth in the form of gold jewelry, and therefore, "The giving of gold has been regarded as the most important form of *dāna* [gift] on all ritual occasions" (Beck 1969: 559). Because of its noble, valuable, and reflective character, gold is not to be worn beneath the waist, especially not on the feet. Gold is also a reflection of pure, auspicious, and elevated qualities. It enhances divine intelligence, goodness, natural loveliness, inner worth, perfection, idealism, and radiant beauty, since as gold reflects light, so too it embodies all material reflections of spiritual qualities (Apffel Marglin 1991).

Gold is closely associated with women as it personifies Lakṣmi, the goddess of wealth; moreover, in Orissa the term "Lakṣmi" also means gold (Mehrotra 2004: 28–29). And Lakṣmi the consort of Viṣṇu is also Sītā the wife of Rāma, who is Viṣṇu's avatar. And Sītā, as we shall see, turns the entire world golden.

Saffron and turmeric, both very cooling substances, are yellow or gold. "Turmeric is often rubbed on a young woman's body before her bath to cool her and to remove pollution. Turmeric is also placed on animals before they are sacrificed, and on new clothes, before they are presented as gifts, a piece of turmeric may be used in place of a wedding necklace" (Mehrotra 2004: 28–29).[8] More generally, this spice has a very strong association with fertility and prosperity. Moreover, married women wearing the turmeric on their faces ensure the transfer of their auspicious energy or *śakti* and therefore their husband's well-being; it is so auspicious that widows are not allowed to use it (Tapper 1979: 10).

The goddess Gangamma of Tirupati in Andhra Pradesh is kept in kitchens in the form of a mound of turmeric, called *pasupu*. By applying *pasupu*, women become golden; it is a beautifying but also a cooling agent. The essences of the goddess, indeed of all females, are said to be *pasupu* and *kunkum*, respectively of golden and red color (Burkhalter Flueckiger 2005, 2013). Women gather more of the quality of goddesses when applying turmeric every morning. However, women need not "become" the goddess, as on some level they already are the goddess, an identity marked performatively through the substance of turmeric shared between women and goddesses. Women must take the turmeric off at night to return to their humanness. They are not transformed by the simple turmeric application but simply recognized for what they are already sharing in the nature of the goddess (Burkhalter Flueckiger 2005; see also Menon 2002 concerning the gap between the power of women embedded in *śakti* that they share with the goddess, and their subdued social position).

The goddess Paiḍitalli of Vizianagaram in Andhra Pradesh is covered in gold during part of her ritual, which serves to complexify, and to intensify, her presence and thus to reveal more of her, creating a profoundness within her: "Turmeric, though applied to the exterior of the female, to her skin, enlivens her interior life, *layering* her from within, adding depth and texture. She glows more intensely from within, a self-shining burning with the brightness of life-force, itself focused by the dot of vermilion on the forehead. Her self-shining seems also to signal the *intensification* of coherence and integrity, the qualities of selfness, the qualities of depth" (Handelman 2014b: 136–137). The goddess's face is made of black stone, so while the turmeric hides that black face, her features are revealed through the bright yellow color. Black and golden are complementary aspects of goddesses. Pārvatī also holds within herself the facets of the two goddesses. During one of her fights with her husband, Śiva, she splits into two women, one golden, the other black (O'Flaherty 1980: 111).

Although colors reveal different facets of goddesses and the cosmos, they cannot be said to be contrary to each other. Rather, they are pairs of colors that are very close to one another. Black and gold reveal the goddess's nature, they share a certain glow, a luminosity that emanates from within; red and white are both the fertile substance of seed blood. Yellow and red are also very close—both the yellow coloring of the face and the red smear on the parting of the hair on a married woman's forehead exteriorize, and emphasize, her feminity and divinity—moreover, the two colors are even interchangeable since both are designated by the same word in Tamil, as well as in Malayalam.

Color is a powerful affect, made of intensity of luminosity, that tends to produce profound changes, intensifying one thing or another without altering identity—a practical tool made of gradations that encourage change through pure difference. Red and Yellow have no clear separate identity that supports distinction, antagonism, and other oppositions. In the two cases at hand, they enhance the spilling over of energy to intensify the cosmos in different ways, "shading off into each other, overlapping, circling back and looping into one another, popping up inside each other" (David Shulman, personal communication).

Like the black goddess covered in gold to reveal her features, and at the same time to cover her blackness, when Sītā renders the cosmos golden, the intensity of this woman-cum-goddess flows into the world revealing her profound and layered strength, divinity, and femaleness, while concomitantly masking other of her potentialities. It is said that during their time in the forest Rāma and Sītā refrained from sexual intercourse so that not only the ascetic life but also abstinence would increase Sītā's power—she is as pure as a virgin (Erndl 1991: 82). Through the fire ordeal, her beauty spills over into the world, revealing the power of her generative sexual potentiality unsoiled, and she shares this auspicious state with the world. Moreover, even when gruesome red Śūrpanakhā is led into the *Kūttambalam* spreading her blood as she advances, she gives out a hint of yellow. Since turmeric is a major ingredient in the concoction that is used as her blood in the performance, she spreads an invasive, fresh and strong aroma of wet turmeric that fills the theater; this aroma is saturated with *śakti* life energy, since it invokes the smell of perspiring women wearing turmeric on their faces.

## Śakti

*Śakti*, the power stored especially in the goddess and women, can move from auspicious to inauspicious and from growth to maturation and decay. Just as the flow of time, so too can *śakti* both destroy and renew. Like life itself, *śakti* is anti-hierarchical, not the power over others, but the power of bare life. In a conjugal or other sexual relationship, however, *śakti* in females is stabilized as auspicious. The danger, however, comes with unfulfilled sexualized women, such as virgins and widows; in other words, the dangerous *śakti* stems from celibacy (Apffel-Marglin 2008: 49, 51, 61, 70, 71; Menon 2002).

*Śakti* is the power of the goddess; it is the goddess herself, the cosmic energy that propels the world's activity, the force to enable.[9] It is the energy of the universe stored mainly in females; the energizing principle without which there would be no motion; it is strength and creative essence, the source of life and vitality, a condition for life, and its loss, and therefore can also herald disaster and death (Wadley 1975: 55; Obeyesekere 1981: 34). The goddess is process, movement, and her form-changing constitutes the universe (Beane 1973: 66). *Śakti* is the goddess's "univalent, ambivalent, and multivalent character," emphasizing her potentialities of "cosmogenesis, devigenesis, and cosmoredemption" (Beane 1973: 55). *Śakti* refers to the coexistence of the benevolent and malevolent facets of the goddess; to the timelessness of the goddess, who has always been, and will always be, and concomitantly enables events to occur and thus enables the flow of time, which entails homogeneity as well as change.

*Śakti* can create anything, and take many forms, it can even take the form of innumerable bees (Beane 1973: 81n168), and can give birth to *śakti* itself. She is the cause and the effect even of her self. Burkhalter Flueckiger (2013: 2–3) suggests that the goddess Gangamma is excess, surplus, overflowing—she is too much to bear. Indeed, the power of the goddess and the female must be excessive since in order to create something where nothing existed before, such as a new human being, surfeit is necessary. Yet this same capacity of the goddess is also anger; it is thus a delicate, complex, and dangerous task to benefit from excess without becoming prey to its wrath. In Kerala, *śakti* is both a surfeit and a capacity to create and maintain life, and specifically the productively feminine (Jenet 2005: 37n8).

*Śakti* may also be understood as the dynamic of action that combats nonaction or inertness and enables the world to do what it does. Were *śakti* to disappear, all would congeal (Handelman 2014: 4). Both Śūrpaṇakhā and her apparition as Lalitā can be seen as the manifestations of the two facets of the same woman-goddess-demon, the fierce and the docile sides of female energy. This double-faceted goddess is not unique to this story; the goddess Bhagavatī, a popular goddess in Kerala, changes her forms throughout the day, such as from quiet goddesses like Sarsvātī to the fierce Kālī (Caldwell 2001).

According to the Purāṇa, the god Murugan married two women—one of a high caste and the other of a low one. Together all three wielded three sorts of *śakti* and lived together in harmony like the three eyes of Śiva. The three *śaktis* are set in hierarchical order, each encompassing the lower one. The lowest *śakti* is *Icchā śakti*, the power of desire, will, and delusion that is passionate and disintegrative. *Kriyā śakti* is the power of motivation of work and action, and of maintenance. The most distant and abstract, *Jñāna śakti* is likened to Śiva's third eye, the transcendent power of perception and discrimination; it is wisdom that encompasses the two other *śakti*s and so equilibrates the cosmos (Handelman 2014: 47, 59).

Certain circumstances are required to experience this lifeforce and harness it for human benefit. Through ritual, *śakti* can be funneled into the human world and used to the advantage of both men and women; thus, all may gain the power of the goddess (Jenett 2005: 37n8). Many rituals are intended to release the goddess's *śakti*; and women also can dispense it naturally, especially powerful women who suffer, since through self-sacrifice women come closer to becoming a goddess themselves, and thus can become healers who channel *śakti* (e.g., Burkhalter Flueckiger 2013: 148). The ability to wield *śakti* by Tamil married women, to use it as action and power—which holds potential to heal, hurt and divine—can become more controlled by those who are out of the ordinary in their self-sacrifice. Mastering *śakti* by women depends on rebellion and on suffering, which is considered an ascetic practice, *tapas*, and yields heat. Particularly, *śakti* can be controlled through suffering at the hands of men and especially husbands—yet also through childbirth, and through self-inflicted restraint or pain. The latter often takes the form of self-inflicted poverty and the loss of body mass, namely, extreme thinness (Egnor 1980: 15–20). Moreover, *śakti* can also be spewed forth as a result of excessive desire; and if such a desire is not satisfied or pacified, it may develop excess and overflow dangerously (Burkhalter Flueckiger 2013: 30).

Both Śūrpanakhā and Sītā disseminate *śakti*-type energy into the world as a result of severe somatic conditions: Śūrpanakhā is mutilated, and Sītā is (almost) burned alive. Both their sufferings result from a male's sexual rejection, yet the energy disseminated by the disfigurement of Śūrpanakhā has a different dynamic and intensity than the one let loose by Sītā's self-sacrifice in the fire ordeal. The energy spewed forth by Śūrpanakhā is the consequence of her excessive desire—to mate, to eat—it is over-sized, over-activated. Śūrpanakhā's mutilation speeds up time, activating the world into constant movement, quickening the pace of life to the edge of war.[10] The red world resulting from Śūrpaṇakhā mutilation is of the powerful yet inauspicious energy of an unattached, sexually mature woman, a widow. Sītā's ordeal gives way to a calm and wondrous world, the auspicious married loyal wife slowing down time. The golden world that ensues is one of equilibrium and auspiciousness, giving the cosmos a leisurely glitter.

## Śūrpaṇakhā—White, Black and Red

The performance of the last night of *Śūrpaṇakhākhāṅkam*, the bloody *niṇam*, is extremely popular with the Kerala audience. Although throughout the week of performance the audience was small, for the last night's performance, the *Kūttambalam* was packed; all came to attend Śūrpaṇakhā's tragic-comic fate—to laugh at black Śūrpaṇakhā and watch with apprehension and horror her progression through the *Kūttambalam* after her mutilation.

Śūrpaṇakhā is fierce, powerful, and dangerous, a mistress of *māyā*, driven by a carnal desire for sex and food, her femaleness overwhelming. She is a widow looking for a new husband, and widowhood, as mentioned, is a dangerous and inauspicious state in Kerala, especially for a fertile woman (Caldwell 2001: 123). Her husband Vidyujjihva, who, she tells us, played with her to her great satisfaction, was killed by Śūrpaṇakhā's brother Rāvaṇa, the mighty king of Lanka. On an expedition to the netherworld fighting another army of demons, Vidyujjihva was a soldier in Rāvaṇa's army. But when the opponents started losing Vidyujjihva felt that it was not fair, and immediately changed sides. Rāvaṇa did not recognize him; he saw only an enemy soldier, and so Vidyujjihva found his death at Rāvaṇa's sword. Now Śūrpaṇakhā is looking around contemplating the gods who abide in all directions of the universe, but she finds fault in each of them.

Śūrpaṇakhā looks at Indra, the king of gods, and thinks, *he is not worthy to be my husband*. He is Ahalyā's illicit love. She goes on to Agni, the god of fire, and thinks that he is too hot, and thus not suitable. She continues to Antaka, the god of death, and thinks that he is very cruel—so no, not him. She then considers Nirṛti, but believes his deeds are not suitable, so not him either. Seeing Varuṇa, the god of water, she thinks he is Gaṅgā's husband, so not him. She sees Vāyu, the god of wind, and thinks that he is always traveling—thus, not him. Seeing Vaiśrāvaṇa, the god of wealth, she thinks he is her own brother, so he cannot be the one. She then looks over Lord Śiva and thinks he is the enemy of Kāmadeva, the god of love, and so definitely not him. "None of the gods are suitable for me," she says.[11] Then seeing Rāma she decides to marry him.

But then Śūrpaṇakhā experiences a reflective moment. She understands that Rāma is young, and she is old, his stomach is small while hers protrudes, she is ugly, and he is glowing. So, if she is to stand a chance with him, she must disguise herself. While Śūrpaṇakhā is seeking a new husband, Rāma is living with his wife Sītā in the *Parṇa-śālā,* the forest hut carefully constructed by Lakṣmaṇa, and this is where Śūrpaṇakhā sees him. She transforms herself through *māyā* into Lalitā, a beautiful and elegantly adorned lady, and walks into the forest to meet Rāma.

Up to the seventh and last night of the act, we have seen Śūrpaṇakhā only as the elegant white lady Lalitā, equal to Sītā in beauty and elegance, played by an actress who speaks in mudrā gestures. Perhaps she is the incarnation of the demoness's ambition and attempt to meddle with, and possibly usurp, other worlds, or, perhaps, if accepted, she could have remained in her docile avatar, a faithful and proper wife like Sītā.[12]

But Lalitā does not fit—indeed, what would an elegant, beautifully adorned lady do all alone in the demon-infested forest? This attempt to belong to the humans-cum-god's family is doomed to failure, and with the crumbling of *māyā,* disarray ensues. For "the attempt of the asuras to ascend the hierarchy, by usurping the natural location of the gods, turns cosmic order into an incoherent aggregation of disconnected elements—in other words into ramified disorder" (Handelman 2014b: 59). Now Lalitā is rejected and her *māyā* revealed. She is discombobulated, and is about to return to demon form; she is seized by an entrancing dance, going through the same series of emotional expressions, each series three times. From love to sadness, to anger, then again, love, sadness, anger, and once more. While her dance becomes wilder and wilder, she gathers emotional momentum for the transformation. Her effort of reflexivity that turned her into a suitable mate for princes has failed,. and she reverts to her black, demonic form.

Now she is ugly, performed by a male actor, black with white tridents painted on her face, her mouth red and exaggerated, her nails very long; she is wearing a straw skirt, and sports enormous protruding pointed conical breasts that are as long as her forearm. Śūrpaṇakhā is bare-breasted, which was typical of lower-caste women, who were not allowed to cover their breasts (e.g., Gentes 1992: 311), a trait that also corresponds to her low-caste speech. As she tells her story, black Śūrpaṇakhā often fondles her pointed breasts. The conical form of her breasts can be associated with rice and fertility. When the great goddess Bhagavatī is drawn into a *kaḷam*—a sacred drawing which is her—raw rice is piled up as her breasts. Those conical mounds of rice echo the common sight in the season after the monsoon when the fertile soil is piled up in small red conical mounds (Caldwell 2001).[13]

Now Śūrpaṇakhā does not speak in mudrā gestures but talks in Malayalam. The other character in *Kūṭiyāṭṭam* who typically speaks in Malayalam is the funny and abusive Vidūṣaka, glossed over as a clown. He too appears on stage without a shirt, and he too is a blend of the funny, the provocative, and the intimidating.[14] Śūrpaṇakhā's voice is an unpleasant screech, her speech distorted. She speaks in a low-caste vernacular, her shrieking voice changing every "sh" into a "ch" so that her name becomes Chūrpaṇākhā.[15] The royal brothers describe her features to each other—Lakṣmaṇa says: "How is she? when she raises her hands they touch the clouds, and when they return, the earth seems to go up and down. When she comes towards us her mouth is open to eat us, it looks like a castle with its spacious door open."[16] Black Śūrpaṇakhā is both fierce and ridiculous. These seemingly contrary attributes were accentuated in the rendition by Raman Chakyar of Black Śūrpaṇakhā in Killimangalam. As he was talking in Śūrpaṇakhā's ridiculous voice, describing the silliness of her husband, making the audience laugh, he was moving around constantly, suddenly throwing to one side and the other angry, urgent, menacing looks that already hinted at her becoming aggressive, thus infusing thrills of laughter with thrills of fear.

When she was contemplating which man to choose as her new husband, Śūrpaṇakhā understood that in the form of a demoness she could not please. But now she loses all reflexive considerations, becoming craving incarnate. Now she is utterly satisfied with her looks, and with herself—and she is hungry. Śūrpaṇakhā means "sieve nails," while Vidyujjihva, her husband's name, means "tongue of lightning"; both names include protruding body parts. These ridiculous names indicate their demonic and dangerous capacities, pointing particularly to a central trait of demons: their proneness to follow their bodily cravings without restraint.[17] Śūrpaṇakhā is a highly sexual being, missing her silly husband for his satisfactory playfulness, and she covets Rāma while fondling her breasts. She is gluttonous, and now lacking social limitations of etiquette, she desires to eat Lakṣmaṇa. She already imagines the sounds his bones will make when she grinds them between her teeth, making "pata pata" and "kulu kala" sounds, imitating the noise of eating, breaking bones, and sucking juices out of her prey. Seeking to avenge her rejection, she captures Lakṣmaṇa and takes him up to the sky to devour him.

Lakṣmaṇa appears on stage with a sword, and as he is lifted to the sky by the ogress he fights back and cuts off Śūrpaṇakhā's breasts and nose. The nose is the organ associated with honor, while the breasts—especially in South India, where motherhood is valued over the role of a wife—are the essence of femininity (Erndl 1991; Caldwell 2001; see also Pasty 2012). So, the mighty Śūrpaṇakhā loses her honor and her womanhood, as her female organs and blood are tossed around from the sky, dropping and dripping, filling the world. Significantly, when the mutilation is performed at a temple dedicated to Lakṣmaṇa, it is the temple priest rather than the actor who goes to the backroom, the dressing "green" room, and there he is the one who cuts off Śūrpaṇakhā's breasts and nose. The "green room" has the properties of a temple, and the mutilation is itself an act of ritual transformation. Therefore, it is performed by the god himself through the hands of his priest.

Tearing off women's breasts is a powerful combustive act: Kaṇṇaki, another South Indian widow, is an enraged woman. Upon hearing that the king of Madurai has unjustly executed her (albeit unfaithful) husband she tears off her left breast and throws it at the city, burning it down. Kaṇṇaki has the power of a chaste but fertile widow (Caldwell 2001: 129; Ilango 1965). She became the goddess Pattini, enshrined in the temple of Kodungalur in Kerala.[18]

Yet, as she is losing her blood and organs, Śūrpaṇakhā is irrigating the world with a powerful generative essence. Blood in Kerala is a central medium of life, a fertilizing fluid holding procreative potentialities, as do sexual fluids, which fertilize as they are exteriorized, propelled into the world (Caldwell 2001: 113). Blood sacrifice is also an act of quenching the earth's thirst to permit renewal and growth. This is why female blood of menstruation or childbirth is not polluting; rather, given its strong generative potentialities, it is powerful and therefore can be dangerous (O'Flaherty 1980: 41).[19] Śūrpaṇakhā unleashes a certain potentiality of female blood sacrifice. Instead of drinking Lakṣmaṇa's blood to add to her own strength, and instead of using her female blood to create new life, Śūrpaṇakhā is oozing, filling the world with gore, rendering everything red. Rāma does not understand the change that suddenly occurs in the cosmos, and says to Sītā, "What is this? Does water flowing from the rivers to the forests get this red color as it touches the mountains? Do the clouds of the flood season pour down red-blood, as done by the rising sun?"[20]

At this point, the anticipation in the *Kūttambalam* is at its peak. Everyone knows that the most impressive, gruesome, and surprising event is on its way, that the mutilated Śūrpaṇakhā is going to appear. The day before the performance, a specialist came to brew Śūrpaṇakhā's blood. He cooked curcuma, lime, and rice powder for several hours to create a bright red, wet, lumpy, and sticky texture.[21] We were warned beforehand that our clothes may be stained by the concoction and that we should wear old clothes for the occasion. Now, in anticipation of the appearance of the mutilated demoness, the children, who were already frightened by the squeaking black Śūrpaṇakhā, are hurried away. Meanwhile

Figure 4.1. Madhu Chakyar as black Śūrpaṇakhā. *Source*: Nepathya Centre for Excellence.

Rāma, Lakṣmaṇa and Sītā are talking in mudrā gestures on stage, but no one is paying any attention to them.

The plastic chairs of the audience are pushed aside, and many of the people who crowd the theater are standing and looking at the entrance of the *Kūttambalam*. The stage has two low doors leading from the green room—an actor will always come on stage through the left door and leave through the right one, but now the mutilated demoness will enter through the main door leading to the *Kūttambalam* facing the stage, the audience entrance. Despite the anticipation, and although the entire audience knew what was coming, the effect of Śūrpaṇakhā's arrival is overwhelming. The electric lights are turned off, and torches carried by five men accompanying Śūrpaṇakhā emerge from the audience entrance. Nowadays, the use of torches in public theaters is considered unsafe, so the use of fire for this extraordinary entrance is rare. Red Śūrpaṇakhā is also supposed to exit the *Kūttambalam* to enter

Figure 4.2. Madhu Chakyar as red Śūrpaṇakhā. Photo Sahapedia. *Source*: Nepathya Centre for Excellence.

the green room from the wrong entrance—namely, the left door—but on this occasion, she exited from the right. Śūrpaṇākhā enters from outside with her insides on her outside, scattering disorder, entering and leaving through the wrong aperture.

She is a gruesome sight—a monstrous apparition of mutilation, hurt, and shame, and she is shrieking like an animal. She is draped in a dripping wrap drenched in blood. As she advances in the *Kūttambalam*, she fills the floor with spatters of her bright red blood; she opens her wrap to show her bloody chest and missing breasts, and then closes it around her body, shrieking in blood-freezing anguish; her nose is a chain of cotton dripping with blood, and her face seen intermittently in the torch fire is red. The men holding the torches are supporting her while she stumbles and falls down, howling, wailing, and spraying the audience with her blood, leaving puddles of blood where she falls. She takes several long minutes to traverse the entire *Kūttambalam*, swaying as she advances, while the audience recoils from her and her blood. Yet, the spectators then advance to get a better look, thus creating waves of movement correlating with her advance. The theater is filled with the smell of curcuma, a pleasant, clean smell of good food. Meanwhile, on stage, the other protagonists continue telling their story, moving their hands to the sound of the drums. All of a sudden, the beautiful, well-contained mudrā world seems too elegant and neat; its affect is effaced in contrast with the mess Śūrpaṇakhā strews in her path.

Lalitā, the white, *māyā* Śūrpaṇakhā, is reflexive; she is capable of following the decorum of a delicate noble lady, yet she is still a misfit, out of place in the forest. Black Śūrpaṇakhā is, in the literal sense, naked of the illusion (*māyā*) that turned her into Lalitā, yet, too, she has lost any hope to marry Rāma or his brother Lakṣmaṇa. Her illusion lost, she becomes a ludicrous woman. Everybody in the *Kūttambalam* finds her funny—frightening but ridiculous. Red Śūrpaṇakhā is disembodied, destroyed, ruined. She is reduced to utter desolation; she has lost parts of her body, her breasts, her femininity, her nose, and her face—her self is distributed all over the world. Red Śūrpaṇakhā is horrifying, disgusting, and menacing, while no less pitiful. An aching, disfigured demoness, she is still powerful, rendering the entire world red, as she fills the cosmos with red wetness, irrigating it. Blood is dripping from the sky, scattered organs falling on everyone in the cosmos of *Kūṭiyāṭṭam*. The downpour is contaminating, smearing everyone with the affect of demonesses. Caldwell (2001) describes the killing of the demon Dārika by Kālī at the end of the dry season in Muṭiyēṯṯu, a temple drama in Kerala. She describes the effect of the demon's bloodshed on the earth: "The sacrifice of the male blood-seed to the hot and thirsty feminine body is the act which enables the perpetuation of life" (2001: 113). Śūrpaṇakhā, too, irrigates the world and thus activates it.

## Sītā's Fire Ordeal

In the seventh and last act of the play, another female is in danger of destruction: Sītā was saved from Rāvaṇa's captivity through a full-fledged war. But now in the presence of her husband, Rāma, she is threatened by another form of ruin. Rāma does not believe that Rāvaṇa—who was full of love and lust toward her and held her captive in his garden—did not defile her. Moreover, like Lalitā before her, Sītā does not fit. She is clean and adorned with no signs of weariness after living in the forest and captivity, and that too arouses suspicion. Like Lalitā, the beautifully elegant and adorned Sītā is also a result of *māyā*, for she was granted a boon from Anasūyā, a sage's wife, so that her dirt would look like ornaments in her husband's presence; now this boon, as we can see her saying to herself on stage, has turned into a curse. To prove her innocence, she undertakes the fire ordeal. She will step into a large fire, a funeral pyre, and surviving that, will prove her innocence.

Whereas red Śūrpanakhā is oozing blood and filling the air with her shrieks, freezing and melting the hearts of the audience at the same time, Sītā's triumph is not experienced by the audience. Rather, it is told to Rāma by his brother Lakṣmaṇa, who has been transformed by the experience to become "wondrous Lakṣmaṇa." He now has red flowers on his face, and his entrance is accompanied by a shower of white flowers that are then left on the stage.

As Lakṣmaṇa is relating the events, Rāma keeps asking over and over, "And then what happened?" "And then what happened?" We experience this cosmic event indirectly through the eyes of Lakṣmaṇa, a second-degree telling by a male. "Wondrous Lakṣmaṇa" describes with amazement, how as Sītā was gently lifted from the fire by Agni—the god of fire—she remained unharmed. In Kampaṉ's Tamil version of the *Rāmāyaṇa*, the decision by Sītā to go into the fire puts the cosmos into distress. Agni does not simply take Sītā in his hands as a merciful act to reinstate justice, but rather he himself is scorched by the goddess's presence within him. Fire burns fire: Agni lifts Sītā to avoid his own pain, while she herself is in a watery state so that even the beads of sweat on her forehead were not dried by the fire (Shulman 1991). In the *Kūṭiyāṭṭam* version, Lakṣmaṇa tells Rāma that Sītā went into the fire "like a person suffering from the torture of extreme heat entering water." The fire cools her. Sītā is a powerful goddess—of a cool substance.

South Indian goddesses, as Handelman (2014b) claims, are interiorized, sunk into themselves, with floating unfocused awareness, and that is where the cosmos grows, "within depth, emerging from inside, from the interiority of interiority" (Handelman 2004b: 117). They are deep inside themselves so that they must be coaxed in different ritual ways to come to our world and bestow their energy on the world. Sītā is such an interiorized goddess, glowing from within, and within her depth, she enters the fire. She does not become unstable or exteriorized; from within herself, she is powerful, and thus, we, the world, are included in her, within her complex interiority, through the fire ordeal.

The entire world was affected by the ordeal; nature was calm and happy. Lakṣmaṇa tells Rāma that, "It is then that the bees that were inebriated after sucking nectar to their fill from the tree by the ocean rose up the tree top and enveloped the sky in a flight of blue.[22] Why did they fly in this manner? They had seen the most fragrant flowers of the heavenly Kalpaka tree falling and were reaching out to drink from it." Then, as the brothers both experience the world turning gold, they see "the glow that is spreading all around, the sky and earth are now very different. How is this possible? The mountains along the coast are golden-hued now. The forest is like a garden in bloom like the Kalpaka Garden in heaven."[23] The golden world is a result of the skies opening to leave no border between the world we live in and the gods' abode.

Once again, femininity is disseminated throughout the world, yet this time it is Sītā's pure and serene power. And as a result, the gods' world is opening onto the mundane one so that the bees can drink from the flowers of the heavenly Kalpa tree, and humans can meet with gods and with the deceased. Lakṣmaṇa and Rāma experience great emotional upheaval when they can meet their ancestors, particularly their dead father. In the *Kūttambalam*, this was a very emotional moment because Lakṣmaṇa and Rāma were played by two actual brothers, Madhu and Sajeev Chakyar, whose deceased father was also their guru. Tears were running down their cheeks, drawing grooves in the green color covering their faces. The golden world of beauty incarnate is completely fluid, capable of erasing the borders between heaven and earth and of reversing the affects of death, so that the living and the dead may meet.

## Two Females, Two Cosmic Events

According to O'Flaherty (1984: 83), "both Sītā and Śūrpanakhā have the potential of violent, destructive action, and both are beautiful and seductive, but Śūrpanakhā cannot control her passion, while Sītā can." The two women are two sides of the female. They relate

Figure 4.3. Brothers Madhu and Sajeev Chakyar as Rāma and Lakṣmaṇa. in the *Agnipraveśāṅkam*, when the sky opens and they see their father. Author photo.

to each other just as the auspicious Lakṣmi—who is Sītā in another avatar—relates to her inauspicious sister Alakṣmi (Erndl 1991: 84), not different in their suffering, but only in the consequences of their emotional manifestation. In this sense, Śūrpanakhā is an aspect of Sītā's emotions, perhaps her shadow side. Śūrpanakhā is enraged by the rejection of Sītā's husband; perhaps the ordeals of all women infuriate her. Śūrpanakhā is not black, nor white, nor red; Sītā is not the pure, radiant, and obedient wife nor a fierce goddess. No form is truer than the other; rather, the two females are unfoldings of intensities, of different potentialities of *śakti*, the energy necessary for the world to keep living, to be active, to sustain movement and to generate connections, to be fertile.

Both Śūrpaṇakhā and Sītā experience a vertical movement. Both go up and come down again, yet whereas Śūrpaṇakhā's movement is abrupt as she lifts herself up, holding Lakṣmaṇa in her grip, then tumbles down spreading her blood and organs, Sītā is gently lifted out of the fire by Agni and then carefully put down again. While Śūrpaṇakhā is eruptive, Sītā is contained. As the demoness's femaleness rains down wet and sticky, turning her flesh inside out so that she is made of raw flesh both inside and outside, Sītā remains intact; she is glowing from within herself, her energy smooth and liquid, changing the laws of the flesh so that it remains wet amid fire.

The two cosmic events shape the world and propel it forward into new trajectories, each bringing forth other events of intensification that are on the way to others, and on, and on, ensuring life's continuation. The result of the mutilation of Śūrpaṇakhā, expressed by Rāma in the last sentence of the *Śūrpaṇakhāṅkam,* is a bloody feud between the two royal families, Rāma's and Rāvaṇa's. Sītā's proof of purity will be followed by the return of Rāma as king of Ayodhya. Both events have cosmic consequences; they both propel the world into different dynamics and bring forth distinctive intensities.

While Śūrpaṇakhā's redness and injury are shocking, disgusting and frightening, directional and energetic, Sītā's is subtle, soothing, and generates extreme well-being. The golden goddess's energy is channeled inward, into order and quietness that permits a convergence of the worlds of gods, humans, animals, and the dead within a moment of harmony, while the demoness's undoing is erupting outward generating disorder, yet creating a multitude of intersections that open up potentialities. The dynamics of the demoness's transformation from white to black to red unleashes her fierce female energy, whereas the unchanging Sītā results in the glowing open universe. Meanwhile, something is happening to time as well; whereas Śūrpaṇakhā's undoing is giving time an urgency, Sītā's ordeal slows down time.

When Gregory Bateson's daughter wonders, "Why do things get into a muddle?," he tells her that there are infinite ways in which things are muddled, whereas there are only a few ways in which things are tidy (Bateson 2000: 3–8). That is, disorder is normal because statistically messiness is more prevalent in the world than orderly arrangements. Disorder, according to Bateson, is a result of atrophy, a normal side effect of life, while order is the result of intentional human effort. Order in such a world is a desired state of affairs that ensures its efficiency. The cosmos of the *Āścaryacūḍāmaṇi,* however, is not constructed in the same way. In it, both order and disorder are beneficial and necessary. Neither order nor disorder is a situation that can be calculated statistically. They are dynamic directions in which the world is propelled. This world is in constant movement, moving in perpetual trajectories that must not be allowed to congeal and stop. Both chaos and harmony are generative; both are female forces of the goddess or demoness, the auspiciousness of calm, and the scattering motion of acute disorder. These two types of energy are not opposed; rather, they are complementary, two extremes on the same trajectory, two intensities that make a difference, two facets of the goddess, and both are necessary for the cosmos to act.

The events described here produce the forces that set a multidimensional pendulum into motion. These two females give a push to the world, set it on a trajectory that will increase energy—the red world reorders inside and out, by displaying the bloody inside on the surface, and the golden generates profoundness out of surface. Atrophy, the result of the daily grind, of the even flow of time, limits the scope of constant motility, while the cosmic events encourage them to move more vigorously between the speeding of time through chaos and the slowing of time through harmony. These are two of the world's profound dynamics: the red frenzy of activity and the golden world of impeccable calm and beauty.

Both types of movement are propelled by excess, generating too much of the demoness and the goddess by driving those females into distress, thus eclipsing other colors, other diversities. The overflow pushes the universe into total fluidity, which may result from eruption as in the red cosmos, or from calm and quiet in the golden one, both reinforcing the world's constant shifting.

Chapter 5

# *Cūṭala-k-kūttu*

## Performing at the Cremation Grounds

Upon the death of a Nampūdiri, a Kerala Brahmin, the *Cūṭala-k-kūttu* is held at the cremation grounds. During this ritual, the entire story of Lord Kṛṣṇa is performed by a Naṅṅyār. Although it has not been held in 150 years, the *Cūṭala-k-kūttu* was performed again recently in March 2013, and again in August 2021. It is indeed a rare ritual, since for it to be called for, many very specific conditions must come together. The main condition is that the deceased must have been the sacrificer in the grand Vedic sacrifice, the construction of the altar of fire—the *Agnicayana*—in his lifetime. As a result of the grand sacrifice, the sacrificer was elevated to the state of Agnihotri and tended to three ritual fires at his home throughout his life. The second determining condition is that his widow must survive the Agnihotri. In effect, the *Cūṭala-k-kūttu* is the ritual act that concludes the *Agnicayana* and is performed in front of and for the widow.

The *Agnicayana*, the building of the fire altar—perhaps the oldest ritual in the world (Staal 1979b: 2)—was renewed in 1975. In fact, for the twice-born Brahmins of Kerala, the Nampūdiris, the only manifestation of gods and the oldest one is the fire itself; no images are required (Tarabout 2004). The *Agnicayana* is grand in scope, time consuming, demands great expertise, and costs 6 *lakh*—600,000 rupees[1]—to perform; it is very expensive, in Indian terms. Perhaps for these reasons, the last *Agnicayana* prior to 1975 was performed in 1956 (Staal 1976). Nevertheless, although the *Agnicayana* has not been performed for many years, it was kept alive in the memory of the Nampūdiris, and so it could be revived through European initiative and funding led by Dutch Sanskritist Frits Staal. Staal explains why he thinks the *Agnicayana* is a rare occurrence: "The tradition is on the verge of extinction because of waning interest, rising costs and because it has become increasingly difficult to find the four Samavedins[2] required." Namely, he claims that the tradition has not passed over to the next generation. At the end of Staal's film on the *Agnicayana,* he correspondingly states that this is probably the last time such a ritual will take place (Staal 1979a). The Nampūdiri Brahmins of Kerala took this statement as a challenge, and since 1975, the *Agnicayana* has been performed nearly every year.[3]

The *Cūṭala-k-kūttu* is a renewed tradition in two respects: first, because the *Agnicayana*—that awarded the old Nampūdiri who passed away his title of Agnihotri—was not performed for a long time, but since its renewal the Agnihotri has resurfaced, and so, too, the need to perform the *Cūṭala-k-kūttu* after his death. Second, since no one remembers the ritual performed 150 years age, the Naṅṅyār had to reconstruct the ways of performing this ritual by drawing on her and her colleagues' erudition. Moreover, she did not rely on the way *Naṅṅyārkūttu* (a single actress's performance) is performed today, but attempted to undo earlier renovations in *Naṅṅyārkūttu,* and reconstruct the ritual in the older fashion, close to the way it was supposedly performed 150 years ago.

As in many renewed traditions, the *Cūṭala-k-kūttu* in particular and the *Naṅṅyārkūttu* in general draw on profound and ancient roots. As in other renewed traditions it too is influenced by the changes in life brought about by the opening of societies to other cultures, and by modern life and opportunities (e.g., Friedman 1990). Yet, although the renewing of the *Cūṭala-k-kūttu* came about as a result of the intervention of Western scholars, through their funding of a renewed *Agnicayana,* it does not enhance any national or ideological tendency brought about by modernization as other renewed traditions tend to do. Rather, it is performed in a very circumscribed ritualistic context, within the confines of the concerned families alone. The *Cūṭala-k-kūttu* is a renewed tradition, yet it is hardly an "invented tradition." The popular term "invented tradition" assumes that the "invention" is contrived and serves a purpose, such as economic gain, building national ethos, or cultural survival (Hobsbawm and Ranger 1992). In the case of *Cūṭala-k-kūttu,* such straightforward functionalist reasons are missing. The specific ways in which this ancient tradition is renewed organize a cosmos, one created by the artists-cum-ritualists, and one relevant to participants today despite great changes in their lifestyles.

Both the *Agnicayana* and *Cūṭala-k-kūttu* bring together a myriad of connections and traditions, some of which are no longer respected, while others may never have been practiced at all. Yet all are included in the reverberating ripples and shimmerings of the ritual, both apparent and concealed. As a result of the changes in lifestyles, many traditions that are at the root of these rituals are not practiced anymore, such as Nampūdiri and Naṅṅyār marriage patterns, the seclusion of the Nampūdiri women, and the terms of the Nampūdiri encounter with impure substances and people. Nevertheless, the renewal of practices permits ancient feelings, dynamics, and devotions to travel to today's world.

Many Nampūdiris Brahmin families were rich landowners in Kerala and were a powerful group in all respects before the land reform act of 1963 stripped them of much of their landed wealth. The *Cūṭala-k-kūttu* involves two Kerala high castes: the patrilineal Nampūdiris and the matrilineal Nambyār/Naṅṅyār temple assistants. However, while the Nampūdiri part of the ritual is documented and detailed in the family book of the deceased, the *grantha,* the explicit role of the Naṅṅyār was lost. The Naṅṅyār who performed the *Cūṭala-k-kūttu* 150 years ago was a member of the Viluvattam-family (Irinjnalakkuta), and this family still keeps the presents received on that occasion as a memento (Moser 2008). So, the name of that Naṅṅyār who performed 150 years ago is known, but obviously no living Naṅṅyār has ever witnessed it. Moreover, no *āṭṭa-prakāram* (manual) has survived to instruct the actress how to perform Kṛṣṇa's story on such an occasion. Although all *Naṅṅyārkūttu* tell the story of Kṛṣṇa, the Naṅṅyārs today, even at temple rituals, perform only the first half of the story; no *āṭṭa-prakāram* for the second half of Kṛṣṇa's story remains. This is why the Naṅṅyār who performed the ritual in March 2013, Aparṇa

Naṅṅyār, was compelled to reconstruct nearly every detail of how to perform the *Cūṭala-k-kūttu*.

Although the origins of the *Cūṭala-k-kūttu* are ancient, and the ritual is a sacred duty fulfilled by the sons of an Agnihotri, and although it is clearly related to the deceased's liberation from the cycle of life, and to his surviving widow, the precise role of this ritual, its exact goal or mechanism, are not explained. This is also true for the *Agnicayana* itself, which led Staal (1979b) to declare that the *Agnicayana* is "meaningless." Ritual, says Staal (1979b: 3; 1986) about the *Agnicayana*, is self-contained and self-absorbed. "The performers are immersed in their complex task"; it is orthopraxy, an activity governed by rules. Ritual is an internal process, generating a specific dynamic that serves no purpose external to itself. Indeed, he claims, all rituals are by definition meaningless, and tautological in the sense that they are done only because they have to be done and can serve no other purpose. Furthermore, if they did serve a practical purpose, they would no longer be rituals. They are performed "because," as one of the Nampūdiris central to the *Agnicayana* of 1975 told Frits Staal, "it is our tradition" (1979b: 4), and "the fruit of ritual activity is—temporarily—unseen." It's result may become apparent only later, after the Agnihotri's death (1979b: 6). The rituals, Staal concludes, "have to be performed for their own sake" (1979b: 7).

Indeed, like the *Agnicayana*, the *Cūṭala-k-kūttu* does not symbolically represent anything, and it is not said to attain a specific goal; in it, as Staal insists, a precise way of *doing* is at the forefront. However, that does not render this ritual "meaningless," as Staal claims. For rituals that place practice at their center,[4] the practice itself, the *doing* of ritual in a certain way, entails consequences in and of itself. As a ritual is performed, a certain discernible world emerges, while other potential worlds are subdued and eliminated. Within the ritual, a cosmos is fashioned to favor the formation of a desired cosmology.

Further, in this regard, there is no difference between a ritual that has an explicitly declared goal and one that has no identified aim. Even if a ritual is performed specifically to achieve a certain goal—such as the safe passage of an Agnihotri into his new existence, health, the birth of a male child, winning a court case, healing or the well-being of the community—a certain cosmic constellation must be produced and put into action to coax the desired outcome, to fashion a favorable space for that occurrence to come to be. This is abundantly clear for both the *Agnicayana* and the *Cūṭala-k-kūttu*; they both create, each in its own way, certain combinations of deeds and words at determined spaces that draw a cosmological constellation into existence in which new potentialities open up, options that were obstructed in everyday life.

Since *doing* is at the forefront of the *Cūṭala-k-kūttu*, analyzing the ritual in its own right (Handelman 2004b; Shapiro 2015), as it was in fact put together, reveals the complex ways in which it works. Regardless of whether the ritual had been performed continuously or has been renewed perhaps in a slightly altered way, the specific ways in which it was carried out in March 2013 generated a particular cosmos that permits certain potentialities to come to life. The organization of space at the Nampūdiri family property, the personae active in it, and the performance itself generate a delicate process that activates dynamics of reverberation between the protagonists of the ritual. This results in the augmentation of certain potentialities that are in turn harnessed to permit separation between the living and the dead, and to ensure that the Agnihotri is ushered into a new existence. Meanwhile, the deceased's relations to his household, including his widow, his sons, and the sacred fires, are radically altered.

The information concerning the *Cūṭala-k-kūttu* that took place in March 2013 was collected mainly from Aparṇa Naṅṅyār in two interviews. I was first introduced to her and informed about the renewal of the ritual in January 2015 in Trissur; I knew from literature that this ritual was performed in the past (Moser 2008, 2011; Paniker 1992) but did not know that it had been reenacted. So, I asked to talk to Aparṇa about it, and we met again for a long interview in Irinjalakuda in August 2016. David Shulman and Yael Shir participated in the interview and were of great help concerning the detailed information on Sanskrit literature. During our conversation, she provided many details, in her soft and delicate manner of speech, and also showed us some nonprofessional photos of the event. More information was collected about this ritual in particular, and the Naṅṅyār tradition in general, in informal interviews with Madhu Cākyār and Indu G. at their home. Madhu Cākyār is an authority on current temple *Kūṭiyāṭṭam* (Margi 2015), *Cākyārkūttu* and *Naṅṅyārkūttu*, and has assisted Aparṇa in reconstructing some of the ways of enacting the rite.

## Renewing the *Cūṭala-k-kūttu*

Three months before the performance, the dead Agnihotri's family came to see Aparṇa's father Ammanūr Kuṭṭan Cākyār—a famous temple performer and teacher in Irinjalakuda—who is married to a Naṅṅyār, and whose daughter Aparṇa, therefore, belongs according to the matrilineal tradition to the Naṅṅyār/Nambyār group, and who is also an accomplished temple actress.

The Nampūdiri family of the deceased owns a *grantha*—a family book—that indicates in detail what rituals the family should observe on certain occasions. The book indicated that if the dead family member was an Agnihotri, *Naṅṅyārkūttu* must be performed after his ashes have cooled. The *grantha* indicated in detail how to perform the ritual but specified only what the Nampūdiri family must do: how to organize the space of their house, the cremation grounds, and the room in which the ritual fires were kept during the father's lifetime, as well as where the stage for the performance should be placed. It also specifies the rituals that the sons of the deceased are to perform during the *Cūṭala-k-kūttu*. But the old Nampūdiri *grantha* included no specification concerning how the *Naṅṅyārkūttu* should be performed. It mentions only that the Naṅṅyār should perform the entire story of Kṛṣṇa.

Since Aparṇa is a Vedānta teacher at the Sankaracharya Sanskrit University in Kaladi, as well as a highly trained actress, she was well equipped to deal with this complex task. The cremation took place in January 2013, and the *Cūṭala-k-kūttu* in March, so Aparṇa had little time to get ready. As she was preparing for the ritual, she faced many obstacles. She needed to find a drummer who, like her, belongs to the Nambyār group. She also needed a Naṅṅyār to sit at the side of the stage and play the cymbal (*tāḷam*), and chose her mother for that role.

More difficult was finding a text: she intended to reconstruct, as close as possible, the way *Naṅṅyārkūttu* was performed 150 years ago, and to try to eliminate the changes that had occurred since. She started to research the matter by contacting all the families who were engaged in *Naṅṅyārkūttu* to find out if they had a manual or any other details, but she found nothing. She thus had to write an *āṭṭa-prakāram,* a manual that tells in detail what text to utter, how to perform it and, which *kriyā*—dance steps that invoke the gods—should be performed on this occasion. The story must span from Kṛṣṇa's birth until the last story, the *Daśamakūttu.*[5] So she consulted a Sanskrit drama teacher at her university, as well as other *Kūṭiyāṭṭam* actors, such as her father and Madhu, who belongs to the same family and *Kūṭiyāṭṭam* tradition. She ended up with a text including more than 250 *ślokas,* an enormous amount to memorize in such a short time, or, as she put it to express the effort she had to muster: "It was too hard."

## The *Cūṭala-k-kūttu*

As mentioned, several conditions must be met for the performance of the *Cūṭala-k-kūttu.* First, the deceased must be a Nampūdiri Brahmin, and an Agnihotri—that is, he must have been, during his lifetime, at the center of a grand ritual, the *Agnicayana.*[6] The *Cūṭala-k-kūttu* is said to be performed for the widow, so a second condition is that the widow must be alive, and must be present throughout the ritual. Third, the body of the dead must be intact; for example, if he dies a violent death, such as in a road accident, the ritual will not take place.[7] And finally, this ritual remains only in the tradition of the Nampūdiri families in the Irinjalakuda region.

For a Nampūdiri man to become the sacrificer at the *Agnicayana,* he must be married, so that the surviving widow becomes the last remaining element of the *Agnicayana.* The wife must be present at the *Agnicayana*—albeit covered with a parasol—at the site of the construction of the altar of fire throughout the ritual. Moreover, she is the only woman who has a role in the ritual. The altar that was carefully constructed during the ritual was burned at the end of the ritual, but three components of the *Agnicayana* remained: the Agnihotri, the sacred fire, and the wife. The Agnihotri is now dead, and the fire is united with the dead since it served to burn his body at the cremation site, and so now is also extinct—only the wife remains.

During the *Agnicayana*, the entire complex of altars was built according to the body size of the sacrificer. His body becomes literally the measuring stick for the edifice—or otherwise put, the altars are made of his body multiplied. To ensure that the deceased moves on safely to his new existence, his body must be treated carefully after his death; it must be destroyed until it is completely annihilated (for an account of the complex relation between the fire altar and the body of the Agnihotri, see Holdrege 1998: 358). Accordingly, the funeral rites of an Agnihotri are elaborate and complex, and like funeral rites of other important Nampūdiri, take a full year to complete. Yet the rites for a deceased Agnihotri are somewhat different from the rites for any other Nampūdiris. For other dead Nampūdiris, the bones and ashes remaining after the cremation are placed in an earthen pot that is closed and buried under a specific tree (see Parpola 2000: 242; Davis 1988). For an Agnihotri, however, the bones will undergo additional grinding until no human form can be seen and only thin ashes are left, and the earthen pot in which his remains were initially kept is also pulverized.

Vedic traditions concerning the funeral of the Agnihotri found in very ancient texts point at elements that occur in the *Cūṭala-k-kūttu*. In them, one who had performed the *Agnicayana* or *agniciti* ritual was entitled to a special funeral monument, a *loṣṭaciti*, in which lumps of earth (*loṣṭa*) are piled up into a funeral monument, a kind of survival of the ancient Aryan kurgans or funeral mounds in the Eurasian steppes. The erection of this funeral monument was preceded by certain dramatic acts: these resembled those acts performed at the culmination of the horse sacrifice,[8] when the horse, who had just been put to death, was performing the "sacred marriage" rite with the chief queen of the sacrificing king. These dramatic acts in the funeral rites of the person who had performed the fire altar ritual apparently became obsolete early on. In them, the dancer is Śiva, but several females are performing the "fanning" dance in the Vedic funeral with *loṣṭaciti* (Asko Parpola, personal communication).

*Cūṭala-k-kūttu* means in Malayalam "dance [or drama] in the burning ground," *Cūṭala* being "burning ground" (from the verbal root *cuṭu*, "to burn"). The Malayalam lexicon glosses *Cūṭala-k-kūttu* as "(Śiva's) dance in funeral grounds," and records *Cūṭala-māṭan* as "a form of Śiva (as dancing in funeral grounds)" and as "an evil spirit supposed to be residing in funeral grounds" (Paniker 1992: xxii).

Today, too, other special funeral rites for the Agnihotri are maintained. For example, before the cremation, a cleansing ritual was held by five Brahmins, and between the *Cūṭala-k-kūttu* and the pulverization of the remains, a white horse must be present at the compound of the family's property.[9] Thus the *Naṅṅyārkūttu* is only a small part of the sending-off rituals for the Agnihotri. The *Cūṭala-k-kūttu* takes place after the cooling of the ashes but before the grinding of the remains. This way, during the ritual, the deceased's human form is still present to some degree.

The March 2013 *Cūṭala-k-kūttu* was completed in six sessions that lasted three hours each and was performed over three days; on each day, a morning session and an evening session were held. Performances took place in a rectangular yard situated between the Nampūdiri family house on the one side and the family cremation ground on the other. The stage, constructed especially for this ritual, was situated at a right angle to both the house and the cremation ground. Aparṇa requested that a white sheet be hung to divide the stage into front and back, so that the back part could serve as a "green room" where the make-up and costume were put on, where she could retire and be out of view, and where she could complete her ritual duties by repeating the text in mudrā gestures after each performance.[10]

Facing the stage, at the other end of the yard, was the room in which the ritual fires were kept before the death of the Agnihotri. The Agnihotri was cremated with the sacred fires that he kept for his entire life ever since he was at the center of the *Agnicayana,* and then with his cremation, the fires were extinguished. Another fire may be kept in that room in the future by the eldest son after he takes over the household. The widow was seated at the entrance to the room of the ritual fires, facing the stage, watching the performance. Her two sons were seated in the yard, facing the cremation ground, their backs to the house. Everyone else, friends and family in the audience, could sit on the balcony of the house, viewing the stage at an angle.

The ashes and remaining bones of the dead Agnihotri were placed in an earthen pot on an elevated stool in the yard between the two sons and the widow. Ritual tools and materials necessary for the rituals to be performed by the sons during the performance were also kept in the yard, as well as a lamp lighted during the performance. No one else was allowed in the yard. The sons performed rituals three times at each performance: before the performance, in the middle during an intermission, and at the end. Although the yard is sunken in relation to both the stage and the room of the sacred fires, only the sons were seated low, while the earthen pot of the husband's ashes, placed on a high stool, was at stage level.

To recapitulate, the rectangular space was organized in the following manner from the Naṅṅyār's point of view, facing the yard: on the left of the house where the audience could sit, the stage was erected and the *Naṅṅyārkūttu* was performed; to the left of the stage is the family cremation ground; and to the left of the cremation ground, facing the stage, is the ritual-fire room where the widow sat. Enclosed on four sides, in the middle, is the yard. The remains of the Agnihotri were placed on a high stool together with a lamp, while his sons sat on the ground and performed rituals. The Naṅṅyār on the stage, the earthen pot containing the cooled ashes of the Agnihotri, the lamp, and the widow, were raised, while the sons and ritual tools were on the ground of the yard, seated about one meter lower.

Both the beams of the house's balcony and those of the stage were covered with white cloth. This cloth is a usual feature of temple performances, and traditionally constituted the Naṅṅyār and Nambyār's payment for the performance. The Nambyār drummers are responsible for providing and folding the sash placed on the Cākyār's lower back, which is made of several meters of folded white cotton cloth so that the white cloth covering the beams would serve for that as well. Meanwhile, the white cloth separates the compound from its mundane appearance and insulates it by wrapping it and hiding its true colors and contours.

The ritual is very strenuous for the Naṅṅyār, as she must comply with many rules and restrictions during the ritual. She must bathe in the Nampūdiri family water tank before and after each session. In the olden days, a little hut would be erected for the Naṅṅyār, and she would stay inside the compound for the three days duration of the ritual. Another hut would be erected for the audience so that no one would leave the compound during the days of the performance. But as Aparṇa told me, she lives close by, and of course, transportation has radically changed, so she went home every evening, which rendered the ritual bath necessary. Another restriction is that she is not allowed to eat or drink after waking up in the morning until she takes the second bath after the performance. Indeed, not a drop of water should pass her lips.[11] She must also change her clothes after the first ritual bath to wear the performance costume, and after the second bath to wear her own clothes.

The performance costume was also different from the one customarily used today, for two reasons. First, because she wanted to replicate the old tradition, but more importantly, because after the performance at the cremation grounds the costume could not be purified. Therefore, as much as possible, only natural materials were used. The headgear was made of carton, cloth, and flowers, and the earrings and necklace were made of silver (which can be purified in water). The old-fashioned make-up was prepared on a ghee basis instead of the water basis used normally today, and the oily substance rendered the application of the make-up more difficult than usual.[12] When leaving for the last time, all items of her costume had to be treated before they could be taken out of the compound. The cloth, carton, and flowers were burned, and the solid jewelry was purified by water.

After each performance, Aparṇa was required to repeat the entire performance again without utterance, only in Mudrā-words, not in front of an audience, but alone in the green room. Moreover, after the whole ritual was over, the same performance was done once again at a Viṣṇu temple, this time without the presence of the widow since she is confined to her home for a year after the death of her husband. It is said that the performance at the temple is a compensation for the performance at the cremation grounds; that is, since it is somewhat inauspicious to perform at the cremation grounds, the second performance in front of the god negates the possible inauspicious consequences of performing at the cremation ground. At the temple it was not possible to perform twice a day, so the performance took six days.

Viṣṇu and his avatar Kṛṣṇa are connected to liberation,[13] and perhaps that is also why a Viṣṇu pūjā is performed for the Agnihotri. It is better, Aparṇa says, to do the second performance after the

*Cūṭala-k-kūttu* in a Kṛṣṇa temple rather than a Viṣṇu one, since it is his story that is told. Aparṇa feels a special proximity to Kṛṣṇa, especially when she is performing his life story. Indeed, he is a lovable, playful, mischievous, sensuous god who embraces spontaneity and vanquishes his enemies with ease; a master magician, he is also an accomplished dancer full of youthful vigor (Kinsley 1975: 13; see also Singer 1966). This is also why *Naṅṅyārkūttu* seems to generate a very different atmosphere than the rigid, Vedic rituals, and particularly those of funeral rites. Whereas the Vedic rituals seem monochromic, the Kṛṣṇa story danced on stage with the elegance of *Naṅṅyārkūttu*, the *Nannyar* dressed in red, is replete with the multiplicity of life's hues.

A Naṅṅyār performance as ritual is *Darśan*, an eye sacrifice (Eck 1998), and since the Naṅṅyār is performing it on behalf of the Nampūdiri widow, the Nampūdiri family must buy the sacrifice and pay the actress. This particular family had little money, and Aparṇa did not specify a price, but the family did pay her something.

## Naṅṅyārkūttu

The entire tradition of *Naṅṅyārkūttu* has undergone intensive changes; it has been revived and adapted since women were admitted to the *Kūṭiyāṭṭam* section of the Kalamandalam school of Kerala arts in the 1970s. Today more actresses—many of whom do not belong to the Naṅṅyār families—are performing *Naṅṅyārkūttu*, and more female roles have been written or revived, and introduced into *Kūṭiyāṭṭam* outside the temples. Even the female costume used today was introduced at the Kalamandalam (see also Casassas 2012; Johan 2014). Before the renewal at the Kalamandalam, only certain female protagonists were played by women, and others were played by men, who told the female part of the story; at other times, a woman's presence on the stage was a lamp, and the women's lines were recited by the Naṅṅyār playing the cymbal (*tāḷam*) at the side of the stage, at times draped with a red scarf. But, as Aparṇa said, only the female protagonist can know her own thoughts, so no one else can relate roles where women's thoughts are expressed. These roles can be played only by actresses (see also Johan 2011a).[14] Only

Cākyār families who performed in temples together with Naṅṅyārs could stage such acts. In other families that had no connections to the Cākyārs (such as Aparṇa's grandmother), the Naṅṅyārs would only play *Naṅṅyārkūttu* alone at the temple.[15]

From the beginning of the twentieth century until the revival of the 1970s, most Naṅṅyārs who performed at temples were not actresses in the full sense. They knew the text, the chanting, and the mudrā gestures, but they did not dance or perform the different *rasabhāva* (facial expressions of moods). Moreover, their costume did not permit lifting legs, so their dancing was restricted (Moser 2011a: 180). But this was not always the case: a story tells of a king who wanted to improve the skills of his three *Kathakaḷi* actors, so he sent them to be trained by a famous Naṅṅyār. When the candidates arrived, the Naṅṅyār was busy in her yard, but she reluctantly agreed to let them audition. She asked them to perform the famous scene of Rāvaṇa lifting Mount Kailāsa. Ultimately, she kept as her student only one of the *Kathakaḷi* actors, saying that he, at least, could lift a hill.[16] This story tells of a period when not only could the Naṅṅyār perform with talent and vigor, but some of them were considered better actresses than even the male Cākyārs (e.g., see Paniker 1992; Moser 2008, 2011).

Today the young, temple Naṅṅyārs are influenced by the changes in style, costume, and expression brought about by the Kalamandalam school of Kerala arts. The older Naṅṅyārs knew the Sanskrit texts of all plays by heart since they had started their training at a young age,[17] whereas the younger generation must prepare before each performance; yet today's Naṅṅyārs are better-trained actresses. Despite the changes, the rules at the temples remain strict, and only a daughter of a Naṅṅyār who is married to a man of a correct (same or higher) caste can play at the temple. This rule created a great shortage of actresses with the correct lineage, and today it appears that Aparṇa is the only well-trained actress of the correct family linage who can perform the ritual.[18]

A woman from a Nambyār family must go through the initiation ritual, the *araṅṅēṯṯam,* to be permitted to use the name Naṅṅyār, and only after the initiation may she participate in a temple performance (Daugherty 1996: 56). The *araṅṅēṯṯam* traditionally occurred before her first menses, when she was about ten years old. Like the Kumari—the living Hindu goddess of Nepal—who becomes the goddess when the special makeup is painted on her for the morning pūjā,[19] the Naṅṅyār too becomes close to the divine by the application of makeup. To purify herself, the initiate fasts after waking on the morning of her *araṅṅeṯṯam*. Continuing the series of purification rites she will undergo, she bathes after arriving at the temple. She is given new cloth with which to fashion the costume. It will be washed on the second day of the initiation by temple launderers, who also wash the deity's clothes. One of her uncles, the drummer who will perform that day, lights the dressing room lamp with a light brought from the lamp in the *sancta sanctorum* and, subsequently, lights the lamp on the stage. As the rite goes on, the young girl receives privileges that are usually limited to Brahmins and Cākyārs in costume, such as sounding the bell, thus announcing the presence of the god at the temple and receiving *prasad* directly into her hand (for a detailed description of the initiation ceremony, see Daugherty 1996: 57–60).

In Kerala, not long ago, many temples had *devadāsīs*—called in Kerala *teviṭicci* (Paniker 1992: 21)—dancers who are consecrated to the temple and to the god. The *devadāsīs* were outlawed at the middle of the twentieth century because they were associated with sexual promiscuity, and thus their behavior was considered morally corrupt and an obstruction to the modernization of India (Soneji 2004, 2012; see also Ramberg 2013; Coorlawala 2004). However, the Naṅṅyār escaped such associations since, although they too are dedicated to the temple, they are always accompanied by their menfolk, the Nambyār, who are the drummers and are responsible for additional ritualistic elements in *Kūṭiyāṭṭam*. And, because they are married to the gods, these dancers are always auspicious and can never become widows (Paniker 1992: 14; about *devadāsīs*, see Apffel Marglin 1985, 1990; Kersenboom 1991; Soneji 2012; for historical references to the Naṅṅyārs, see Moser 2011a, 2008).

Today's *Naṅṅyārkūttu* is attributed to the play *Subhadrā-dhanañjayam*, which tells the story of Subhadrādha, Kṛṣṇa's sister, who falls in love with his friend Arjuna. She is then abducted by a demon and rescued by a man with whom she falls in love without knowing that he is, in fact, Arjuna. A brassiere (*gātrikā*) that can reveal the truth is involved in the resolution of this conundrum, but the Vidūṣaka, as Vidūṣakas tend to do, muddles things up. Between the first and the second acts of this play, five days of *Naṅṅyārkūttu* present a flashback (*nirvahaṇam*) enacted by the Cēṭī, Subhadrā's maid. The Cēṭī tells the story of Kṛṣṇa up to the point in which the second act of the play *Subhadrā-dhanañjayam* starts[20] (Moser 2011a: 170–171; see also Daugherty 1996: 55; Unni and Sullivan 2001). Since this flashback tells the story up to the point where the day's act begins, today's *Naṅṅyārkūttu* tells only half of Kṛṣṇa's story and goes no further. A few generations ago, the *Naṅṅyārkūttu* lasted twelve days. This was reduced to seven days and has now, in most temples, been cut to a three-day performance that usually includes the *purappatu* (invocation) and the first thirty-six verses (Daugherty 1996: 62).

Since *Naṅṅyārkūttu* performed at temples is *Darśan*, it is always auspicious to see (Daugherty 1996: 55; Madhavan 2012); in general, a Naṅṅyār at the temple is always auspicious. Although she is never possessed, the Naṅṅyār is of the domain of the god; she is with godly power (Daugherty 1996: 60). Her exact relation to the gods takes many forms. She is a Cēṭī maid to Kṛṣṇa's sister, Subhadrā; consecrated to the god, she is a *devadāsī* who is married to the god; as an *apsara*, she is a celestial dancer; and sometimes she is considered a goddess. When the Naṅṅyār has finished her makeup and put on her attire, it is said that she is considered to be the Bhagavati, the mother Goddess (Paniker 1992: 48). As such, she is the female entitled to the highest degree of proximity to the gods at the temple, second in Kerala only to the *nāga* (snake gods) priestess (Daugherty 1996; Madhavan 2015: 347).

According to Paniker (1992), the evidence concerning the performance of Kṛṣṇa's story dates back to the ninth and tenth centuries. *Cūṭala-k-kūttu*, the only ritual a Naṅṅyār performs outside the temple, is at the center of an origin story of the *Naṅṅyārkūttu*, which is included in the *Bhāgavata Purāṇa*, as part of the story of Kṛṣṇa. In this origin story, Brahmā asks Lakṣmi Nārāyaṇa, herself an *apsara*—a celestial dancer—to perform a ritual dance, but a ghost of a Brahmin interrupts the dance, and the performance is stopped. Brahmā is furious over this and casts a curse that the dancer should die. After supplication, the curse is modified, and the *apsara* is condemned to perform at the cremation grounds for one hundred *yāgas*—for Brahmins who keep the ritual fire all their lives—before she can be released from the curse. The Naṅṅyārs are said to be the progeny of Lakṣmī Nārāyaṇa and they, therefore, inherited the curse and must perform at the cremation grounds.

This version of the *Apsara* story was related by Aparṇa. Another version of the story appears in Kālidāsa's play *Vikramorvaśīyam*, which tells of the divine nymph Ghṛtāci, created by Brahma. She was disturbed during a performance by the arrival of the soul of a deceased Agnihotri-Brahmin. Brahma cursed her because she paused and, as punishment, she was reborn as an actress in the human world. She begged Brahma for mercy, so he promised her that she could return after having performed the Kṛṣṇa story 101 times on the burning ground of an Agnihotri-Brahmin. The Naṅṅyār are considered to be the terrestrial descendants of Ghṛtāci, who continue the art of acting (Moser 2008: 95–96fn3).

Rao and Shulman (2009), in the introduction to their translation of Kālidāsa's "How Urvasi Was Won," tell a similar story of the Apsara Urvaśī, who while on earth as a result of the curse had a child with the king but separated from him—yet if the king should see their child, she would become an *apsara* again. In her divine state of *apsara,* she cannot feel emotions such as love, jealousy, or regret. Nonetheless, as she falls in love with the king and develops the desire to live with him, she descends closer to a human condition that enables her to live on earth. Thus, the curse is transformed into a desirable state. Contrarily, the condition that would lift the curse—namely, if the king should happen to see their child—would itself turn into a curse since it would separate the lovers; moreover, it would deprive Urvaśī of her human emotional world. Note that here, in Urvaśī's story, the curse and the lifting of the curse are reversed: instead of aiming to return to the *apsara* celestial condition, Urvaśī desires to stay on earth. The same may be true for the Naṅṅyār. As a woman, she can perform with feeling and emotion that the goddesses and *apsara* cannot express, and thus through her double state she can cajole the departed Agnihotri from his human state to a godly one.

Performing at the cremation grounds, however, is polluting and inauspicious, indeed a curse. *Cūṭala-k-kūttu* became rare, it is said, out of fear for the safety of the Naṅṅyār, and the dread of arousing the wrath of the gods and causing a similar curse as a result of the smallest faux pas the actress might make. Indeed, as Aparṇa testifies, it is an eerie feeling to have a dead person as the audience at the performance.

Apffel-Marglin (2008: 59–62) draws a distinction between the pairs of purity and impurity, on the one hand, and auspiciousness and inauspiciousness on the other. Purity and pollution, or impurity, are hierarchical. They are relative to each other since what is impure for one is pure for another, according to the degree of pollution a group is susceptible to. A certain situation or substance can be at the same time polluting for one, but pure for another—or, even what is pure in one situation is polluting in another. Auspiciousness, by contrast, has no hierarchical relation to inauspiciousness. Something can be auspicious and polluting or inauspicious and pure. Moreover, the same act can have both auspicious and inauspicious consequences, so that the mixtures and combination of these attitudes toward people, things, or entities provide the ground for a variety of ritual behaviors. What is more, Apffel-Marglin states that the "coexistence of both auspiciousness and inauspiciousness has a transformative effect of renewal" (2008: 49).

At the *Cūṭala-k-kūttu*, the auspicious presence of the Naṅṅyār is blended with the inauspicious state of widowhood (Caldwell 2001: 123) and the impure presence of the dead. The Nampūdiri themselves belong to the most easily polluted group, the Brahmins. Ṇearly everything pollutes them. The Nampūdiri of Kerala were considered so easily polluted that to prevent pollution they had roads to themselves that were forbidden to everybody else (Parpola 2000[21]). At the *Cūṭala-k-kūttu*, the presence of a dead human is now impure but on his way to a higher existence in the domain of the gods, together with the Naṅṅyār who at times belongs to the domain of the gods. During the ritual, the Naṅṅyār moves back and forth between domains; between the gods, the *apsara* and humans; between the curse, working toward untying it and the benefits of humanity while under the spell of that curse; between auspicious and inauspicious; and between purity and slight impurity, while constantly purifying herself. This is how she acquires qualities of a psychopomp, generating a complex weave of forces that can propel the Agnihotri and his family to a new state of being.

## Liberating the Agnihotri

The fruits of the *Agnicayana* are not visible during the life of the Yājamān—who for the rest of this life becomes the Yāga (Agnihotri). After the ritual, he continues his life as usual, for the change will come only after his death (Staal 1979b: 6[22]). The funeral and post-funeral rites constitute, therefore, the final portion of the *Agnicayana*. At death, the Agnihotri moves from the domain of the humans and mortals into a domain of the immortals, closer to the gods. Yet he cannot achieve this transition alone; rituals must be performed that will sever the dead man's connections with members of his family and retie them in a new and different way. In particular, his sons must exchange places with him to become the heads of the family, and his wife, turned widow, must set him free and sever all ritual connections with him. Since this concerns the reconfiguration of the ties within the family, the rites must be performed exactly as the family tradition indicates.

The year-long careful and meticulously performed rituals, intended to liberate the Agnihotri and send him away to his new existence, comprise many steps and details. These include, among others, his cremation, the pūjā performed every day during a year, the white horse that roams the family's property, the crushing of his bones into dust, and the widow's confinement to her home for that year. These funeral and post-funeral rites for the Agnihotri in general, and the *Cūṭala-k-kūttu* in particular, are part of the process of ushering the Agnihotri into his new existence.

In the film documenting the *Agnicayana* of 1975, the older Nampūdiri, who explains the events, calls the Agnihotri's new existence after death "immortality." That is, if all the rites are accomplished as they should be, the Agnihotri may be liberated from the cycle of rebirth and pass into a higher existence, that of a Pitṛ. Saindon (1995) elaborates on the potentiality of the Pitṛ, the ancestors who acceded to a higher level. The Pitṛ is entirely benevolent; he is an ambivalent entity since he is connected to the gods and capable of receiving sacrifices—yet he is not a deity (Saindon 1995: 111). Becoming a Pitṛ depends on the dutiful completion of the post-funeral ritual performed by the sons, for during these rites the roles between the sons and the father are reversed. As the sons once depended on their father, now the father depends on his sons. For him to traverse into the realm of his ancestors and subsist there as a Pitṛ, the sons must complete the post-funeral rites, and then they will feed their father with sacrifice (Saindon 1995: 105). The sons liberate their father from his role as father and reinforce the chain of exchange between the generations of the lineage while, recursively, the consequent liberation of the sons after their death depends on their ushering their father into becoming a Pitṛ after his own death (1995: 107–108).

The first element of the funeral rites is the meticulous treatment of the body. In some Indian rituals, particularly in Tamil Nadu, "under certain conditions the individual body and the universe are thought to actually merge" (Beck 1976: 214). This is also true for the *Agnicayana*. During the *Agnicayana*—which is exceptional in that it summarizes or includes all other fire rituals (Saindon 1997: 66)—a world is created, one that stems from the specific body of the sacrificer. The merging between the world and a specific body is achieved through reenacting the original man's (Puruṣa's) dismemberment. Within the *Agnicayana*, it is the Nampūdiri at its center that is a sacrifice, who, in turn, is also the original body, yet during the *Agnicayana* his death did not yet occur (see Beck 1976: 224n18; Staal 1983; see also chapter 1 in this book). Puruṣa sacrificed himself to produce the world and then was reconstituted by Agni. By the same token, a son who performs the funerary and post-funerary rites for his father rewards his father with life after death by enabling him to fully become the sacrifice of the *Agnicayana*. His father is transported to a new existence after having sacrificed himself and being consumed by fire (Saindon 1997: 66).

At the *Agnicayana*, the dimensions of the bird-shaped altar dedicated to Agni, as well as its bricks—considered to be solidified fire (Saindon 1997: 67)—are based on the bodily dimensions of the Brahmin sacrificer, the Yāgamān, who later becomes the Agnihotri (Staal 1983). During the *Agnicayana* his physical body is a measure that turns into the space of the world. This sacred body of the Yāgamān is indeed sacrificed, albeit replaced by goats, that in turn were replaced at the *Agnicayana* of 1975 by vegetarian offerings. However, once dead, a man's body can be properly sacrificed—now his dead body can become food for the gods. Thus, his cremation itself is a sacrifice. In the Vedic sense of the term, cremation is a sacrifice in which, like Puruṣa, the dead person is both the one who sacrifices and the victim who is offered to the sacrificial fire. This transformation is carried out by Agni, the god of fire, who transports sacrifices to the gods (Saindon 1997: 57–58). After his death, the Agnihotri has become a true sacrifice that does not need to be replaced, since the cremation pyre is correlated to the altar of the *Agnicayana* (Saindon 1997: 67), and the fire is the same fire, kept alive at home over many years.

In order to pass on to his next existence, the Agnihotri's body must remain intact at death. This is a condition for the *Cūṭala-k-kūttu*. The body that was multiplied to construct the altar of Agni must be fit for sacrifice at his death, and only if his body remains intact at death is he fit to become a sacrifice. Agni passes the body into the domain of the gods; and, to complete the passage, the ashes and bones that remain of the body are later pulverized into dust so that none of it keeps its human form—all of it passes to his new existence.

Within these series of funerary and post-funerary rites, the *Cūṭala-k-kūttu* is directed to the widow, who must be present. The *Agnicayana* can be performed only on behalf of a Yajamāna who is married and whose wife is present. She must be an *antarjanam*, an "inside person," that is, a high-caste Nampūdiri lady (Staal 1983: 314). During the ritual, the wife (called Jagamānapatni), covered with the parasol, is seated next to one of the three fires, the domestic fire, brought from the Yajamānapatni's home (Staal 1983: 44). Thus, the sacrificer, his sacred domestic fire, and his wife were ritually bound together. If the wife dies, she is cremated with the household sacred fire, and a new fire must be kindled if the sacrificer remarries; and when a sacrificer dies, his body is cremated by his household fire, and then that fire is extinguished until the new house owner creates his own new fire (Jamison 1996: 36–37). So, of the inseparable unit of three born from the *Agnicayana*, the dead husband becomes one with the household sacred fire, which is extinguished, yet a critical problem remains since the wife must be separated from the triad.

Whereas a Nampūdiri boy becomes a true Nampūdiri after his initiation rite (*upanayana*), or the tying of the thread, there is no puberty rite for Nampūdiri girls. A woman becomes a full Nampūdiri through marriage. After marriage, a Nampūdiri wife can assist her husband in rituals, and in particular, she can help him tend to the household's sacred fire (Parpola 2000: 144). She cannot, however, perform the recitations that accompany the rituals, since Nampūdiri women are not taught the Vedas (Staal 2008: 68). Nevertheless, a total ritual amalgamation is generated between the Nampūdiri woman and her husband; she even uses the same terms for his relatives as he does. They are like "the two halves of a block" (Staal 2008: 165).

## The Widow

Nampūdiri women in the olden days lived very secluded lives; and when I suggested an interpretation I had heard, that perhaps the *Cūṭala-k-kūttu* is meant to entertain the widow and make her feel better after the death of her husband, Sudha Gopalakrishna—who is a great patron of Keralan arts, an author of a book on *Kūṭiyāṭṭam*, and a Nampūdiri widow—dismissed this possibility. She claimed with profound hurt that the Nampūdiri women are among the most limited of women with regard to freedom of movement and prospects, moreover insisting that they are the most oppressed among the women of Kerala.

Whereas the men conduct many rituals, the women are not involved in any of these. Moreover, to prevent the parceling out of property, only the eldest Nampūdiri son could marry; he could take up to four Nampūdiri wives, and he could also form an alliance with a woman of a matrilineal house. Although strict conventions are employed in a Nampūdiri marriage, the rules that apply to the creating of liaisons, *sambandham*, were much more lax.[23] The relations between the Nampūdiri families and the matrilineal ones were such that the children of these alliances did not belong at all to the father or his family, so that a man could even form an alliance with his half-sister (Mencher and Goldberg 1967: 87). On the other hand, the Nampūdiri women could rarely leave the house. A Nampūdiri woman must not be seen by other men, so she could only go out covered and under an umbrella (*marakkuṭa*), accompanied by lower-caste women. Indeed, in the olden days, a Nampūdiri woman could leave her house only with a chaperone, only if covered from head to toe, and only to go to the temple (Parpola 2000: 175).

Since they could not marry a close relative, Nampūdiris preferred wives from distant *Illams* (Nampūdiri households), a woman who was expected to observe the same funeral pollution as himself. Thus, Nampūdiri wives were secluded from their natal families, but they had daily contact with women from matrilineal families who often worked at the *illam* or would come to visit their Nampūdiri partners and could chaperone the Nampūdiri ladies (Mencher and Goldberg 1967: 97). So, despite the relations that may resemble those between co-wives, the Nampūdiri women were close to the women of matrilineal families. A Nampūdiri widow, however, is taken out of the ritual and social roles after the death of her husband, and is supposed to dedicate herself to fasts, offerings, prostrations, and penance, although theoretically she may remarry (Parpola 2000: 229–230).

## The Dynamics at Work in the *Cūṭala-k-kūttu*

*Cūṭala-k-kūttu* is a purification rite that counters death pollution "to ensure purification of the soul of the dead and the place of cremation" (Paniker 1992: 28); it is part of the rites intended to ensure the safe passage of the Agnihotri to his new existence, his liberation. Since the widow is at the center of this ritual, amongst the year-long rites that accompany the Agnihotri after his death, the *Cūṭala-k-kūttu* specifically is a sort of divorce,[24] one aimed to separate the widow from her ritual connection to the Agnihotri, from the family sacred fires, and from the *Agnicayana*. The playful story of Kṛṣṇa may be meant as entertainment to cheer up the widow. Nonetheless, since all of the Agnihotri's progeny are present at the ritual, they are in a way parts of his body still alive that need to release him. Thus, although today the traditional marital arrangements no longer exist, the matrilineality of the family onstage, and in particular the matrilineal young actress, sever ties with possible progeny an Agnihotri might have fathered with matrilineal women (e.g., see Parpola 2000: 191).

The *Cūṭala-k-kūttu* is dangerous for the Naṅṅyār, who as a ritualist belongs to the domain of the deities and is always auspicious. The death of an Agnihotri is polluting yet auspicious because it provides the opportunity to reap the fruit of the *Agnicayana*. Yet ensuring the safe passage of the father into his next existence is a complex and delicate matter that depends on the living, and the meticulous exactness of their rituals. Moreover, this is dangerous for the living because the faults of the dead can cause misfortune for the living through occult powers, should they not honor the dead "through a proper display of respect, offerings, and gifts, or through various forms of expiation" (Tarabout 2000: 654). The task of pulling the Nampūdiri property into purity and auspiciousness, and of managing the forces of the impure death and the inauspicious widow, impacts on the Naṅṅyār. When the Naṅṅyār enters the Nampūdiri compound, she sheds all of her mundane connections. She takes a ritual bath, changes her cloth, does not consume any substance from the exterior—neither drink nor food pass her lips—and when she leaves, she goes through the reverse process. At the end of the three-day performance, her ritualistic-self inside the performance area is burned together with her clothes as she returns to her daily life. The entire ritual draws the Naṅṅyār towards inauspiciousness; moreover, as she purifies the cremation grounds, she takes impurity onto herself. Many of the actions meant to move the Naṅṅyār into her ritualistic self are also meant to guard her auspiciousness and purity. Her frequent baths, her fasting, the burning of her costume, and particularly the repetition of the performance in the green room through mudrā gestures after each performance, and then the subsequent performance in the temple.

The dynamic intended to thrust the household into movement in this multidimensional space is created by employing playfulness and reverberation as its propelling forces. The playfulness of Kṛṣṇa dissolves borders and obstructions. Play sets a dynamic into movement that then follows its own meandering route, which can lead to construction or destruction. Handelman and Shulman (1997), while considering Śiva's game of dice, show how play can become a world-building tool. While playing dice, Śiva exteriorizes the world itself, the moon, the sun, the mountains; yet he cannot win. Since everything is within him, by losing parts of himself to the world, Śiva separates from his wife Pārvatī, and keeps losing to her while adding elements to the world. "Indic cosmology is imbued with playful properties of ludic paradox.[25] These playful qualities of processuality are embedded in cosmogenesis" (Handelman and Shulman 1997: 37; Handelman 1997). Through play, Śiva is moving parts of the world from one reality to another, from his dense interiority into the more fluid exterior world.

Play and ritual can engender transformation in a world that has no rigid boundaries between aspects of reality. They enhance smooth passages from play and entertainment to grand ritual such as the *Agnicayana* to the mundane reality of widowhood, from the realm of the gods to that of the Pitṛ, to that of living humans. Play (and ritual) set into motion different dynamics; and indeed, Kṛṣṇa's playfulness and mode of cosmogenesis, which is at the center of *Naṅṅyārkūttu*, is different from Śiva's game. Whereas Śiva's game of dice is a stern game, involving exterior powers that propel the dice and lead them, Kṛṣṇa's playfulness is sheer careless enjoyment stemming from within. Since Kṛṣṇa has play—*līlā*—embedded within himself, both the cosmic and the mundane are part of his making.

When his adoptive mother opens Kṛṣṇa's mouth to see whether he stole a butterball, she sees the entire universe inside, including himself. His playfulness has reverberation or resonance embedded within, since the world including him is inside his mouth, and the Kṛṣṇa inside the world inside his mouth also has Kṛṣṇa inside his own mouth, and so forth, and so on, interiority within interiority. He is an infinite god, yet in his human form he is embedded in a finite and sensuous body. He is a "beautiful youth playing the flute, frolicking with, and seducing the village girls. He is the misshapen, monstrous, primeval Jagganāthā" (Handelman and Shulman 1997: 56–57). Kṛṣṇa saves through death even the meanest of creatures and allows the liberation of demons such as Pūtanā, who is sent to kill him as a baby by feeding every baby she finds from her poisonous breasts. While nursing baby Kṛṣṇa, she herself is poisoned and killed, and thus liberated. Although Kṛṣṇa breaks the rules by stealing, seducing married women, and more, he does not arouse anger or revenge but rather instills harmony (Hawley 1985: 109; Pitkow 2001); these transgressions are his play, which permits his ever-changing form.

Much as the infinite worlds of interior depth found within Kṛṣṇa's mouth, *Darśan* generates infinity in its reflective, reciprocal gaze—looking at the god, while the god is looking at you. *Darśan* is a "representation of the cosmos as a whole. But where, then, is that whole? Is it like a series of receding mirrors? Individuals, in worship, orient themselves towards foci of divine power greater than themselves. Those foci are again oriented to face still greater forces. Thus, the containment principle is many-layered. What is outside and facing the self from one perspective is the self from another"

(Beck 1976: 241). *Darśan* has reverberating embedded in itself since the worshiper is looking at the god looking at her or him, so that they are both reflecting each other's gaze, and that reflection also reflects. These echoes of reflections render the space between them fuller, denser. Resonance as the generator of difference through repetition is a simple thing; it connects two sides of a repeated movement and can systematically bring together the two sides of a valley through the oscillating movement of an echo. It has no content in and of itself; it is only a becoming of relation, determining an uncomplicated to-and-fro connectivity. This is why Gilbert Simondon calls resonance "the most primitive of communication tools" (Massumi 2002: 273n48, 34–43); thanks to its very simplicity, resonance can link together very different things and through its repetition enhance the connectedness (Bar-On Cohen 2014).

Naṅṅyārkūttu as Darśan generates this reverberation among the Naṅṅyār, the widow, and the Agnihotri in the presence of gods residing in the lighted lamps. Two lamps are lighted in the ritual space: the three-wicked lamp on the stage and the lamp in the yard. In the three-wicked lamp, the gods summoned on the stage are present; the wicks are also said to resemble the three sacrificial fires of the *Agnicayana* (Daugherty 1996: 58). The burning stage-wicks are facing the three extinct Angi fires where the widow is sitting, while the lamp in the yard invokes Viṣṇu as liberator.

The *Cūṭala-k-kūttu* is organized to generate transformation through reverberation. The ritual enhances resonances that will encourage separation by mirroring. The lighted lamp and the extinct fires; the lively Kṛṣṇa and the deceased; the auspicious Naṅṅyār and the inauspicious widow—auspiciousness, inauspiciousness, purity, and impurity are reflected in each other through the shimmering of homology and play.

Looking at the enclosed space at the Nampūdiri property reveals that the *Cūṭala-k-kūttu* is organized along two axes at a right angle to each other: one between the house and the cremation ground (right to left from the Naṅṅyār's vantage point), and the other (front and back from the Naṅṅyār's vantage point) between the stage and the room where the sacred fires were kept and the widow is sitting. The space is also divided into two strata vertically.

The right-to-left axis is the trajectory of the male and oscillates between the house of the living and the cremation grounds of the dead. The deceased father was moved from the house to the cremation ground, and then was placed at the center of the compound in the yard for the time of the performances, awaiting his final departure. His sons move in the other direction to become the masters of the house; and they too are seated on this axis facing the cremation grounds. The front-to-back axis is female. The Naṅṅyār is facing the widow on this axis, which oscillates between the auspicious Naṅṅyār and the inauspicious widow, between the patrilineal Nampūdiri women and the matrilineal Naṅṅyār and her family, including her mother playing the cymbal, as well as an uncle, or another male from her mother's family, a Nambyār playing the drum. Whereas the widow has no ritual standing separate from her husband, the Naṅṅyār has a very high ritual position, nearly the highest of any woman in Kerala (Daugherty 1996: 60). The Naṅṅyār therefore is pulling the widow and the dead Agnihotri into auspiciousness, so that they can go their separate ways and the Agnihotri can enter the auspicious domain of the deities.

The third division of the Nampūdiri property is vertical. The higher level includes all the active protagonists—the stage, the widow, the remains of the Agnihotri, and the lamps—yet this higher level excludes the sons and their rituals. These are placed on the submerged ground of the yard. The sons are very active in the funeral and post-funeral rites during the entire year, which is their filial duty, and at the *Cūṭala-k-kūttu* too they are present but placed on a lower level. There they continue their pūjā during the intermissions. Relatively disconnected from the performance, they are made to wait. Seated on the lower level, they are excluded from the actions taking place on the higher level between the Naṅṅyār, the widow, the father, and the gods. The remains of the dead husband are placed on a high stool, between the Naṅṅyār and the widow, so that he is present in all axes; he is a fixed point around which the entire event is revolving, and the aim of the ritual is to eliminate this fixed point and send it on its way.

In the corpus of austere, male Vedic rituals, the auspicious *Cūṭala-k-kūttu* stands out amidst the gruesome location of the cremation grounds. The colorful, feminine, and elegant *Naṅṅyārkūttu* brings to life Kṛṣṇa, the most positive, naughty and sensuous of gods, a hero that wins cosmic victories (Hawley 1979). Her performance, like Kṛṣṇa himself, is playful and mischievous, powerful and generative. With its lively attributes within the grim surroundings, the *Cūṭala-k-kūttu* generates a dynamic that blurs distinctions, opening passages through the potentiality embedded in playfulness for reversal and reverberation that intensify movement, encouraging passage from one state of being into another. Kṛṣṇa, brought into the cremation grounds by the Naṅṅyār, propels the small enclave of the Nampūdiri property in a new direction, replenishing emotion and devotion, and transforming the Nampūdiri family and their cosmos. The ritual links the world of the deities to that of the living, and the death of the husband to the subsequent renewal of the widow's life, while concomitantly severing the ritual continuity between them to allow him to set on his new way.

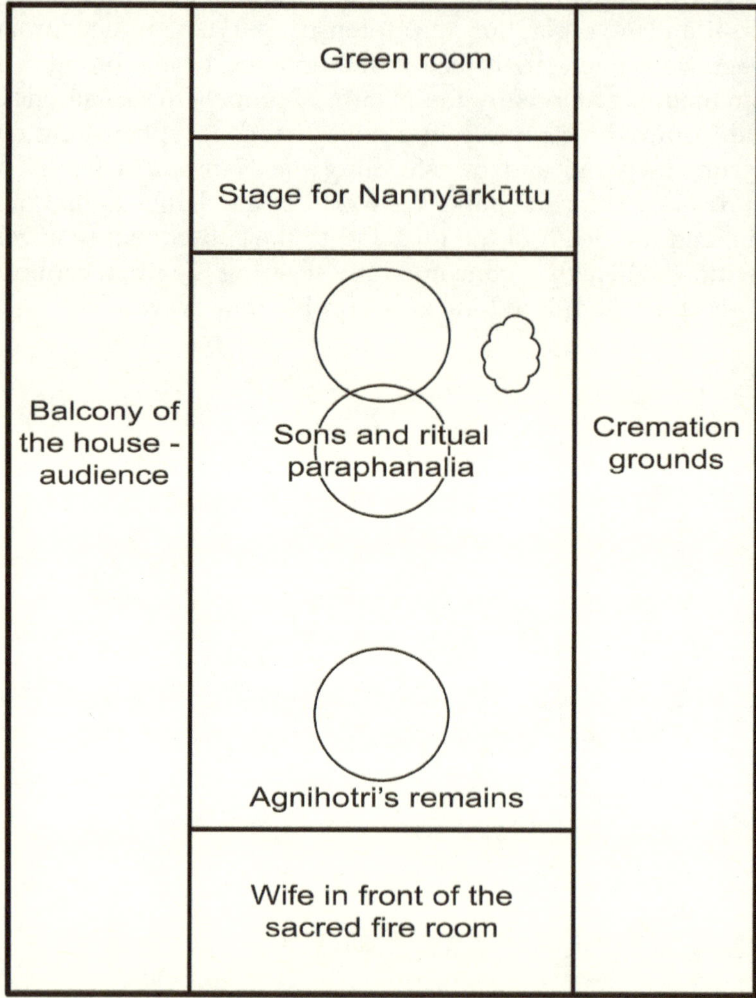


Figure 5.1. Cūṭala-k-kūttu—The Nampūdiri Property. Diagram created by the author.

Chapter 6

# The Vidūṣaka—and the Connectivity of Human Frailties

One evening, during a performance of *Nāgānandam,* I befriended a retired headmaster and teacher of mathematics, a Nampūdiri. He told me of a ritual held at the vast temple in Trichur (central Kerala): when Kochi still had an active king, the king would come to the temple to receive *prasad* from the chief temple priest. The only other person allowed into the sanctum during that ritual was a Cākyār, fully dressed and made up in performance costume as a hero in green makeup. "The king," added my new friend half in jest, "awarded him such an honor, because he was afraid that the Cākyār might make fun of him when he performs as the Vidūṣaka." The Cākyār was probably an important part of this ritual for other reasons too, but this explanation emphasizes the prominence of the role of Vidūṣaka. Within this hierarchical setting, the Cākyār—standing at the temple between the highest of Brahmins and highest of aristocrats, dressed for performance as a hero—is still identified as a Vidūṣaka, a status that awards him on-stage license for social and political critique. The Vidūṣaka, himself a foolish Brahmin, can even criticize the king—"one set of social elites (the Cākyār caste) satirizes another (the Brahmin caste) for the amusement of a third (the royal caste)"—and perhaps even point out hypocritical and unjust behavior of those castes, while the audience is made up by members of those same castes (Davis 2014: 94).

The Vidūṣaka is, indeed, central in the Cākyār professional life, since, although the actors follow no formal training for this role, the first performance of an actor (*araṅṅēṯṯam*) is as the Vidūṣaka. A *Kūṭiyāṭṭam* actor is trained by learning the stances, Mudrās, chanting, and movements necessary for playing heroes, gods and demons; yet all these skills are not used while playing the Vidūṣaka. Despite the difficulty, complexity, and the need for improvisation, there is no specific training for this role. The necessary skills are learned only through watching the performance of gurus, and other actors. On his first performance (*araṅṅēṯṯam*), the actor is set loose on stage as the Vidūṣaka, to follow his thoughts and feelings, employing his own humanity as his sole tool.

Due to his humoristic and transgressive behavior, the Vidūṣaka is often identified as a clown. Like a clown, he reverses everyday etiquette and displays a coarse gluttonous behavior. Indeed, the Vidūṣaka is a fool, a clown, a buffoon, a trickster, a royal jester, and a shaman, embodying traits of each, yet he cannot be reduced to any of these. In his subversive role, the Vidūṣaka goes well beyond the burlesque, far surpassing the liminal role recognized in clowns.

The Vidūṣaka's thought processes seem skewed and funny and are made amply clear with an endless flow of words and stories in Malayalam. He is a Brahmin, albeit an ignorant one, who does not know even one Veda; for him, "no problem is too thorny to be solved by a feast" (Shulman 1987:158). Accompanying his friend, the aloof prince, in his journeys, the two experience the same reality in completely different ways. While the prince overflows with pure and beautiful emotions, the Vidūṣaka cares only for prosaic affairs.

The Vidūṣaka is allowed to make fun of everything and everybody, and draws his popularity from the audience's expectation he will do so. The Vidūṣaka is funny because he makes fun of the audience, because he is oblivious to the unfolding drama in which his friend, the hero, lives, and because he is always hungry. He is constantly thinking and talking about food, about the prospect of food, plenty of good food. He has no ethical concerns to speak of, only a voracious desire to fill his stomach. Through this crude somaticity, this primary, fundamental aspect of the human condition, he drives human potentialities to its utmost limit. Thus, the Vidūṣaka distills the prosaic messiness of human life into a generative force that can stimulate cosmological transformations.

The potentiality embedded in his stubborn, unmitigated humanity is practice-oriented. Personal devotion or religious sentiment cannot describe the cosmic affect embedded in the Vidūṣaka's extreme humanity. Piety is frequently understood as a method of inner contemplation, but the Vidūṣaka's cosmological role may come closer to the prosaic: "public acts and visions of devotion that are inscribed on and which transform the body and the landscape" (Narayanan 2021: 199). The force of the Vidūṣaka is "more than human," similar to ascetics or monks who devote their lives to becoming "more than human," the Vidūṣaka can accumulate the force associated with piety or devotion, albeit through a far different path.

The Vidūṣaka enhances connectivity within the continuum of living entities—deities, humans, heroes, demons—to engage with his own transformative capacities. His concentrated, unwavering humanity is equal to demons and gods in its intensity. The Vidūṣaka's power is the power of the human, emanating from perceiving the world through human fleshiness and frailty. He brings the human and the mundane closer to the divine. The Vidūṣaka can traverse the border between worlds to erase straightforward distinctions, and can thus embrace the members of the audience, the humans at the *Kūttambalam*, and include them within the events on stage.

Moreover, as a go-between, the Vidūṣaka is made of much the same cultural logic as the Cākyār community. And fittingly, when performing *Cākyārkūttu*—a single actor telling stories—the actor is dressed as a Vidūṣaka. The Vidūṣaka embodies on stage many of the dynamics that the Cākyārs, and *Kūṭiyāṭṭam* itself, set into motion through their ritualistic performance. The role of mediation between the Brahmins presenting the *prasad* bestowed by the deities to the royals at the Trishur temple, and more generally, he permits binding connections between the realm of the gods and that of humans in the audience since he can directly address both. The Vidūṣaka ties knots within the plot, reverses the order of things, jumbles matters up, and thus—as does *Kūṭiyāṭṭam* itself—permits real-live penetration between the worlds of the play and those we currently live in.

Whereas the hero, like all *Kūṭiyāṭṭam* characters, relies on his eyes as an aperture to the world, the Vidūṣaka relies on his mouth as the gateway to the interiority of his body. He is constantly chewing paan, talking, searching for food; he is a vast vessel that can contain the world itself within his body, a vessel that is never full. He is always seeking to fill himself with food, and all the while emptying himself with incessant talk. By living in a parallel world to the purely emotional and spiritual one in which the prince is sailing through the world, the Vidūṣaka's coarse, somatic humanity too—like the purity of love, and the power of heroes, gods, and demons—acquires a transformative capacity, influencing the world through what is lodged in the body.

## The Vidūṣaka

In the summer of 2013, the second act of the *Nāgānandam* was presented during eight nights by Nepathya in Moozhikkulam.[1] *Nāgānandam*—written in the seventh century by King Śrīharṣa Deva (Alyar 1992; see also Unni 1990)—is the only Buddhist play enacted on the *Kūṭiyāṭṭam* stage. However, it is not part of the temple repertoire and, thus, was not presented as an offering. The act tells of the true, unadulterated love between a prince and a princess, who encounter many obstacles and adventures before their ultimate union. The story is situated at a mountain hermitage, where the prince, traveling with his companion and friend the Vidūṣaka, sees a princess and hears her play the veena. Unbeknownst to one another, they secretly fall in love with each other, and after a series of tormenting misrecognitions, misunderstandings, a suicide attempt enacted with a theatrical stunt, dramatic heartbreaks, and revelations, they are allowed to marry. It is said that the play is part of *Kūṭiyāṭṭam* repertoire only because the beautiful princess is Malayali. Although Ātreya, the Vidūṣaka, plays a less crucial role in the unfolding of the story in Śrīharṣa Deva's original play, on the *Kūṭiyāṭṭam* stage he takes up much of the performance, including many nights in which he alone comes on stage.

To better follow the workings of the Vidūṣaka, I also watched with joy and attention the recordings from 2012 at Nepathya of Margi Madhu performing Vidūṣaka's entry in the play Subhadrā-dhanañjayam. Unlike *Nāgānandam*, in Subhadrā-dhanañjayam, the Vidūṣaka does play a central role in the plot when he misplaces the brazier that can untie the misunderstanding that plagues the lovers. Also, unlike *Nāgānandam*, which features only humans, in Subhadrā-dhanañjayam gods, demi-gods, Apsaras (celestial dancers),[2] and demons are present. Another brief performance of a Vidūṣaka was held at the Sankaracharya Sanskrit University in Kaladi. Madhu demonstrated *Kūṭiyāṭṭam* in front of an audience of students, and unlike the two performances at the *Kūttambalam*, in which the audience merely chuckled from time to time, the short demonstration at the university provoked abundant and rolling laughter.

## The Vidūṣaka Arrives on Stage

The second act of *Nāgānandam* begins with the prince—dressed as a hero—musing about the beauty of the young woman he saw and heard play wonderful music. He describes her body from top to bottom, showing her marvelous eyebrows, eyes, cheeks, ears, nose, earrings, breasts, navel, thighs, shanks, and feet—and then he is struck by the arrows of *Kama*, hitting him again and again, until he swoons unconscious. He then wakes from his stupor to find he is painfully in love. He pleads with *Kāma* to stop shooting his futile arrows since he is already profoundly in love. The hero displays his noble—even if slightly obsessive—love for the unknown beautiful girl, and the deeds of *Kāma*, many times over during the days of the performance. But although the original play concentrates on the prince's love, here again, the *Kūṭiyāṭṭam* manual, the *āṭṭa-prakāram*, takes great liberties with the Sanskrit play, accentuating the role of Vidūṣaka, which skews and overshadows the love story. The Vidūṣaka enters the stage and massages the hero's arms, ventilating the prince.

The Vidūṣaka's presentation immediately reveals his main concern. He enters carrying a banana leaf folded into a cone, and while chewing paan—his entire face convulsing unevenly in rhythm with the drums—he rubs his stomach and extends the banana leaf toward the audience, indicating his urgent demand to fill his empty leaf and stomach. He shows his shameless displeasure, perhaps even disgust since his leaf is still empty. He joins his fingers together and opens them with a sharp movement as if shaking something off, and then thrusts his palms toward the audience. The audience chuckles uneasily. Then he turns around with his back to the audience and extends the leaf again—in the hope that if he doesn't see who is giving him food, he will be more successful—but again when he turns the leaf upside down, he finds it empty. The audience still chuckles quietly. And again, holding his midriff, he is begging for food. Indeed, the Vidūṣaka is a hollow abdomen with an endless capacity to be filled. When the banana leaf fails to provide him with food, he sticks it in his ear.

Then he stops chewing and puts his hands in front of his body, holding his Brahmin thread in both hands, and starts his invocation steps (*kriyā*); his palms are now facing each other, coming together, and spreading apart with the thread in between, slowly, horizontally. After his last invocative step, he turns around to face the audience with his hands over his face and then, revealing his face, he starts chewing again, and again starts a movement of separating his hands and bringing them together with the thread between the thumb and the palm, this time a vertical movement, picking up speed, his hands separating in larger and larger movements, from the side of his head to his hip, gathering momentum, and now the movement includes more of his body, his head tilting in rhythm, his back bending with the drums. All the chewing, the hand movement, seems nearly ecstatic. Then suddenly it all stops. Out of this orgiastic convulsion, the Vidūṣaka emerges, pops out, born.

Now he needs to clean and purify himself, so next the Vidūṣaka starts his morning rituals: he takes off his sash, folding it and ventilating himself with it, and then he combs his hair with his hands, the hair made of red yarn. When a hair gets stuck on his fingers, he attentively wraps the loose hair around one finger and tosses it into the audience. A loose part of his human body is shared with the audience. The Vidūṣaka then precedes to wash his sash and ring it, waving it dramatically under his armpits and discreetly over his behind. While going through his toilet, he is rhythmically chewing paan, his whole face distorting in rhythm with the drums.

The Vidūṣaka cuts a figure far different from the other characters in *Kūṭiyāṭṭam*. The faces of the other protagonists on stage are completely covered with a basic color (red, green, orange) with perfectly symmetrical black, red, and white lines, dots, and a white paper beard. Only the Vidūṣaka's eyes and mouth are painted, rimmed with a thick black frame; the remainder of his face is visible, covered with crisscrossed thin lines of white paste and red circles the size of ping-pong balls at the intersections of the lines on the tip of the nose, on the cheeks, forehead, and chin, creating a perfect square with the nose at its center. His block-painted mustache is asymmetrical, dropping on one side; like other men in the temple, his torso and arms are naked, painted with the same white lines and red circles pattern. The dots make a pattern of four directions, with centers on the face and chest. Four more dots are painted on his arms, pointing in four additional directions. The design of his face and body, taken as a whole, can be seen as an eight-direction mandala, with the direction drawn as roads between two parallel white lines, leading from the two centers (nose and chest) to the eight cosmic directions, while the centers and directional points are drawn as red circles.

Figure 6.1. Sreehari as Vidūṣaka. *Source*: Nepathya Centre for Excellence.

Whereas Hanūman in the sixth act of *Āścaryacūḍāmaṇi*[3]—who like the Vidūṣaka appears on stage alone for hours—keeps losing himself in the folds of the stories, to emerge somewhere else in a continuous effort to recognize himself and his capabilities, the Vidūṣaka is born on stage fully formed, fully present. Hanūman is on stage, while the actor is hidden within him; the Vidūṣaka, on the other hand, does not hide the actor. While he is on stage, the actor is also present—his skin, his face, and his colloquial speech.

He is always in movement, slowly walking to and fro, crossing behind the lamp in his path. He is constantly using his hands; they are spread apart, slapping his thighs; he is leaning forward toward the audience, posing his hand at his side for support; he is arranging his red hair back on the crown; he is clapping, or else holding his hands together behind to support his heavy belt resting on his lower back. His facial expressions are exaggerated; he is showing emotions concerning the stories he is telling. His own expressions are mainly joyous expectations for food, sometimes with a little dance, song, and clapping. He has a white sash that he wraps and unwraps constantly around his hips, reflecting in a way the behavior of Kerala men who keep folding, tying, and unfolding their dhoti. In stark contrast to the other actors who are stationary when another is talking, saving their highly stylized hand and eye movements to express their text, the Vidūṣaka is constantly moving around, chewing paan, waving his hands. Often, when the hero and the Vidūṣaka are both on stage, the Vidūṣaka touches the hero's arms, holding and massaging or just tapping on them, waving his shawl to ventilate the hero, pulling his fingers, massaging them, rearranging his breast jewelry, then tucking his head under the prince's immovable extended arm. The contrast between the free movement of the Vidūṣaka and the static posture of the hero opens up a different sort of *Kūṭiyāṭṭam*; the hero seems, all of a sudden, encased within his role, within the story, within his love, while the Vidūṣaka is free of such constraints.

The Vidūṣaka is notably different from the other protagonists in many respects, whereas the others talk with mudrā words—taking their time to express every word meticulously, articulating deliberately, every inclination, repeating it in different ways and stopping to play out the meaning of the words—the Vidūṣaka utters a stream of Malayalam words flowing with no interruption.

Whereas the other actors must look at the lamp and avoid gazing at the audience, the Vidūṣaka not only stares at the audience but addresses it directly, asking spectators for food and mocking audience members. All *Kūṭiyāṭṭam* protagonists enter the stage smiling, whereas the Vidūṣaka is not smiling—he is chewing paan, while his demeanor is serious, slightly urgent, and bewildered; the others may brush against each other occasionally, but they are instructed to avoid touching one another,[4] whereas the Vidūṣaka enters and immediately touches the hero. The Vidūṣaka initiates contact, both physically and verbally, with both the other protagonists and with the audience.

Perhaps an even more significant difference between those roles is that whereas the hero as storyteller engages in "exchanging roles," *pakarnnāṭṭam*, playing out other protagonists, entities, and objects—the heroes can become gods, demons, lotus flowers, bees, and deer, and actresses can play men, while actors bring lovely celestial women into the world of the play. This is to say, they experience the world from multiple points of view. Vidūṣaka, on the other hand, adopts no other roles—he has but one point of view: his own.

Only after the invocation steps, the unveiling of his face (his emergence or birth), and his morning grooming does the Vidūṣaka signal to the drums to stop and starts talking. And "when the Vidūṣaka starts talking," Madhu says, "he cannot stop." "He treats the audience to a feast of satirical and ironic comments, self-conscious parody, and spontaneous wit" (Shulman 1987: 175). Indeed, the Vidūṣaka is hyper-chatty, talking and telling stories for hours. First, he points at one of the men in the audience, shooting his darts, aiming a prickly remark at him. One evening he pointed at Yigal (a Sanskrit professor) and said, "he thinks that Sanskrit is everything." Teasing Yigal for thinking that he will understand everything by studying the Sanskrit verses seriously, while according to Vidūṣaka/Madhu this endeavor is ridiculous and doomed to fail, perhaps an indication that Sanskrit is not the only important aspect of *Kūṭiyāṭṭam,* that there is much more to *Kūṭiyāṭṭam* than poetry. Madhu would never have uttered such a remark to a distinguished scholar and a guest, under any other circumstances; only as the Vidūṣaka can he express such sarcasm. On another occasion, after another bout of the prince's detailed description of his loved one's body, and *Kāma*'s vicious attack on him, the Vidūṣaka, played that evening by an older actor, turned to a gray-haired man and said, "Your hair is white so you can no longer understand such [sexual] desire"—that is, this man is too old for the sort of passion displayed by the prince; his days of acute sexual desire are over. This kind of remark is the criticism that my Nampūdiri friend referred to as having the potential for social, political, or even personal offense.[5]

The Vidūṣaka's introduction (nirvahaṇa) is a parody of the philosophical pillars of life. It focuses on four mock goals of human life: entertainment, or enjoyment of pleasures; deception; feasting; and service at the court.[6] The wholesale parody of the classic series of desire, personal profit, duty and righteous behavior, and finally release (Unni 1990: 8). To illustrate the enjoyment of pleasures, the Vidūṣaka, in the longer version of the second act of Nāgānandam, would tell of the escapades of some knaves in their pursuit of prostitutes. After their visit to the whore they have chosen, the knaves steal from her, thus illustrating the principles of enjoyment of pleasures and deception. Then a story is told of a banquet in a Brahmin house that describes the principle of feasting. Finally, the host of the feast dies, and then the fools choose one member of their group to perform services at the court; thus, the Vidūṣaka is chosen to accompany the prince (Unni 1990: 8). However, only the feast and choosing of the companion were presented on the Nepathya stage. Perhaps sexual innuendoes were avoided because they seemed inappropriate today.[7]

The Vidūṣaka is a philosopher of sorts. At the beginning of his ongoing monologue, he asks the audience about karma: Did any of you ever see karma? What is karma? He goes on to tell the story of a man who fathered only girls, every year a new girl; he gave them all the same name, but there were so many of them that it became confusing, and he had to name them "the big one," "the big-small one," "the small-big one," and so on. Then finally a boy was born. But when one of the girls was looking at her image in the well, the boy also wanted to look; he fell into the well and drowned. The Vidūṣaka covers his hand and draws air loudly in an exaggerated gesture of grief—for the lost child, for the father whose karma is unclear. Was it to never have a son or was it to have one and then lose him—which turns the gesture into a slightly humorous one. Here too the audience chuckles uneasily.

Even the gods have karma, he goes on to say, and it is a tough one: "It is not easy for Brahma to create a world; or for Viṣṇu to change avatars all the time, to meet with ignorant Vedic scholars who cannot even recite one mantra; it is difficult to be Śiva, wondering covered in ashes with a bowl stuck to his hand."[8] Then, moving on to his own karma, the Vidūṣaka speaks of his poor and ignorant village, "foolishbrahminville."[9] The Vidūṣaka as Brahmin acquires special significance since, traditionally, Brahmins were extremely powerful in Kerala; they owned most of the lands while observing strict proximity laws and ritual power—they even traveled on special roads to ensure they would not encounter people from lower castes (e.g., see Osella and Osella 1996). Yet the Vidūṣaka together with the prince has traveled from elsewhere, a place where Brahmins can be ṣilly, and as Gitomer remarks, "a dirty Brahmin is always funny" (1991: 82). Up to this point, the presentation of the Vidūṣaka is common to all plays (Unni 1990: 9).

In contrast to the distant princely hero searching for (Buddhist) justice for living creatures, profoundly in love with the girl he had only a fleeting glimpse of, the Vidūṣaka's interests are down to earth. He repeats the *śloka* chanted by the heroes and comments on them, explains them to the audience, but his comments emanate from his own take on the situation, many amounting to misunderstandings of the text, puns between Prakrit and Malayalam, as well as associations from his imagination and reminiscences. Two simultaneous events are developing on stage, one between the heroes as the plot unravels, and the other between the Vidūṣaka and the audience. The heroes, however, are not aware of this parallel reality. Although they may be on stage at the same time, they do not hear what the Vidūṣaka is telling the audience about his life; about the hardship of the travel; about his gluttonous desires; nor do they hear the bantering between the Vidūṣaka and the audience. The heroes may not even be aware of the audience at all.

Vidūṣaka means "a spoiler," and indeed he spoils the formal and ceremonious protagonist of the play, as well as the delicate and noble emotional display of erotic love, "the high-flown sentiment of the hero wedded to the absurdly human, earthy, and corporeal attitudes" (Shulman 1987: 160, 162). After the prince dreamily meditates yet again on the beauty of his loved one and the arrows of *Kāma*, the Vidūṣaka describes a dream in which he saw his sweetheart Cakki husking rice, and her limbs are nothing like those of the beautiful flawless princess. In his dream, she is scolding him for failing to be at her side: "She was waiting by the side of a torn mat and tattered pillow always keeping her broom nearby. Her thighs are visible through her torn loincloth, and her breasts hang suspended touching her navel." Her hair has not seen oil in many days, while her squinting eyes and irregular teeth add to her great beauty (Unni 1990: 13).

When Malayavatī, the Malay princess, in a rare acrobatic gesture[10] of attempted suicide, hangs herself from a liana, by falling from the height of two stools positioned one on top of the other on the stage, hanging by a rope that is wrapped around her throat, her maid is crying for help. The Vidūṣaka thinks that the maid is crying because Malayavatī did not eat that day and thus does not understand the urgency of the situation. Meanwhile, the audience, impressed by the dramatic-romantic event, is immediately transported into a slightly humorous and absurd mode, perhaps reflecting on karma and human frailty and messiness. The Vidūṣaka is pocking holes in the world in which the heroes of the play are evolving, through which he can peek outside and make connections.

Unlike other jesters, the Vidūṣaka does not play pranks or slapstick tricks. His stories have no moral; he is neither cunning nor manipulative; his bantering is not malicious; he is good hearted and wants to help, albeit in a quaint, foolish, irresponsible way; he does not steal;[11] his body is not deformed; his thinking is skewed only in relation to the hero. His humor on stage is not lighthearted or easy-going and rarely provokes open laughter, so that his appearance does not provide relief but rather a restrained, uneasy, chuckle. It is often double-edged: the Vidūṣaka draws a funny expression when talking about the dead boy in the karma story, but of course, a dead boy is never really funny; he thinks the princess is hungry when her life is at stake, again funny but also dangerous because this misunderstanding can prevent urgent help for the damsel in distress.

The Vidūṣaka's stories may be closer to the stories of clowns told in the Iranian rural theater, which have no end, so they can be stopped at any point (Beeman 1981: 512). Like life itself, in which stories have no natural end, but rather the storyteller prescribing their "point," and therefore, also their end, the Vidūṣaka cannot stop talking. He is never stationary, always in the process of doing, of living. Reality itself exceeds categorical thinking, abrogating prescribed order (Shulman 1987); the Vidūṣaka is defying order and border in a setting that specializes in exactly that: dissolving boundaries to encourage dynamics of becoming something more.

## Clowns

Like other clowns and tricksters, Vidūṣaka is entertaining, funny, awkward, and his figure is incongruous with the other "serious" protagonists of the play; he is awarded a license to behave outrageously, to mock others, to be vain or vulgar without shame (Mitchell 1992: VII), and to voice pointed personal and social comments. Looking at other traditional clowns displays the varied and complex behaviors clown types are licensed to adopt in different settings, while foregrounding commonalities and differences between Vidūṣaka and those other clowns.

Since tricksters are breakers and rebels; through their crooked manner of thinking, and grotesque body, they are personae of the boundary (Köpping 2002: 164). Moreover, they are made of the material of the boundary itself (Handelman 1998). Much like children, clowns are considered socially irresponsible (Beeman 1981: 525) and are forgiven for their misinterpretation of social situations, being rude or inconsiderate. Clowns hold a liminal role at the periphery, and as such, they may also contract the image and status of the outsider, the other, whose behavior is clumsy, and who perhaps does not understand social situations well, and can be mocked and degraded, but is also slightly and at times—like native American ritual clowns—greatly feared (Boyer and Boyer 1983; Makarius 1972).[12]

Anthropologists have often concerned themselves with the social aspect of the clown and claim that clowning is a critical practice for voicing social failures (Mitchell 1992), and that clowning is subversive or anti-structure (Köpping 2002; see also Vizenor 1990). The clown's "illusiveness, hybridity or transmutability may form a critical counterpoint to rigid social homogeneity or ideological dogma," unmasking society and confronting its falsehoods and fears (Robb 2007: 1). The clown's healing powers emanate from treating breaches in social norms. When such a breach occurs, the telling of a parable creates a response of laughter, which restores the social equilibrium. A clown can overcome unconscious psychological or social censors (Beeman 1981: 507). Laughter provides a cathartic, cleansing effect, which shakes loose the body as well as social hardships through letting off social pressures. Clowns are social critics, albeit under limited and manageable conditions, and thus they rarely yield any genuine social mayhem or change; rather, from a functionalist perspective, they are understood as a sort of vent, letting off social steam. The relief provided by humor alleviates pressures but leaves social arrangements intact.

Two Tamil clowns are said to express social discontentment. Seizer (2005: 177–201), looking at a buffoon, who performs at a goddess Māriyamman temple in Tamilnadu, centers her attention mainly on the text he utters and describes it as a critique of the changing gender roles in today's society. Tĕnāl Rāma, a Tamil traditional jester, aids the powerless against the powerful. He overcomes the prohibition on criticizing the king by concocting a metaphor that is in fact an anti-metaphor, aimed to reveal to the king himself the silliness of his decision, to persuade him to change it and to save the people from the king's foolish and harmful ruling (Shulman 1987: 180–200).

Many clown types are associated with religious practices, even clowns that have been considered light entertainment, as the clown (chou) in Jingju (Beijing "opera"), who is associated with the origin of Chinese acting, his performance showing a fundamental relationship between the clown and shamanism through drumming. This clown's comedy may emanate from exorcism since patterns of percussion that are played for the clown are also used to gather and subdue demons (Thorpe 2005: 269).[13]

The native American clowns—such as the Capakobam of Sonora, in Mexico—are aggressive, abusive, and highly sexuated (Lewis 1982). Sacred Clowns such as the Chiricahua and Mescalero Apaches are associated with the trickster coyote[14] and with ashes (Boyer and Boyer 1983). Indeed, some of these clowns are the ritual counterpart to a central character in Native American myth: the trickster "who is obsessed with satisfying his almost constant hunger or his seemingly uncontrollable desire for sexual intercourse" (Carroll 1981: 305). These clowns may violate taboos and engage in all manner of profanations; they are dangerous and must be obeyed (Makarius 1972).[15]An interpretation of the native American trickster and his counterpart, the ritual clown, influenced by Freudian thought, claims that his role is to sustain two incompatible, mutually destructive, yet necessary elements—uncontrolled sexuality, which ensures the continuation of the species, and culture, which regulates the smooth working of the species—by implying control over sexual and other somatic urges. According to such a view, a universal unresolved conundrum is embedded in the trickster's central civilizatory role (Carroll 1981).

The comic in Sinha demonic exorcism in Sri Lanka fulfills a rather straightforward role. The "comic is the performativity genre through which the "normal" hierarchical order is restored into their proper place in the scheme of things"; through the comic, the demons "cease to be awesome and become ridiculous." Comedy thus "destroys the demonic and unmasks its illusion" (Turner in Kapferer 1991: xxiii). The demons are masters of illusion, and through illusion they bestow misfortune and disease. By making fun of them, their masks are unveiled, so their illusion is destroyed, as well as their malfeasance (Kapferer 1991: 285). At the Thakurani Jatra in Orissa, abusive behavior of costumed men promotes mayhem, restlessness, even fright among onlookers participating in the festival; the ambiguity of these men concerns their motives for asking for money—are they, in fact, collecting for the goddess, who is venerated in the festival, or for their own benefit? (Hauser 2006: 140).

Ritual clowns are often comprised of contradictions; they may say the opposite of what they mean. Their names indicate traits that are contrary to their role; they eat what should be discarded, such as bodily ordure, as do the Tewa clowns in training, while claiming it is good (Handelman 2008), and they present gender incongruities. The clown in a Pakistani wedding is a woman dressed as an old man, a dirty old man (Handelman 1998a: 238–239); the classic Naven uncles described by Bateson (1958; also, Mitchell 1992: 3), who, to honor the achievements of their sister's child, are dressed in tattered and dirty women's dress, to become "mothers" demonstrating their femaleness via grotesque attitudes with their spread legs, meanwhile encountering screams of laughter from the village children. Those performances contain blunt sexual allusions that are permitted only through cross-dressed clowns (for forceful photos of cross-dressing comedy in Sri Lankan actor exorcists, see Kapferer and Papigny 2002). The striking contradiction between proper modest behavior and clowning, as witnessed in Papua New Guinea, when parents in law shame themselves by publically displaying their genitals to honor their son in law, provoke bales of laughter (Mitchell 1992: 145–166).

## The *Kūṭiyāṭṭam* Vidūṣaka and his Hair

Vidūṣaka is a well-known figure in Sanskrit drama, who "enters the past with mythological or historical characters and with the same ease comes out of it to comment upon contemporary life" (Varadpande 1987: 11). He is a social rebel of sorts, an anti-hero that shows the flaws in social life; though he is "intelligent, his humour is usually crude and spiced with eroticism, sometimes he uses humour as a powerful instrument of social, even political criticism" (Varadpande 1987: 11). He is in the play, and *of* the play—since unlike other protagonists, he is not a mythological or a historical character but appears only as part of the drama. Concomitantly, he is also not quite within the play. The Vidūṣaka devours the world, with verbal narrative being his forte; and takes up a position somewhere between the onstage and offstage worlds, while not belonging entirely to either (Varadpande 1987: 11). The Vidūṣaka is also associated with the ambiguous Varuṇa, who is an *asura* as well as the deva, or a demon that became a god (Kuiper 1979). The gods and the demons are foes, but Varuṇa is both god of the water and demon of the night. Like Varuṇa, the Vidūṣaka is an in-between persona, a "frame shifter" (Gitomer 1991: 94). The Vidūṣaka is the Vedic paradigm of *jumbaka,* a deformed scapegoat and representative of Varuṇa, which also redeems Varuṇa. A Brahmin who takes his place in the Vedic ritual is immersed in water as a sort of sacrifice to the element of the ocean, Varuṇa's domain. So, the Vidūṣaka, a Brahmin who, while purifying, can take impurity onto himself, is associated with the earnest sacrificial transformation of a demon into a god (Kuiper 1979: 217–222; Sullivan 1995: 47). As a trickster, the Vidūṣaka is capable of transgression, of passages from the higher world of the gods to the lower world of the demons. Thus, the Vidūṣaka has a central role in the cosmology of Indian drama—he connects humans, gods, and *asura*.

Although the *Kūṭiyāṭṭam* Vidūṣaka shares many traits with other Vidūṣakas in Indian classic theater, he is put together in a slightly different manner, and those differences determine his particular dynamics.[16]

The *Kūṭiyāṭṭam* Vidūṣaka is very popular with the audience and draws crowds. In Moozhikkulam, too, when the Vidūṣaka is expected to make an appearance the *Kūttambalam* is full; everybody loves him and listens to his witticisms, laughing at his insatiable exaggerations. His popularity stems from his multifaceted role; he is central in rendering the performance accessible to the audience. He translates the *śloka* from mudrā gestures and Sanskrit to spoken Malayalam. He is also a commentator; after repeating each *sloka* and translating it, he provides an interpretation—a strange and skewed one, but nonetheless an elucidation of sorts, a "transformative translation" (Gamliel 2016: 17). A *bricoleur*, he collects food wherever he can find it; he provides comic moments within the seriousness of the situation. "His control over language and his association with its limits; his critical capacity; and his penchant for satire, irony and stark inversion of whatever is given" constitute a wholesale "violation of the norms" (Shulman 1987: 180, 182). He connects the mundane reality of the audience to that of the heroes; while a character in the play, the protagonist's friend and companion, he is also free to comment, interpret, parody, and elaborate on the events and statements, as if he is outside the play (Narayanan 2006: 146). Through his amalgamated behavior of comic and seriousness, of the reality of the heroes and that of the audience, he plays a role in the dramatic and ritualistic affect of the play, of countering the main mood, or *rasa*, of the play in order to showcase and enhance it (Shulman 1987: 157).

Although the Vidūṣaka on the *Kūṭiyāṭṭam* stage is crude, he is also kind and loyal, and his "violation of norms" does not appear to present acute social criticism as such (Richmond 1989: 73). His "comic powers are rarely self-consciously directed at his companion, the nāyaka—the play's hero, often royalty. The Vidūṣaka is funny despite himself, often against his will" (Shulman 1987: 156).

His physical aspect in *Kūṭiyāṭṭam* is less fierce than in some Indian theater forms. In other Indian theater traditions, the Vidūṣaka is balding from the repeat tonsure of his hair; he resembles a demon or a monkey. "The Nätyasästra describes his appearance as dwarfish, hunchbacked, baldheaded, red-eyed, and having big teeth—not unlike some descriptions of rãksasas [demons], and clearly a distorted, comic body when set against the smoothly perfected nûyaka and nãyakt [hero of the play] of Sanskrit poetry and drama" (Gitomer 1991: 87; see also Siegel 1987; Tarabout 1998). While the hero is handsome, the Vidūṣaka is ugly; while the heroin is attractive, Cakki (Vidūṣaka's loved one) is repelling.

In *Kūṭiyāṭṭam,* Vidūṣaka is not deformed, and does not sport animal traits; rather, the Vidūṣaka on the *Kūṭiyāṭṭam* stage shares characteristics common (strangely enough) to demons and Brahmins. His red hair stored in a knot on top of his hat is reminiscent of the demons in its color, and concomitantly also alludes to the Brahmin men, who "were expected to shave their heads but leave a tuft of hair, the topknot, unshaved. This topknot was generally kept tied in a knot when a Brahmin appeared in public" (Hiltebeitel 1998: 15). Some Brahmin Vedic experts retain a topknot still today. Vidūṣaka's constant hunger and gluttony is also a trait common to both Brahmins and demons. Demons are known to be gluttonous and follow their bodily cravings, but the Nampūdiris too as a high and rich caste are known to be fond of leisure activities, while "for the delights of the table they show undistinguished weakness" (Staal 1983: 168).

Another character who, like Vidūṣaka, draws crowds is Śūrpaṇakhā, the ugly mutilated demoness. Indeed, Vidūṣaka and Śūrpaṇakhā have much in common, both appear bare-breasted, both speak in Malayalam with their own voice, and both are the only two characters allowed and encouraged to look directly at the audience. Moreover, both share parts of their body with the audience. While Śūrpaṇakhā fills the *Kūttambalam* with her blood, the Vidūṣaka throws hair at the audience.

Both blood and hair can be separated from the body under healthy and natural conditions, and then regenerate. Menstrual blood leaves the body without causing damage, and hair is detached from the scalp while combing, but as blood spoils after leaving the body, hair can be kept intact. Moreover, both blood and hair are ambiguous according to Indian traditions; both are polluting, and both are strongly connected to fertility, and therefore, both can also be auspicious. Detached parts of the body are potentials for sorcery because they can be extensions of a person into space through intrinsic connections between the detached parts and that person, their name or image, and can thus transport intentions and emotions and collect transformative power (Keen 2006: 523). Body substance can also be pure and replete with forces, material for the creation of relics. Whether invigorating or dangerous, when detached from the body, human substances are powerful and can be used to heal, harm, or make fun.

After combing his hair with his fingers, the Vidūṣaka flicks the hair that got stuck on his hand at the audience. Hair is as complex as the Vidūṣaka: Indian tradition affirms that "sins become lodged in the hair. Thus, a person who wishes to expiate sins should shave the hair," and also "flying hair may indicate the demonic." "Most ancient Indian sources require that people throw away any food contaminated by hair. Hair in this sense is equal to excrement." Yet hair can become offerings to the gods (Hiltebeitel 1998: 26, 16, 28). Hair is so powerful that at times it is dangerous to look at; it is wild like an animal, and brushing hair may disseminate pollution, so hair can store up both pollution and the divine life energy (Shweder 1987: 40–41). Anthropologists of India and Sri Lanka (especially those adhering to psychoanalysis) assume a close connection between hair and sexuality. Untamed, matted hair becomes live matter; it becomes cobras or penises on the heads of ascetic women, which goes together with refraining from sexuality, pushing away the husband's penis, as Obeyesekere (1981) puts it. However, the devadāsīs consecrated to the goddess Yellaman, some of whom engage in prostitution, also keep their hair matted, so their matted hair is closely associated with active sexuality (Ramberg 2009;[17] Assayag and Jeanne Ferguson 1988).

Like many of the Vidūṣaka's actions, throwing the loose hair is powerful yet highly ambiguous. Vidūṣaka is born on stage hungry, and he immediately and insistently asks the audience for food; he has an urgent need to eat, and in exchange, he gives the audience his loose hair. This gesture has potential for disrespect, even close to ensorcelment, and also of sharing his most profound emotions, motivations, and intentions, of sharing life energy, and his karma with the audience. Sharing with the audience his human body creates a physical somatic connection; he draws us into his human world through multifaceted connectivities.

## Symbolic Type and Becoming Human

As becomes clear even from these brief examples, ritual clowns do more than merely entertain. Their role also exceeds regulating social pressures, and their eccentric and comic streak does not always provide social relief. Although being "not serious" seems an essential part of their description, ritual clowns may become quite serious. Moreover, although "comedy has many features of an 'anti-rite'" (Kapferer 1991: 285)—while ritual is considered serious as opposed to comedy, and since clowns are iconoclasts that make fun of norms and rules—clowns and comedy may fulfill indispensable transformative roles in ritual itself, such as breaking down complex emotions and dealing with transitions between life situations, for example, the passage from mourning to mundane life (Mitchell 1992: 30), fending off suffering (Bala 2010: 51). Their role gathers cosmic ramifications when tackling forbidding situations.

This diversity in the making of clowns within different social environments calls for an alternative anthropological approach—one that forgoes the search for universal social or psychological motivations for the appearance of clowns. And rather than assuming that they mainly play a social role within society at large outside the setting in which they appear, consider how exactly they are constituted and operate, what they do within the enclave of the event or ritual in which they are active (Handelman 2004b). The workings of "symbolic types" are particularly suitable for an approach that looks at the "logic of composition" of each clown, and the dynamics it engenders, precisely because they are autonomous to a great degree from their social context. By analyzing each through their practice in its own right, and in particular scrutinizing their interaction with the audience and with the other elements present upon the appearance of the clown, the dynamic of their mode of operation surfaces.

Like other symbolic types, such as tricksters, fools, contortionists, charismatic leaders, and clowns (Handelman and Kapferer 1980; Handelman 1985, 1991, 1998b), the Vidūṣaka lives out an extraordinary sociality. He stops the mutuality of everyday life to replace it with his own perspective. The prominent features of a symbolic type are "its closure to negotiability, its lack of mutual tending, and the relative absence of give-and-take in its relationship to roles, personae, and context. Instead, the symbolic type is consistent and wholly true to the logic of its own internal composition" (Handleman 1998: 244). The symbolic type is thus capable of imposing his point of view on the social context, molding it according to his interior consistency.

No single definition can account for the clown type[18] because, as mentioned above, the term "clown" englobes a variety of personae, and following the diversity in what strikes different groups and people as incongruous or funny, wields divergent cultural dynamics. However, clown types often share a certain internal composition that is a "contradictory juxtaposition of humor and gravity" (Handelman 1981: 366). Mixing sacred and profane, auspicious and inauspicious, and more, while the clown types include, within their maladjusted composition, traits of playfulness and mirth, they continually oscillate between poles, consistent in their inconsistency (Handelman 1998b: 236–265).

The most salient trait of a clown type is embodying irresolvable contradictions. The clown type can render oppositions, such as between "serious" and "not serious," "man" and "woman," or "rampant sexuality" and "culture" (Carroll 1981) embedded in one persona. By embodying contradictions, clowns can overcome obstacles and borders, and also communicate between incompatible worlds. The potency of ritual clowning, therefore, claims Mitchell (1992: 30), "is in its metamessage, often submerged in ambiguity but nonetheless communicated in practice."

Thus, the meta-messages of clowns are submerged in ambiguity, which the clowns themselves do not solve. Indeed, the insolvable conundrums are their raison d'être; they continue to live within them while disregarding the mixture of incompatible oppositions. Clowns, like other symbolic types, do not alter their behavior, even when faced with changing conditions. They force the situation into their own perspective; that is, they remain within the conundrum, managing it in different ways to entertain the insolvable oppositions while giving them no respite or solution.

A meta-message is the way to resolve a paradox, and other coexisting antagonistic realities, such as those personified by a clown. According to Mitchell, only a message that is situated on a higher (meta) order can disentangle a paradox and dissolve the coexistence of two incompatible truths (Bar-On Cohen 2011; for an understanding of the trickster as paradoxical, see Köpping 1985). Gregory Bateson (2000), in his communication theory, first suggested that a meta-message is the solution to a conundrum—such as the ambiguity that exists between a nip and a bite: though they look the same to the bystander, they are in fact not the same. For dogs, therefore, to determine whether they are playing and nipping, or fighting and biting for real, a meta-message is necessary. The meta-message or captions are more abstract and encompassing than the act of nipping or biting itself; the announcement "this is play" or "this is serious aggression" indicates to the participants in an interaction whether an action is "play" or "serious."

Nevertheless, the world of the Vidūṣaka, as well as many other ritual clowns, does not support paradoxes at all. Domains or plateaus do not encompass but rather penetrate one another, involuting into each other and promoting smooth passages. The Vidūṣaka does not solve an unsurmountable border between "serious" and "not serious" or between sacred and profane because these dichotomies did not exist in the first place. Within inclusive worlds, cosmological premises that promote paradox and the need for meta-message solutions are missing. The hierarchal cosmological organization of the encompassing orders separated by solid (ontological) borders, together with a binary structure of mutually exclusive oppositions, are absent from the cosmologies that yield ritual clowns. Within a continuous cosmos, such as the cosmos of the Vidūṣaka, there is no hierarchical ordering between practice and its abstract symbolic summation, so that the solution of a meta-message to a paradox, which assumes that the abstract is on a higher order than the practical, does not hold. In an organic, inclusive cosmos, since domains of the world and consciousness are not organized hierarchically, nor are they separated by unbreachable borders, the relations between incompatible yet coexisting truths are not paradoxical—rather, such conundrums energize and add depth to the world on stage.

## Becoming Intense

In more dynamic terms, the processuality of the "symbolic type" is a "becoming-intense," "becoming-animal," "becoming-different," as Deleuze and Guattari thought of those notions. These dynamics of change, of presentation anew, account for internal processes that do not result in identity alterations. Violent somatic dynamics of transformation—like the gradual augmentation of pain, cold, or starvation—do not change anything but intensity, yet they change experience and reality in profound ways. They depend on time itself, as "becoming different is its own time, the real time in which change occurs" (Stagoll 2005: 21–22). Deleuze and Guattari (1987: 232–309)[19] describe the dynamics of "becoming-animal" while scrutinizing its potentiality in litterateur. The process of "becoming-animal" occurs when a man[20] meets an extraordinary singular member of a pack, a swarm, a flock, or a herd—a member that is of the border, brave, intelligent, reflexive, daring, an intellectual animal of sorts. Through the tense, intense, and at times obsessive relation that develops between this singular member and that man, the man can become included and follow the ways of the animal, their movement, their reasoning, their bodies, and himself "become-animal," joining the pack, the swarm, the herd for a while.

"Becoming" is pure movements, and as such does not evolve within time but rather *"is its own time"* (Stagol 2005: 21, original emphasis). Deleuze and Guattari (1987: 232–309) use the processual terms "becoming," "becoming-intense," and "becoming-animal" as contrasts to the stable terms "identity" and "being." For them, becoming-animal is a process that suggests something between imitation (like an animal) and being within a fixed category (being an animal); it concerns alliances, it is communication, or contagiousness (Deleuze and Guattari 1987: 238). Deleuze and Guattari describe the process and dynamic of becoming mainly in negative terms: "A becoming is not a correspondence between relations. But neither is it a resemblance, an imitation, or, at the limit, and identification. . . . Becoming lacks a subject distinct from itself." Becoming is an involution and symbiosis, and involution is creative (as opposed to evolution and filiation). Becoming-animal can happen only between packs, populations, "modes of expansion, propagation, occupation, contagion, peopling," and by infection, which is "interkingdom" (Deleuze and Guattari 1987: 237, 238, 283, 242).

Becoming is a real somatic dynamic of intensity and thus depends on the body and what it can do, for we "know nothing of the body until we know what it can do, in other words, what its affects are, how they can or cannot enter into composition with other affects, with the affects of another body, either it destroys that body or be destroyed by it, either to exchange actions and passions with it or to join with it in composing a more powerful body" (Deleuze and Guattari 1987: 257).

The Vidūṣaka brings forth contradictory traits, yet these contradictions are not embedded within him—rather, they frame him. We may be surprised that such a coarse man is a Brahmin; that a Brahmin does not know a single Veda; that within a play about true love such a hungry character occupies center stage; or that an actor on the *Kūṭiyāṭṭam* stage speaks in Malayalam and addresses the audience directly. But these contradictions are exterior to the Vidūṣaka; moreover, he himself is oblivious to them.

The contradictions of the Vidūṣaka are situated on the frame between the multiple realities of the play, those of the audience and the actor's mundane lives, between that of the heroes dressed in costume, speaking in mudrā gestures and the Vidūṣaka. More generally, between mudrā gestures and uttered words; between the mundane Malayalam and the ritualistic Sanskrit; between heroes (whether human heroes as in *Nāgānandam*, or deities and demons in *Subhadrā-dhanañjayam*) and mere humans.

The *Kūṭiyāṭṭam* Vidūṣaka is clearly a symbolic type; he is wholly true to the logic of his own internal composition (Handelman 1998b: 244). He allows no give and take with the play heroes or with the audience, and draws everyone into his own take on the situations, but is he a "clown type"? The Vidūṣaka of other Indian classic theaters appear to be closer to a clown type, but the *Kūṭiyāṭṭam* Vidūṣaka may be closer to what I would call a "human (symbolic) type," following a process of "becoming human" while blocking out anything that is not human, and intensifying the affects of acting within the human pack, of humanness. Pouring the world into himself through his human somaticity to concentrate his humanness until it can draw on the potentialities reserved to the gods. And this is what the Vidūṣaka does: he affects through the potentialities of his human body. Through his gluttonous self, he exhausts the potentialities of being human to the extreme into an intensity of upholding humanness; he lives on stage amid other than humans, which permits him to intensify, even exaggerate the process of "becoming human."

Thus, through the person of the Vidūṣaka, the frame itself loses its solidity, becoming porous, unclear, and recursive, twisting onto itself, involuted, becoming unobstructed, continuous. Through the Vidūṣaka, with "its inversions, its mirror effects, its transformative powers, its ludic approach to the realities of the inner and outer worlds" (Shulman 1987: 153), humanity itself loses its unquestioned self-evidence to require a process of self-formation.

## The Vidūṣaka's Dynamics or How to Become a "Human Type"

The Vidūṣaka as "symbolic type," a "human type," as a carrier of the process of "becoming human" is riddled with discontinuities. He is a constant contrast to the aloof romantic naiveté of the two young princely lovers and their agonizing search for union. Moreover, while spoiling the purity of the young couple's love, he also spoils other illusions, and either places new illusions in their stead or, perhaps, does away with illusion altogether.[21] He spreads disillusion, and shows the centrality of material somatic existence, adding a corporal dimension to the lovers' obsession. Concomitantly, he also spoils *Kūṭiyāṭṭam* itself, the meticulous results of precise efforts—the mudrā words, Sanskrit, facial color, the art of changing characters, and formal movement—all seem overdone, petrified in comparison to his light and free body movements and comments.

The Vidūṣaka does not bend himself to the story and its mood. He does not fall in love, nor try to kill himself; none of this drama concerns him. The Vidūṣaka keeps interjecting unrelated remarks, strewing discontinuity through his misunderstandings and other sidetracking. Although he is hyperactive, constantly moving, his deeds are mundane; they stem from real life, and real-life is often at variance to the claims of order, whether religious, romantic, or political. "Personal experience perceives a world shaken by non-sense, capriciousness and ambiguity" (Mitchell 1992: 36).

Through the incongruity between the neatness and continuity of the emotions of play's protagonists, and the untidiness and discontinuities of everyday life, the Vidūṣaka introduces the power of vitality embedded in daily human messiness. He lives within the deeply puzzling, unsolved conundrums of karma. In this sense, the Vidūṣaka is karma; his is of the logic of karma, not karma as a disembodied philosophical idea, but rather as the fully somatic texture of living as it is lived. The surprises of "real" reality, embedded within the minutia of every day, which "forbids us escaping the reality of our own bodies, and the raucous possibilities of change, decay, and recreation" (Gitomer 1991: 99).

Deleuze and Guattari's understanding of the dynamics of "becoming-animal" occurs when a man meets an extraordinary, singular animal of the periphery. The Vidūṣaka is a singular member at the border of the clan of humanity, at the border between the historical and mythological entities and the audience, between the actor and the character of the play, between the Brahmin, the king, and more. The Vidūṣaka is also like the original man Puruṣa, "the divine anthropos" (Holdrege 1998: 351) whose sacrifice enabled all life, and who was reassembled to allow human existence. Puruṣa and the Vidūṣaka share the urgent need for food. "The Vedic myth of Puruṣa reinforces the same concept that 'food' and the 'enjoyer of the food' are essentially interlinked [. . .] the body as a collection of food-substances" (Timalsina 2009: 45). The Vidūṣaka body and its capacities for doing, enjoying, moving, and failing are his compass and tool. His shameless demand for food, his stories, his behavior while making us chuckle, also unsettles our unquestioned taken-for-granted attitude toward ourselves, our bodies, everyday life, and the discontinuities and potentialities of human life. After placing the messy humanity of humans on a pedestal, the Vidūṣaka embarks on the dynamics of "becoming human." This new presentation of the familiar reveals the dramatic and ritual forces embedded in the human body and existence, its invisible potentially powerful transformative affects.

Like Vālmīki, the scribe of the *Rāmāyaṇa,* the Vidūṣaka breaches the border between sorts of living entities. Vālmīki is a human who appears within his own story, meeting the gods' avatars while also recounting the events, and can, in this way, communicate among the various protagonists of the story, as well as the readers of the Rāmāyaṇa.

Like the Chakiār, both his dramatic and ritualistic power are of the stage, and on it. The Vidūṣaka is human, like the audience: we all are attracted by good food; our partners most probably resemble the lowly maid Cakki rather than the marvelous princess Malayavatī, yet we chuckle uneasily at her description. The Vidūṣaka challenges our humanity. The self-evident becomes questioned and a bit uncomfortable, and concomitantly draws us into a purely human dynamic. Through his endless filling himself with food, chewing, and spouting out words, the Vidūṣaka builds a powerful humanity that matches the capability of gods.

## Chapter 7

# The Gods Are Coaxed into our Lives

> First, we have sound, and seeing the sound; then sight, and seeing the sight and hearing what we see; with this comes thinking sound and sight and all the rest—always together, never alone.
>
> —Shulman, *The Rite of Seeing: Essays on Kūṭiyāṭṭam*[1]

When dealing with magic, religion, or ritual transformation, anthropologists often claim to suspend their disbelief. Naturally, anthropologists, stemming from a different cosmological reckoning, do not believe in local gods and demons, nor the supposed outcome of ritual and sacrifice. But while observing the field, we try to avoid this mistrust and proceed "as if" we do believe in the entities active in the field. Due to our trade, we must award the authority of truth to events and experiences in the anthropological field in the attempt to decipher other peoples' perspectives, but ultimately the task is to explain religious phenomena through sociality alone. So, suspension of disbelief also means that anthropologists imagine what they are seeing to be true, just long enough to understand it. Basically, anthropology is a secular pursuit—that is, a pursuit that uses logic exclusively. It assumes that while attempting to figure out how people make sense of their world, all can be explained without recourse to the occult.

Kapferer (2001) claims that the suspension of disbelief can disentangle the paradox that seriously undermines anthropology, which results from the mismatch between the secular attitude, and the belief in invisible forces. Considering the reality of magic, religion, or gods as a real reality is thus usually outside the purview of anthropology.

Indeed, magic, religion, or ritual transformation can make sense only within a certain environment, and through local ingenuity. However, the assumptions underlining the suggestion to suspend disbelief are not always relevant, and are superfluous in the case of *Kūṭiyāṭṭam*. As mentioned, rituals and other events are not necessarily directly dependent on social order, nor do they imperatively play a functional role in society; the relation between each event and its social surrounding is not a given. If a ritual does play a specific role for social arrangements, this needs to be shown, not assumed (Handelman 2004).

Moreover, three notions at the base of the suggestion to suspend disbelief are not relevant to an inclusive world: paradox, acting "as if," and belief itself. For a paradox to exist, two things must be absolutely and completely mutually exclusive). When other relations between oppositions and binaries are in place, which is a required condition for an event to be inclusive, the paradox melts away. This is why no paradox forms between a secular, or logical, attitude and one that includes invisible forces. Further, the choice of cultural dynamics in *Kūṭiyāṭṭam* does not employ "as if" to distinguish between gods and humans, and thus does not require a semiotic leap of faith, nor an ontological difference of sorts between the real world and a pretended one that dissipates if one does not believe.

More importantly, belief itself is not a universal prerequisite, and in *Kūṭiyāṭṭam* it is not necessary at all. The question of belief or disbelief, therefore, is redundant. The anthropologist need not suspend anything, since this reality relies on body, senses, rhythm, dynamics, differences in their own right, and more, and does not require abstract reconning, such as belief or a heuristic corpus of explanations. The dynamics set out to roam the *Kūttambalam* produce an existence not different from other life experiences.

An inclusive cosmos operates within its interiority, toiling, through establishing complex interconnections, to move inward and generate more and more depth where none existed before. Seeing that the dynamics that enable to achieve an inclusive world are at the center of this book, in lieu of a conclusion, in an attempt to loosely tie together the strands developed above, I will return to the question of how the gods materialize from a slightly different angle and draw attention to the densest locus in the *Kūttambalam*, its central focal point, the space between the actor's eyes and the lamp on stage.

## The Eyes

First, the *miḻāvu* drums invoke the gods, alone on stage, playing the gods' rhythm, the *miḻāvoccappeṭuttal*—the composition which gives the start to every *Kūtiyāṭṭaṃ* performance. The drummer creates an entire universe that is later displayed by the actors on the stage (Pacciolla 2022). Next, the actor arrives and strengthens the presence of the gods with *kryā* dance invocation, and then the eye movements concentrate, deepen, and diffuse this presence.

Shulman (2022) calls his recent *Kūṭiyāṭṭam* book *The Rite of Seeing*;[2] every encounter with the gods at the temple is *Darśan* (Eck 1981), namely, a rite of seeing. In *Kūṭiyāṭṭam*, the performance is *seen*—the words are *seen* in mudrā gestures rather than heard[3]—and during the performance, the actor assumes the role of a god, becomes infused with many of the god's qualities, and as a god, is seen by the spectators. Moreover, in the temple, the god or the goddess is the main spectator. When the performance is held at a temple, the god in his inner sanctum is not only a passive spectator, on some occasions, but also involved in choosing the drama to be enacted in his temple (Sullivan 1995: 46). But, seeing and the eyes themselves are responsible for much more—they bring *Kūṭiyāṭṭam* to life. The eyes are the most significant and active facial apertures. The *ucci*—the highest aperture—is covered to prevent ritualistic pollution as well as possession, and since the actor does not talk, the mouth is closed for most of the performance. Thus, the potentialities embedded in vision and eyes are employed in *Kūṭiyāṭṭam* to the fullest, so that "eye sacrifice" amasses depth (on "visual sacrifice," *cākṣuṣayajña*, see Richmond and Richmond 1985: 54).

The actors use their eyes in extravagant ways, moving, widening, enlarging, and accentuating them with thick black lines stretching to the ears, and coloring their eyeballs red. The actors' eyes communicate, at times adding a second voice to what the hands are saying through mudrā gesture, or even saying something else completely, hinting at a viewpoint that the hands may obscure.

Vision in *Kūṭiyāṭṭam* undergoes a change to include more than what the eyes can see, "through perception of overlapping vectors" (Shulman 2022: 194), seeing the sound, but also turning movement into an organ of perception. In karate training, this potentiality is learned systematically. Training the peripheral vision enables participants, first, to unfocus what is directly in front of them, and then to perceive movement and objects at their sides and to see everything within the widened field of vision calmly and clearly, without concentrating on anything in particular within that field. A sort of meditative, yet completely alert, vision is developed. And then, over time, this vision comes to include everything moving around, and even behind the participant (Bar-On Cohen 2007). Something similar occurs at the *Kūṭiyāṭṭam* performance when movement can be perceived through vision, not specifically through the eyes, but rather through a process akin to unfocusing, which results from the constant movement of the actor, from the beating of the drums, and the flickering flames of the lamp in front of the actor. Seeing extends itself to the periphery of the field of vision and beyond. Movement itself becomes an organ of perception, eyes, ears, and movement, each providing slight differences in perspectives, resulting in the multiplication of space, time, and realities.

This multiplicity, this intimate layering of points of view and realities, recursively changes the vision to include much more than what the eyes perceive: "There is no projected, external Archimedean point. One sees, and sees what one sees, only from inside what is seen" (Shulman 2016: 332). The activity on stage becomes in-sight; it can be found under the observer's eyelids, becoming part of her interiority, as well as her exterior environment. Over many hours and many nights, vision becomes the inner iteration within everybody in the *Kūttambalam*, including more than mundane reality.

## The Eyes and Three Wicks

These potentialities spread from the focal point of the *Kūttambalam*. The entire performance is concentrated and condensed into the space between the actor's eyes and the lamp on stage. Inside the space delineated by the five points—the two eyes and the three wicks of the lamp—a reality that is obscured by everyday life starts to flicker and emerge. Even with the Vidūṣaka, although he does not look at the flames, his whole body reflects the focal points of the performance, as he is covered with Mandala-like dots that form a five-point referring to the eyes and the flames.

The flames should never be left to die out since they are the source from which the deities materialize, while the light of the lamp also shines from the actor's eyes to generate a glow. The eyes and the flames are in movement, flickering, reverberating, and resonating with each other until source and reflection are interchangeable. Moreover, all the movement on stage, the hands in their mudrā dance and the actors moving about, is generated from this focal point, and also recursively returns to it.

Once the actor evokes the gods with *Kriyā* and the Naṅṅyār chanting, on the long evenings of the *Nirvahaṇam*, the actor as storyteller sits on the stool, looks at the lamp, and performs eye acrobatics, rolling his eyes for several minutes, vertically, horizontally, diagonally, and round and round. The trained actor's irises seem to be bouncing around of their own accord, like ping-pong balls, as if encountering a wall and bouncing off it; they become objects detached from the person controlling them, bouncing back and forth. This is an impressive feat that demands long and hard training, and it is also the root of creating the special quality of *Kūṭiyāṭṭam*.

The eye movement condensates the shimmering of the lamp to disseminate its light and the reality emerging from it, and concomitantly concentrates the power of the cosmos and projects it to the lamp. The eyes moving in all directions and around are summoning the gods to that space between the actor's eyes and the three wicks of the lamp, the focal point of everyone's gaze. The actor is looking straight into it, and the audience is looking at the actor and the drummers behind the flames so that their gaze includes the flames in the foreground and the actor in the background, constantly changing their focus. The accentuated movement of the eyeballs expands the space facing the lamp to include more. The actor's eyes adjust to the flames, get in sync with them, and with this intoxicating blurring of vision, a generative intersection is created, activating the gods, coaxing them to the *Kūttambalam*, the movement, energetically expanding to the periphery of the field of vision, to the entire *Kūttambalam* and beyond.

Śūrpanakhā, Rāvaṇa's sister's description of Sītā, causes the demon-king to intensely fall in love with the most beautiful woman in the world, and he then performs the first description of her body head to toe (*keśādipadam*). The image that stems from his imagination becomes a visible description in movement of feminine beauty. And then, when he finally sees her, he again describes her entire body, admiring her beauty, but this time *keśādipadam* is performed through eye movement alone. Upon seeing the real woman, he is overwhelmed by emotion, and the description becomes interior, while the proof of the emotional turmoil can be glimpsed at through his eyes alone. This is a moment of interiority, happening within the demon-king, yet the audience is privy to its unfolding, which can be seen and felt between the actor's eyes and the lamp. We witness a reduction of movement to its core, the embodiment of the thickest of potentialities. Next, the performance is spread out again when Rāvaṇa's ten heads quarrel over Sītā's body and divides it between them. Her body parts are now distributed, with each of the demon-king's heads claiming one of the parts.

More generally, the entire performance follows these same dynamics, as the unfolding starts as a neutral description stemming from the actor's imagination, becomes interior and spreads out again to look at what he has created from afar. Correspondingly, the space and time in the *Kūttambalam* also concentrate and dissipates.

The movement of contraction and expansion—the breath of the *Kūttambalam*, the twinkling and reverberation of the light, which is a birth of sorts—becomes a freestanding live entity. Not a concept or an idea, not a second-degree notion that demands a leap, but rather a concrete, material abstraction that includes more than the story and its telling, more than the eye can see, more even than movement can generate. A surplus of interiority, a bulge of gestation, a child of effort and of the potentialities engaged in that effort. Like the potentialities of the body, the senses, and the world itself, this actuality was there all along; the gods were present even before the drumbeat, but through the movement, their presence comes to life, and becomes thickened to englobe the *Kūttambalam* so that we can feel it and live within it.

## The Gods Are Coaxed into our Lives

*Kūṭiyāṭṭam* multiplies and intensifies to the extreme the potentialities embedded in the human body, while complexifying and deepening feeling and creativity. Lakṣmaṇa can build the *Parṇa-śālā*—a temple in the wilderness—out of invisible branches and twigs. Hanūman can relieve the world of distress and desolation caused by the abduction of Sītā. The world is dimmed, emptied out when Rāvaṇa dies. *Śakti* can fill the air through *Śūrpaṇakhā's* mutilation and Sītā's ordeal. The Naṅṅyār performing the *Cūṭala-k-kūttu* can dissociate the dead Agnihotri from his earthly connections and usher him to liberation. The Vidūṣaka can become a sacrificial human through his waddling in mundane murkiness. All can bring joy and amazement while safeguarding gentile elegance and auspiciousness.

*Kūṭiyāṭṭam* had developed, was reworked and improved, over generations, coming to fruition through intense training to become both an aesthetic masterpiece and a transformative ritual. Manifestly, it is refined, elegant, poetic, and sophisticated entertainment that can unravel profound layers of human sentiment and relations. Deep love, uncanny deception, unbridled devotion, extreme violence, cruel suspicion, divine mischief, female suffering, human folly, and more materialize on stage through exacting ways of storytelling. Concomitantly, through the constant movement of flames, actors, and membranes of the drums, another reality opens up, and all in the *Kūttambalam* are ushered into a cosmos inhabited by humans, gods, and demons.

Within this world we are privy to miraculous events such as demons taking on the appearance of humans, a ten-headed demon-king falling deeply in love, a demoness carrying a man into the sky, a monkey that can traverse the sea to Lanka in one leap, a jewel that can reveal pretense, and a woman going into fire emerges from it unscorched—but that is not all. We all entice, encourage, and draw the gods to improve the mundane world. This is done to advance the goals of the patron, who paid for the performance; to transport a dead man into a better existence; and to concomitantly bestow auspiciousness all around. Even the gods cannot resist the tantalizing affect, grace, and elegance of *Kūṭiyāṭṭam*.

# Notes

## Introduction

1. Also spelled Mūḻikkuḷam.

2. Except for the young students of the Nepathya school. When they want to communicate with one another during a performance without disturbing by shouting to be heard over the loud drums, they use mudrā gestures.

3. From the *Toraṇa-yuddham*, "The War at the Gate."

4. The lamp was not filmed in this video, since the shot was taken from the side, but its constant presence is a vital feature of the performance.

5. I am using the term "lived-in-world"—borrowed from phenomenology—very loosely, since the change *Kūṭiyāṭṭam* brings about depends not on consciousness or perception alone. Moreover, I am using the word "affect" and not "effect" because these changes do not only leave an impression but actually make a difference in reality. *Kūṭiyāṭṭam* changes the world itself in ways that affect the world. However, as an anthropologist and not a philosopher, I am not interested in dealing with the ontology of this world, nor with the question of what is really real.

6. Venkatesan details what she means by the animation of the goddess by a Tamil priest: "First, that processes of animation create new social beings that are both amenable to human projects and un-canny; second, that animated things are recognized by those who interact with them as humanlike but not human; and third, that their other-than-humanness is what renders them both attractive and disquietingly potent" (2020: 1).

7. My attitude is closer to claiming a-duality, namely, a situation in which dual or non-dual is not relevant, because what is usually referred to as non-dual also includes the potentiality of the dual, which in turn promotes strict exclusion of other options. I choose instead to highlight one very general characteristic of such an a-dual world, that of inclusiveness. *Kūṭiyāṭṭam* makes its choices of ways to create such a world, but

other inclusive worlds are constructed quite differently (see, e.g., Bar-On Cohen 2016). The question of dualism and monism has been debated at length both in Western and Indian philosophy; here, however, I am not formulating an argument about the nature of the world, whether it is dual or not, but of differences in cosmologies created through practice.

8. A widespread example of a strictly exclusive logic is bureaucracy that encases everything in neat categories, and, when those compartments fail, new ones are contrived (Handelman 2004a).

9. Repetition of iterations is one hallmark of Deleuzian philosophy; they generate the power of difference, the true drive to change in its own right (see Deleuze 1994). Repetition can change reality in profound ways without altering identity since its terrible power comes from variations within sameness. Through discovery and experimentation, repetition allows both experience and expression undifferentiated and affirms the power of the new and unforeseeable, yielding mutations and transformations (Parr 2005).

10. I found an extreme example of such separation from mundane life in *kyūdo*, Japanese archery. For the archers, everything in the outside world is pushed aside to create a world that is condensed into the eight steps that constitute a shot, including everything that occurs in the fraction of time it takes to shoot an arrow (Bar-On Cohen 2014).

11. I include all these faculties in the "body" not from some monistic attitude that denies "mind" but rather to avoid hard-and-fast distinctions among them; here, physical and mindful faculties nourish each other practically and grow together.

## Chapter 1

1. See, e.g., https://kutiyattam.wikispaces.com/Gestures.

2. See Sara Yona Zwieg's 2013 film *The Backstage of Tradition*.

3. The only difference between the training of male and female actors that I could find concerns massaging. Wearing only a loincloth, the boys smear their bodies with oil as their teacher stretches their limbs. No such practice occurs for female trainees.

4. Amanur is the grandfather of Aparna Naṅṅyār, who performed *Cūṭala-k-kūttu* in the cremation grounds—see chapter 5.

5. I had the privilege of visiting Indu G. at work and meeting with her colleagues and students. This was just before the festivities of *Onam*, the most important holiday in Kerala, celebrated by all religions and communities. A main feature of this holiday is flower arrangements at the entrances of homes, which expand and become more elaborate

each day. The public school at which Indu G. teaches, which accepts children from all walks of Kerala society, is an example of that state's achievements since all Kerala children must attend school. They were all wearing immaculate uniforms, the girls' hair neatly braided. During my visit, every class competed in making large flower arrangements.

6. Other *Kūṭiyāṭṭam* troupes have also been invited to performance tours through other international connections. For instance, another family-based school, directed by Madhu's close relatives, the Ammannoor Chachu Chakyar Smaraka Gurukulam of Irinjalakuda, toured Australia a few years ago. Another group, led by Usha Nangiar, went to Japan in 2017.

7. In 2012, the first fortnight of the performance took place during the month of Rāmāyaṇa; thousands came to the temple as part of their pilgrimage to the four temples dedicated to the four Rāmāyaṇa brothers, one of whom—Lakṣmaṇa—is the patron of the Moozhikkulam temple.

8. In recent years, big projectors have been added to the stage, which unfortunately deter the bats from coming in.

9. The question of language is a bit more complicated in *Kūṭiyāṭṭam*; whereas the lines of the male protagonists are indeed chanted in Sanskrit, the females speak Prakrit, some characters speak a quaint old Malayalam, and the mudrā gestures follow the grammar of Sanskritized Malayalam.

10. Madhu says that the "tying" is like a full stop: the day's segment of the act has been successfully accomplished and completed. Indeed, this day's segment is done and kept safe for the next day.

11. Cākyār actors complain that some members of their community, who are not trained as actors, dress up in costume only to perform for money as a blessing, rendering entire acts, such as the most demanding *Aṅgulīyāṅkam*, in mere minutes.

12. A new, nontraditional way of temple performance was devised to bridge between the strict temple performance as ritual, open only to artists of the correct lineage, and the "new," highly accomplished actors and actresses stemming from other groups. The "new" actors and actresses perform in temples in which the *Kūṭiyāṭṭam* tradition has died out, and in temples without such tradition. This was probably initiated by the Venu family; Kapila Venu, for example, initiated a tour of temples completed in 2019, and performed *Naṅṅyārkūttu* in those temples.

13. I heard slightly differing accounts from various families as to who initiated the modernization of *Kūṭiyāṭṭam* and who objected to it; these stories are by now part of these families' founding myths (for such accounts, see Rajandran 2012: 261; Moser 2013; Lowthorp 2020).

14. The changes initiated by the Kalamandalam School were led by Painkulam Rama Chakyar (see Margi 2015: 23). Many of the female students of the *Kūṭiyāṭṭam* schools stop performing after marriage, so

in many cases, the studies render them keen members of the audience rather than performers.

15. More generally, because of the use of Sanskrit, the high status of the groups involved in this tradition, and its antiquity, *Kūṭiyāṭṭam* is considered "classic" and endangered and was recognized as such by the institutions of the Indian government as early as the 1950s; see Lowthorp (2017). In the state of Kerala replacing the old patronage and its complexities, see Guillebaud (2011).

16. At high schools, too, students have some initiation to *Kūṭiyāṭṭam* and other Kerala stage arts. Yet many of the people I talked to in Kerala did not even know that *Kūṭiyāṭṭam* existed.

17. To the best of my knowledge, the *Aṅgulīyāṅkam*, performed over twenty-eight days, was performed in 2012 by an artist's family in honor of their father. Because it is a single-actor performance and there were not enough actors to divide the exhausting task, the performance included few elaborations. Madhu's family also performed the protracted version about a decade ago, as part of the entire *Āścaryacūḍāmaṇi*, "the wondrous head-jewel," but only once a week and not on consecutive days. Rendering the entire play took two years. I was also told by one of the readers of this manuscript that the Margi school performed the entire *Aṅgulīyāṅkam* in the 1990s.

18. On Rāvaṇa worship, see Burkhalter Flueckiger (2017).

19. In a similar vein, Schieffelin (1998: 194) calls performance "the creation of presence," formulating his idea this way: "'Performance' deals with actions more than text; with habits of the body more than structures of symbols, with illocutionary rather than propositional force, with the social construction of reality rather than representation."

20. Palmer and Jankowiak make a more complex claim when they connect expression (performance) with experience through imagery: "When we observe performances and physical constructions, we experience them as mental imagery. When we self-consciously monitor our own performances, we reexperience the imagery that we think they project to audiences. Thus, performances may weave complex webs of interaction and experience, all mediated through imagery" (1996: 226).

21. Holdrege (1998) uses the notions of taxonomy, categories, and representation, which I extracted from her descriptions. These notions, I think, belong to another world of content.

22. Holdrege (1998) calls this principle "encompassing hierarchy," but encompassment implies a total separation between ordered elements; this is also how she depicts them in her article. I would consider this a porous organization and that the word "encompassment" is better suited to an integrated rather than an intra-grated world (Handelman and Lindquist

2011; Handelman 2014), which is why I have replaced "encompassment" with "inclusion."

23. See chapter 6.

24. See chapter 5.

25. I have advanced the hypothesis that the mudrā language is connected to the noise of the drums. Since these are sacred phrases and must be heard distinctly, and since the drums' noisy beat prevents the human voice from being heard clearly, the mudrā gestures, which are clearly visible, replace the voice. I have not been able to corroborate my hypothesis. Richmond and Richmond found a partial resemblance between the Vedic and Tantric use of gesture and sound pattern transitions (1985: 59n5).

26. Spoken and written words can also act directly on the world without a gap, for example, mantras, depending on how they are used and on the connectivities of words to other phenomena in that same world.

27. Although movement in both the more famous *Kathakaḷi* Kerala theater and *Kūṭiyāṭṭam* is also related to the local Kerala martial art *Kalarippayattu* (Zarrilli 1998, 2000), the two theater traditions, as well as the martial art, have different attitudes toward both body and violence.

28. The Vidūṣaka does not wear a basic color on his face; in general, human characters in *Kūṭiyāṭṭam* are only smeared with ghee, which makes their skin darker and glistening.

29. On other ritual dynamics that permit the construction of inclusive worlds, see, e.g., Seamone (2013) on Pentecostal Christians, and Foulk (2013) on Zen Buddhism.

30. See chapter 4

31. Whether the original setting for *Kūṭiyāṭṭam* was within the temple or outside is not certain. Heike Moser (2008, 2013), who is a trained *Kūṭiyāṭṭam* actress as well as a scholar, and Richmond (1990: 87) both claim that the original form was a ritual. Madhu, however, believes it developed first and foremost outside the temple grounds as entertainment. Narayanan (2006: 141–142) argues that *Kūṭiyāṭṭam* began as a court practice and was incorporated into the temples only later, sometime between the eighth and tenth centuries. One story of origin tells that the *Kūṭiyāṭṭam* performers descend from a line of court bards who drove the battle chariots of the kings (Richmond 1990b: 90). Last, Rajendran (2012: 256) proposes that the Cākyārs stem from Buddhist communities that existed in Kerala. In any case, in recent centuries *Kūṭiyāṭṭam* has been performed mainly within the temples (see Margi 2015).

32. According to Kunjo Vasudevam, three acts were mainly used as sacrifice: *Mattavilāsam, Mantrāṅkam,* and *Aṅgulīyāṅkam.* Until about 150 years ago, during the coronation of the king of Kochi, the entire Rāmāyaṇa was also performed.

33. The connection between the evenings is also achieved through enactment; the final phrase uttered or gesture made on one day is the first presented the next day, leaving the audience with no closing or climax at the end of each day's enactment.

34. On performing obeisance to the gods and other ritualistic preparations for the performance, see Enros (1981). The *Kūṭiyāṭṭam* three-wicked lamp is also referred to as the yāgaśāla, the Brahmin fire sacrifice; for details, see Paulose (1993: xix).

35. See chapter 5.

36. A change may occur even there. It has been debated and may happen in the near future that the son of a Cākyār father may be permitted to perform in a temple, even though his mother stems from a different community.

37. Since the Cākyār and Nambyār families are matrilineal, sons may perform only in the temple of their mother's village. For example, Madhu and his brother Sajeev, whose father was a prominent actor in the Moozhikkulam temple, are not allowed to perform there.

38. Outside the temple, *Aṅgulīyāṅkam* is performed over twenty-eight nights; the temple version takes only twelve nights.

39. Narayanan (2006; 2022) goes to the extreme of accusing Western scholars of denying Indian history: "Perhaps even more importantly, one suspects this denial of history is a denial of the right to history of non-Western societies, a denial of their status as human societies subject to change, development, and transformation" (2006: 142). Narayanan leaps from the tenth century when (he claims) *Kūṭiyāṭṭam* was founded as a Buddhist theater connected to kingship, to the fifteenth century when *Kūṭiyāṭṭam* was according to him first performed in a temple, to today when it is performed both within and out of temples. However, as Sullivan (2010) points out, the *Kūṭiyāṭṭam* rendition of the classic dramas clearly emphasizes the devotional aspects of the plays.

## Chapter 2

1. An earlier version of this chapter was published in Bar-On Cohen (2019). On the *Aṅgulīyāṅkam*, see also Oberlin and Shulman (2019) and in particular Johan (2019).

2. Translated in Jones (1984) as "The Wondrous Crest-Jewel."

3. Binding, tying up, capturing some aspect of the Supreme principle is more generally the purpose of a sacred space such as a temple, a Mandala, or a *Kūttambalam* (Richmond and Richmond 1985: 53).

4. The actor chants only the text of the original play, not the added elaborations that take up most of the time.

5. Although the mudrā grammar is in Malayalam, some Sanskrit is incorporated. For example, in Malayalam, only singular and plural are declined, while Sanskrit has a separate dual declination distinct from other plurals. This dual form has a separate mudrā word.

6. Possession is considered a practice typical of lower castes because they tend to become possessed from the exterior. Higher casts, however, possess an element of divinity within themselves and through (tantric) practice can exteriorize it (Tarabout 1997).

## Chapter 3

1. Don Handelman, *On God, Two Goddesses, Three Studies of South Indian Cosmology* (Leiden & Boston: Brill, 2014b), 60.

2. Whether the Naṭāṅkuśa is a criticism of *Kūṭiyāṭṭam* or, on the contrary, an endorsement of it is not clear (Poulouse 1993). However, the author of the text describes himself as a Nampūdiri and friend of the Cākyār, thus including two of the traits of the Vidūṣaka.

3. In the same vein, the term "non-representation" affirms the primacy of representation, positing every other option as its antonym. However, I have not yet found a notion to replace non-representation adequately. Non-representation is, in fact, world-generating, yet labeling it as such can cause confusion.

4. Shulman talks about the elephant footprints that came before the elephant arrived.

5. The establishment of mutually exclusive binaries is also why paradoxes can be used to overcome binaries in an exclusive system. Paradox, however, is irrelevant in an inclusive world, since nothing entirely excludes anything else; rather, they entertain complex interconnectedness.

6. This is Dumont's view of caste (1980), a hierarchy into which another intermediate rank or caste can endlessly be inserted.

7. In her thought on "concert time," Sheets-Johnstone suggests that body movement is innate and universal (2017: 6). This idyllic viewpoint, still based on the idea that concert movement and movement in general, in contrast to language, does not develop. My argument here is the opposite: movement and concert movement are harnessed by culture and develop into specific highly sophisticated forms in parallel to other aspects of culture. For another, beautiful take on the social and cultural importance of movement, see Mezzenzana (2018).

8. Japanese philosophers Bin Kimura and Hideo Kawamoto also claim that the reflexive cognitive stance toward the world appears when we contemplate what we have done; it is delayed until after the fact of doing, since it is only after doing that we know that we "can do" (Ishii

2012; see also Satsuka 2018). During "doing," "understanding" occurs, and when "understanding" occurs we realize that it can be done and can be repeated.

9. Particularly among the people that Menon (2002) has studied in Orissa.

10. Since emotions are contagious, the North Indian wrestlers that Alter (1992: 107) describes are not allowed to eat street food in the market for fear of contracting erotic emotions, and thus inadvertently losing semen.

11. Chapter 4 is dedicated to two such cases: the demoness Śūrpaṇakhā accelerates the universe through her rage, and the goddess-cum-woman Sītā slows it down by her serenity.

12. Usually actresses do not express "disgust."

13. This is a much-reduced summary of Abhinavagupta. For him, the central aesthetic move, both on stage and in the spectator, is what he calls sādhāraṇī-kāraṇa, "universalization," or depersonalization, in which the individual's egoistic involvement in what happens on stage disappears and the spectator loses his empirical sense of self in the universal pure emotion that is his or her deeper core (David Shulman, private communication).

14. For another criticism of perspectivism, see Heywood (2020).

15. Indrani is Indra's wife; Rohini is married to the moon.

16. I refer here to Jorge Luis Borges's story "The Garden of Forking Paths," in which he describes what would happen if one could avoid choosing one path over another and simply follow all of them (1998). Something similar happens here, as no time-place and no potentiality gains the upper hand.

17. On versions of the story of Śūrpaṇakhā, see Erndl (1991). An entire collection concerning different versions of the Rāmāyaṇa can be found in Richman (1991).

18. The notion of intensity is used widely by Deleuze: intensity as difference in its own right, and as difference in potentialities (Sauvagnargues 2009: 306). According to Deleuze, the enemy of the quantitative is the scale, since scale makes it impossible for the quantitative to make a qualitative difference. The enemy of the qualitative is identity, for when a thing is fixed into an exclusive definition and identity, it cannot be changed by intensity. Deleuze and Guattari's discussion on intensities concerns what they call the Body without Organs (BwO), a holistic body that is made of intensities. For a discussion of "intensity" in Deleuzian thought, see Sauvagnargues (2009: 304–311). For a presentation of BwO on stage, see Bar-On Cohen (2013).

19. Deleuze was labeled the "philosopher of difference." He "is concerned to overturn the primacy accorded to identity and representa-

tion in Western rationality by theorizing difference as it is experienced" (Stagoll 2005: 72). Deleuzian multiplicity is very close to nonlinearity in the context of this book, as it is conceptualized by Lee (1950). In nonlinear dynamics, there is no arrangement of activities or events into means and ends, nor are there any causal or teleologic relationships (Lee 1950: 91). For Deleuze, multiplicity can be glossed as "a complex structure that does not reference a prior unity. Multiplicities are not part of a greater whole that have been fragments, and they cannot be considered manifold expressions of a single concept or transcendent unity" (Roffe 2005: 176). Hence difference yields multiplicity, and, recursively, multiplicity in its turn begets difference.

20. See chapter 4.

21. However, I will abandon the fine-tuning of "counter-cosmogony" and stick with "cosmology."

22. Handelman and Kapferer's idea of "symbolic type" concerns changes in the flow of sociality. The "type" is a case that differs from regular social interaction, since its behavior is unaffected by interaction. The "symbolic type" is so unmoved by its social surrounding that it creates and iterates the context in which it operates, becoming that context itself (Handelman 1985, 1991, 1998; Handelman and Kapferer 1980). The "type" holds consistently in interaction to its own self-presentation. Therefore, other participants in its social setting, in order to interact with the "type," must either accept this self-presentation and its practice or reject it (Kidron and Handelman 2016). In *Kūṭiyāṭṭam*, it is not one person who creates the "type" interaction; the entire cultural enclave sets up an interaction that forces itself on all present and is unaffected by interaction within the mundane world.

23. Coming up with concepts, according to Deleuze and Guattari (1994), is the only aim of philosophy. Concepts are abstract summations; practice, on the other hand, engages in doing and observing what the world does in reaction, and there is more than one way of tuning ourselves to the world in this way. Pickering (2017) thinks that to conceive of and tolerate the possibility of a multiple ontology a shift is needed from representation to practice since representation is "sharp-edged" while the world is "foggy and amorphous" (2017: 136). For another take on ontology in anthropology, see Satsuka (2018).

## Chapter 4

1. Cited in Shulman (2022). This citation describes the frustrated tearing out of breasts, which may calm the devastating fire of love, thus

combining tearing off the breasts as in Śūrpaṇakhā's mutilation, with Sītā's fire ordeal into one fierce, sexualized, and powerful female modality surfacing as a reaction to the unreliable love of the male. For more Tamil examples, see Ramaswamy (2009).

2. The relations between humans, demons, and gods are complex and cannot be summarized as good versus bad, reflexive versus mere bodily desire, or any other binary. In particular, the relations between Rāma's family, a royal incarnation of the god Viṣṇu, and that of the royal demon Rāvaṇa are complex and their fates interconnected. Rāvaṇa was Viṣṇu's guardian, but he insulted a sage by refusing to let him see Viṣṇu, and thus the sage cursed him to become Viṣṇu's enemy during three incarnations. Rāma, in the last *śloka* of the *Śūrpaṇakhāṅkam*, laments that mutilating Śūrpaṇakhā, Rāvaṇa's sister, will bring havoc and cause a disastrous feud.

3. For other examples of nonlinear cultural dynamics such as homology and resonance, see Bar-On Cohen (2012, 2014).

4. For a criticism of color universality not only in its symbolic meaning but also as a way of perception and thought, see Wierzbicka (2008); Saunders (2000); and Hemming (2012) regarding the widespread triad of colors red, white and black. One example of various uses of colors is that in the Japanese aesthetic white is not connected to body fluids but is associated with emptiness (Hara 2014).

5. When I asked Kesavan Veluthat, a prominent scholar of Kerala, about matrilineality, his reply was curt—to wit, matrilineality was abolished in Kerala in the 1960s. And, indeed, according to the law, for all bureaucratic purposes, martilinearity no longer exists. Yet in the private domain, and in temples, matrimonial preferences, in terms of reference for relatives, and more, matrilineality still plays a role in people's lives.

6. Vadakkiniyil (2019) suggests that the black dhoti is worn by the Ayyappan pilgrims since they are in a liminal, transitional state between life and death.

7. Freeman (2016) suggests a connection between the political, religious, and economic traditional upper-caste arrangements of the Kerala society, and within it the centrality of women, as an incentive to the prominence of *śakti* goddesses and *śakta* tantric practices.

8. Today the *tāli*, or wedding necklace, is worn as a golden amulet on a golden chain.

9. *Śakti* is often referred to as a nonphysical force, based on the spiritual, on the power of consciousness (e.g., Wadley 1975: 55). Yet since it actually propels the world, it surely has powerful physical ramifications, and since consciousness is not disembodied, describing *śakti* as nonphysical seems to emanate from another set of concepts. In Kerala,

*śakti* is often connected with the angry side of the goddess (Pasty-Abdul Wahid 2020: 19).

10. In the exquisite wall paintings of the "Dutch Palace" in Kochi, Śūrpanakhā after her mutilation is depicted as a giant—she is perhaps five times bigger than the other protagonist in the scene. In this depiction, she is indeed excess.

11. From the *āṭṭa-prakāram,* the *Kūṭiyāṭṭam* manual, translated by Nepathya Yadukrishnan, Nepathya Viṣṇuprasad and Nepathya Rahul (henceforth the *āṭṭa-prakāram*). When I first encountered this scene of the demoness finding that the gods are unsuitable for her, I found it funny and asked Madhu about it. He assured me that it was not funny.

12. I asked Sangeeth Chakyar, a very talented young actor, whether in his view Śūrpaṇakhā could have stayed in her elegant form had Rāma accepted her as a second wife. He thought that *māyā* was always temporary and that therefore Lalitā would not have lasted. But I am not so sure, for Lalitā displayed genuine love, which could have sustained her in her elegant form.

13. On the history of breasts, see Yalom (1998).

14. See chapter 6.

15. Madhu Chakyar, who played black and red Śūrpaṇakhā said that if Śūrpaṇakhā calls herself Chūrpaṇākha, then that is probably her real name.

16. From the *āṭṭa-prakāram*.

17. Demons are made of pure desire in many places around the world; see, for example, Blacker (1975) on demons in Japan, Kapferer (1987) in Sri Lanka, and Eichinger Ferro-Luz (1998) on Tamil folktales.

18. Folklorist Chummar Choondal, in his discussion on variations of the Kaṇṇaki cult in Kerala, reports that the goddess in rural north Kerala is called *ottamulacci* (the one with one breast) and *ottappalli* (the one with one tooth). The image of *ottamulacci* is placed outside the temple of Kodungallur. Womenfolk among the pilgrims remove their bodices and expose their naked breasts when they start singing and dancing (Choondal 1978: 28; Gentes 1992: 311).

19. There is a profound difference between the South Indian and the Vedic attitude toward menstrual and childbirth blood, yet both coexist in Kerala. Whereas in the South Indian view female blood is dangerous but auspicious, the Vedic view sees it as polluting (see Caldwell 2001; O'Flaherty 1984; Apffel-Marglin 2008). For rituals of menstruation in North India, in Assam and the extremely polluting status of menstrual blood, see Das (2014). Dinesan (2009) proposes that menstruating women visiting the temple of the celibate god Ayyappan may be in danger, which may be the source of the taboo for their visits.

20. From the *āṭṭa-prakāram*.

21. Such a mixture, known as *guruti,* is often offered to the goddess *ghōra/ugra* (terrible, furious) *Bhadrakāḷi* (Patsy-Abdul Wahid 2020: 2, 22). On use of artificial blood substitute in *śakta* tantric rituals in Kerala, see Freeman (2016).

22. Bees are sometimes considered a form of *śakti*.

23. From the *āṭṭa-prakāram,* translated by Dr. P. Venugopalan and Dr. B Hariharan.

## Chapter 5

1. Approximately $7,200 in US currency.

2. The Sāmavedins are ritualists specialized in chanting the ancient vedas who play an important role in the *Agnicayana*.

3. This information was provided by Nampūdiris at the Vedic school in Thrissur, where to ensure the continuation of this tradition, poor Nampūdiri boys are trained in the oral traditions of the Veda.

4. Rituals that Handelman (1998) called "rituals of modeling," rituals that do not reflect the world but rather intervene in them.

5. The stories of Kṛṣṇa from Book X of the Bhāgavata, the *daśama kāṇḍa*.

6. For a very detailed description of this ritual, see Staal 1983; see also, a film made together with anthropologist-filmmaker Robert Gardner: www.youtube.com/watch?v=RYvkYk7GvJ0.

7. Concerning "bad death" in Kerala, see Tarabout (2001).

8. The horse sacrifice, aśvamedha, was supposed to be used in connection to an ancient king's rituals to assert his rule. However, it is doubtful that this ritual ever took place (Asko Parpola, personal communication).

9. A horse was drawn around the altar in the *Agnicayana* as well.

10. Beck stresses the importance of the "green room" in village dramas in Tamil Nadu, which are "traditionally performed on a square stage that is divided along its east/west axis by a hanging cloth. The actors are made up behind this curtain in the so-called green room. When the actors pass around the ends of this hanging cloth at the beginning of a drama, they can be seen to be like the sun at sunrise. They are also like children exiting from a womb. The darkened backstage area is a place of secret growth. It is also the place to which all actors must return, like the sun entering its secret abode again at sunset" (Beck 1976: 235).

11. Refraining from food and drink is also required in temple performance, but Aparna fasts only on the first day for the temple; at the Nampūdiris compound she refrained from food and water every morning.

12. The cone for the traditional headdress was fashioned from the dried sheath of an areca tree. Garlands of tecci flowers were wound around it, and silver ornaments, invariably including a nagapadam (serpent hood), were attached (Daugherty 1996: 69n6). From the first known photo of Kuttyiatam, taken in 1912, we can see that the Naṅṅyār was dressed like the drummers, namely with a white half sari and bare-breasted (P. K. Sreejith and V. Sreekanth 2014). As late as the beginning of the twentieth century, Naṅṅyārs would perform bare-breasted, but modesty standards have changed, so this is inconceivable today.

13. Other gods are also connected to liberation, notably Śiva (David Shulman, personal communication).

14. Traditionally, only five roles were played by Naṇṇyārs on the *Kūṭiyāṭṭam* stage, all from the Rāmāyana: Sītā (Rāma's wife), Maṇdōdarī (Rāvaṇa's wife), Tārā (the monkey-king Bāli's wife), Laḷitā (Śūrpaṇakhā in disguise), and Vijaya (the doorkeeper at the Laṅkā palace) (Johan 2011a: 145–146).

15. Madhu provided this information and also showed me his family manual, where on the first page it is stated how much the Naṅṅyārs should be paid in two cases. They were paid less if they habitually played together, and more when they were only invited to play at that particular performance.

16. The story was told to me by Madhu; see also Casassas (2012: 25n6).

17. At a conference in Trissur in 2015, a Naṅṅyār of the older generation was present, and when one of the actors forgot his line, everybody turned to her, and she immediately reminded him. She can recite by heart not only her own role but the entire text.

18. As in Aparna's case, the Cākyār and the Naṅṅyār can be husband and wife or father and daughter. Usha Nangiar, a great teacher and actress of an older generation, used to perform in temples but married into the wrong family and cannot perform in temples anymore. Thus, for a Naṇṇyār to perform at temples she must be able to engender Naṇṇyār daughters.

19. For example, see www.youtube.com/watch?v=lxCbhJve6Ks.

20. One version of the Kṛṣṇa drama explains why females present his story. It is said that his consorts, the Gopīs, played his role. In his absence, they miss him so much that they impersonate him to bring him to presence (Hawley 1985: 17).

21. For a novel on the fear of pollution amongst Brahmins and the complicated problems that ensue, see Anantha Murthy (1978).

22. Staal (1979) quotes the Mīmāmṣā Sūtra.

23. See chapter 4.

24. In Orissa, a rite called "Vidudala" releases a widower from his dead wife and is considered a divorce, thus enabling the man to remarry (Tapper 1979: 7).

25. The word "paradox" here should be revised, I think, and Handelman (e.g., 2011) indeed revised his view on play and borders. Paradox assumes the coexistence of play bounded within its frame. The border between the two incompatible truths, or realities, is set hierarchically, one encompassing the other in which play is inferior to real reality—it is less real. To undo a paradox, the border between the separate realities must be overcome, and only on a higher frame is it resolved. Here, however, there are no solid boundaries that determine hierarchical relations; rather, the relations between realities are fluid and malleable so that people, entities, and objects can be cajoled through play to move from one reality to another.

## Chapter 6

1. This act traditionally takes sixteen nights. The first thirteen present the lives of the hero and the Vidūṣaka, and only the last three nights present the unfolding of the drama, from day seven until day thirteen. The Vidūṣaka first appears on day six together with the hero (Unni 1990: 4, 9).

2. Subhadrā-dhanañjayam is central to *Naṇṇyārkūttu*. See chapter 5.

3. See chapter 3.

4. There are exceptions, such as the embrace of Rāmā and Lakṣmaṇa after the latter is saved from Śūrpaṇakhā's hands. At the end of the second act of *Nāgānandam*, the two lovers were holding hands. But that, I was told, is a new feature.

5. On Vidūṣaka performing in the royal court of Cochin at the beginning of the twentieth century, see DuComb (2007).

6. The four classic philosophical pillars of life (puruṣārthas) are dharma (lawful duty), artha (proper acquisition of wealth), kāma (controlled pursuit of pleasure), and mokṣa (systematic attainment of liberation). The alternative goals as given by Davis are gluttony (aśanaṃ), kissing up to the King (rājaseva), enjoying prostitutes (vēṣyavinodaṃ), and "stiffing" (cheating) prostitutes out of their money (vēṣyavañcanaṃ) (2014: 95, 98).

7. Some of the Tibetan trickster stories include sexuality, and these cannot be told at home (Kun Mchog Dge Legs, Dpal Ldan Bkra Shis, and Stuart 1999).

8. The citations from the *āṭṭa-prakāram* are translated by S. P. Suresh.

9. One of the Tibetan tricksters resembles the Vidūṣaka since he belongs to a religious community that performs rites at people's homes, but they lack religious knowledge and their chants are a pretense—all they want is money and food. Within iconoclast Buddhism, such behavior gains additional significance of self-reflexivity. Another trickster engages

in profane sexual and eschatological activities in order to awaken people from their dream-like reality into enlightenment (Kun Mchog Dge Legs, Dpal Ldan Bkra Shis, and Stuart 1999: 9; 11).

10. When the seventh act of the *Nāgānandam* is played, an even more impressive acrobatic feat is set in place. This act is performed outside to allow a contraption on which the actor playing Garuda may fly around.

11. On the contrary, in one of the plays (Mantrāṅkam), a Vidūṣaka-like character gets robbed and loses his clothes, forcing him to arrive at his bride's house naked.

12. In psychoanalytical terms, the clown is a sort of alter ego and thus permitted transgression. For a Jungian analysis of the clown, see Bala Michael (2010).

13. Similar characters called "dignitary clowns" are presented in the Szechuan theater. They can be recognizable by the white square painted on their faces; they may, however, start off as regular characters in the play, and their subversive facet is revealed only later, as the plot unfolds (Kalvodová 1965).

14. Other native American tricksters may be associated with coyotes, ravens, hares, and rabbits, mainly solitary animals (Carroll 1981; see also Espírito Santo 2016a).

15. This connection between the trickster and healers can also be found in Africa. On the relations between the trickster and the Kalahari trance practitioner, see Wessels (2008).

16. The elaboration of the role of the Vidūṣaka is recognized as a special feature of *Kūṭiyāṭṭam* and attributed to eleventh-century (?) poet Toḷan, who was known as a royal jester. He is also said to have introduced the Vidūṣaka as a translator and commentator of the play for the Malayalam speaking audience (Shulman 1987: 175, 6).

17. Ramberg (2009) shows how the Indian government together with NGOs cut down *devadāsīs'* matted locks and therefore transforms this material from sacred organs of live material that connect those women to the goddess into unhealthy dirt, and concomitantly turns their sexuality and devotion from "primitive" and abject in their eyes to purified and modern.

18. I am using the terms "clown," "buffoon," "trickster," "jester," and "comedy" interchangeably; they are all clown types, and defining them or entering the distinctions between them does not yield any benefit for understanding the Vidūṣaka. For a comparison between the Vidūṣaka and the "fool," see Jefferds (1981).

19. I am using these notions rather loosely here to suit my understanding of the Vidūṣaka. For Deleuze and Guattari, "becoming" is also equated to time and multiplicity (Stagoll 2005: 21; 22).

20. A man and not a woman, since a man dictates hegemony in society; thus, according to Deleuze and Guattari, there can also be a process of "becoming woman."

21. Shulman argues that the Vidūṣaka "exemplifies the world's status as, *māyā*, at once tangible and real, and immaterial; entirely permeable by the imagination; always baffling, enticing, enslaving, and in the process of becoming something new and still more elusive" (1987: 213). But I feel that he is challenging even *māyā* since he lives in some hyper "real" reality.

## Chapter 7

1. David D. Shulman, *The Rite of Seeing: Essays on Kūṭiyāṭṭam* (Delhi: Primus, 2022), 1.

2. Many more works concerning *Kūṭiyāṭṭam* include the eyes and seeing in their title: Shulman (2016), Madhavan (2012), Rajagopalan (1974a), and Narayanan (2022), to mention only a few.

3. Ingold suggests that seeing is emotionally cold, while hearing is warm (2007: 243–287). If this is so, replacing sight via sound makes sight warm.

# Works Cited


Abramson, Allen, and Martin Holbraad (eds.). 2015. *Framing Cosmologies—The Anthropology of Worlds*. Manchester: Manchester University Press.

Alter, Josef S. 1992. *The Wrestler's Body—Identity and Ideology in North India*. Los Angeles: University of California Press.

———. 1994. "Celibacy, Sexuality, and the Transformation of Gender into Nationalism in North India." *Journal of Asian Studies* 53, no. 1: 45–66.

———. 1996. "Gandhi's Body, Gandhi's Truth: Nonviolence and the Biomoral Imperative of Public Health." *Journal of Asian Studies* 55, no. 2: 301–322.

———. 2000. "Subaltern Bodies and Nationalist Physiques: Gama the Great and Heroics of Indian Wrestling." *Body & Society* 6, no. 2: 42–72.

———. 2004. *Yoga in Modern India*. Princeton, NJ: Princeton University Press.

Alyar, T. K. Rāmachandra. 1992. *Naganandam of Sri Harsha Deva—a Sanskrit Play with English Translation, Notes and Introduction*. Palghat: R. S. Vadhyar & Sons.

Anantha, Murthy U. R. 1978. *Samskara: A Rite for a Dead Man*. Translated by A. K. Rāmanujan. Oxford & New Delhi: Oxford University Press.

Angot, Michel. 2003. "Les corps et leurs doubles. Remarques sur la notion de corps dans les *Brāhmaṇa*." In *Images du corps dans le monde Hindou*, ed. Véronique Bouillier and Gilles Tarabout, 101–134. Paris: Éditions CNRS.

Apffel-Marglin, Frédérique. 1985. *Wives of God-king: The Rituals of the Devadasis of Puri*. Oxford: Oxford University Press.

———. 1990. "Refining the Body: Transformative Emotion in Ritual Dance." In *Divine Passions: The Social Construction of Emotion in India*, ed. Owen M. Lynch, 212–236. Berkeley & Los Angeles: University of California Press.

———. 2008. *Rhythms of Life—Enacting the World with the Goddesses of Orissa*. Oxford: Oxford University Press.

Artaud, Antonin. 1964. *Le théâtre et son double*. Saint-Amand: Gallimard.

Assayag, Jackie, and Jeanne Ferguson. 1988. "The Basket, Hair, the Goddess and the World: An Essay on South Indian Symbolism." *Diogenes* 36: 113–135.

Avorgbedor, Daniel Kodzo. 1999. "The Turner-Schechner Model of Performance as Social Drama: A Re-Examination in the Light of Anlo-Ewe Halo." *Research in African Literatures* 30, no. 4: 144–155.

Babb, L. A. 1990. "Social Science Inside Out." *Contributions to Indian Sociology* 26, no. 2: 201–213.

Bala, Michael. 2010. "The Clown: An Archetypal Self-Journey." *Jung Journal: Culture & Psyche* 4, no. 1: 50–71.

Bar-On Cohen, Einat. 2006. "*Kime*, in Japanese Martial Arts and the Moving Body." *Body & Society* 12, no. 4: 73–93.

———. 2007. "Timing in Karate and the Body in its Own Right." *Social Analysis* 51, no. 3: 1–22.

———. 2009. "Kibadachi—Pain and Crossing Boundaries within the Lived-in-Body and within Sociality." *Journal of the Royal Anthropological Institute* 15: 610–629.

———. 2011. "Events of Organicity—the State Abducts the War Machine." *Anthropological Theory* 11, no. 3: 259–282.

———. 2012. "The Forces of Homology—the 1928 Rites of Succession to the Throne of Hirohito, Emperor of Japan." *History and Anthropology* 23, no. 4: 425–443.

———. 2013. "To Eat, to Speak, to Skirt: Reading the Little Girl's Lips: Sarah Mann-O'Donnell's World." *Anthropology & Humanism* 38, no. 1: 19–35.

———. 2014. "*Kyūdo*—Resonance Involuted and the Folding of Time in Japanese Archery." *Anthropos* 109: 525–537.

———. 2016. "Perfect Praxis in *Aikidō*—a Reflexive Body-Self." In *Reflecting on Reflexivity: The Human Condition as an Ontological Surprise*, ed. Terry Evens, Don Handelman, and Christopher Roberts, 173–198. New York & Oxford: Berghahn Books.

———. 2019. "The World of Hanumān: Creating a Fluid Cosmos on a Kerala Kūṭiyāṭṭam Stage." In *Two Masterpieces of Kūṭiyāṭṭam: Mantrāṅkam and Aṅgulīyāṅkam*, ed. Heike Oberlin and David Shulman, 226–330. New Delhi: Oxford University Press.

———. 2021. "Yokozuna Hakuhō—Japanese Mongolian Hero." In ETHNOGRAPHY. Special Issue: Hand-to-Hand Sports and the Struggle for Belonging 22, no. 3: 334–350.

Bateson, Gregory. 1958. *Naven—a Survey of the Problem Suggested by a Composite Picture of the Culture of the New Guinea Tribe Drawn from Three Points of View*. Stanford, CA: Stanford University Press.

———. 2000. *Steps in the Ecology of the Mind: Collected Essays in Anthropology, Psychiatry, Evolution, and Epistemology*. Northvale, NJ & London: James Aronson Inc. (First published in 1972)

Bateson, Gregory, and Margaret Mead. 1942. *Balinese Character—a Photographic Analysis*. New York: The New York Academy of Science.

Beane, Wendell C. 1973. "The Cosmological Structure of Mythical Time: Kālī-Śakti." *History of Religions* 13, no. 1: 54–83.

Beck, Brenda E. F. 1969. "Colour and Heat in South Indian Ritual." *Man, New Series* 4, no. 4: 553–572.

———. 1976. "The Symbiotic Merger of Body, Space and Cosmos in Tamil Nadu." *Contributions to Indian Sociology* 10, no. 2: 213–243.

Beeman, William O. 1981. "Why Do They Laugh? An Interactional Approach to Humor in Traditional Iranian Improvisatory Theater: Performance and Its Effects." *The Journal of American Folklore* 94, no. 374: 506–526.

———. 1993. "The Anthropology of Theater and Spectacle." *Annual Review of Anthropology* 22: 369–393.

Berthomé, François, and Michael Houseman, 2010. "Ritual and Emotions: Moving Relations, Patterned Effusions." *Religion and Society* 1: 57–75.

Bhattacharya, France. 2003. "De sang et de sperme. La pratique mystic *bāul* et son expression métaphorique dans les chants." In *Images du corps dans le monde hindou*, ed. Véronique Bouillier and Gilles Tarabout, 241–274. Paris: Éditions CNRS.

Blacker, Carmen. 1975. *The Catalpa Bow: A Study of Shamanistic Practices in Japan*. London: Routledge.

Borges, Luis Jorges. 1998. *Collected Fictions*. London: Penguin Classics.

Bouillier, Véronique, and Gilles Tarabout (eds.) 2003. *Images du corps dans le monde Hindou*. Paris: Éditions CNRS.

Boundas, V. Constantin. 2005a. "Intensity." In *The Deleuze Dictionary*, ed. Adrian Parr, 131–132. Edinburgh: Edinburgh University Press.

Boyer, L. Bryce, and Ruth M. Boyer. 1983. "The Sacred Clown of the Chiricahua and Mescalero Apaches: Additional Data." *Western Folklore* 42, no. 1: 46–54.

Burkhalter Flueckiger, Joyce. 2005. "Guises, Turmeric and Recognition in the Gangamma Tradition of Tirupati." In *Incompatible Visions: South Asian Religion in History and Culture. Essays in Honor of David M. Knipe*, ed. James Blumenthal, 35–45. Madison, WI: Center for South Asia, University of Wisconsin-Madison.

———. 2013. *When the World Becomes Female: Guises of a South Indian Goddess*. Bloomington: Indiana University Press.

———. 2017. "Standing in Cement: Possibilities Created by Ravan on the Chhattisgarhi Plains." *South Asian History and Culture* 8, no. 4: 461–477.

Caldwell, Sarah. 2001. *Oh Terrifying Mother: Sexuality, Violence and Worship of the Goddess Kāli*. Oxford: Oxford University Press.

Carroll, Michael P. 1981. "Lévi-Strauss, Freud, and the Trickster: A New Perspective upon an Old Problem." *Ethnologist* 8, no. 2: 301–313.

Casassas, Coralie. 2012. "Female Roles and Engagement of Women in the Classical Sanskrit Theatre *Kūṭiyāṭṭam*: A Contemporary Theatre Tradition." *Asian Theatre Journal* 28, no. 1: 1–30.

Colas, Gérard. 2003. "Variations sur la pâmoison dévote. A propos d'un poéme de Vedāntadeṣika et du théâtre des *araiyar*." In Images du corps dans le monde Hindou, ed. Véronique Bouillier and Gilles Tarabout, 275–314. Paris: Éditions CNRS.

Coorlawala Uttara, Asha. 2004. "The Sanskritized Body." *Dance Research Journal* 36, no. 2: 50–63.

Daniel, Valentine. 1984. *Fluid Signs: Being a Person the Tamil Way*. Berkeley: University of California Press

Darmon, Richard A. 2003. "Vajrolī Mudrā. La rétention séminale chez les yogis *vāmācāri*." In *Images du corps dans le monde Hindou*, ed. Véronique Bouillier and Gilles Tarabout, 213–240. Paris: Éditions CNRS.

Das, Mitoo. 2014. "Performing the 'Other' in the 'Self': Reading Gender and Menstruation through Autoethnography." *Indian Anthropologist* 44, no. 2: 47–63.

Daugherty, Diane. 1996. "The Nangyār: Female Ritual Specialist of Kerala." *Asian Theater Journal* 13, no. 1: 54–67.

———. 2004. "Documentation of "Koodiyattam" by Margi." *Asian Theater Journal* 21, no. 2: 220–221.

Davis, Donald R. Jr. 2014. "Satire as Apology: The Puruṣārtthakkūttŭ of Kerala." In *Irreverent History: Essays for M.G.S. Narayanan*, ed. Kesavan Veluthat and Donald R. Davis Jr., 93–110. Delhi: Primus Books.

Davis, Richard H. 1988. "Cremation and Liberation: The Revision of a Hindu Ritual." *History of Religions* 28, no. 1: 37–53.

De Bruin, Hanne M. 2006. "Donning the Vēṣam in Kuṭṭaikkūttu." In *Masked Ritual and Performance in South India—Dance, Healing, and Possession*, ed. David Shulman and Deborah Thiagarajan, 107–134. Ann Arbor: University of Michigan Press.

Deleuze, Gilles. 1994. *Difference and Repetition*. New York: Columbia University Press.

Deleuze, Gilles, and Félix Guattari. 1987. *A Thousand Plateaus—Capitalism and Schizophrenia*. Minneapolis: University of Minnesota Press.

———. 1994. *What Is Philosophy?* New York: Columbia University Press.

Desjarlais, Robert, and C. Jason Throop. 2011. "Phenomenological Approaches in Anthropology." *Annual Review of Anthropology* 40: 87–102.

Dinesan, Vadakkinyil. 2009. "*Teyyam*: The Poiesis of Rite and God in Malabar. South India." PhD diss, University of Bergen.

———. 2019. "Mahishi's Rage: Communitas and Protest at Sabarimala, Kerala." *Anthropology Today* 35, no. 5: 16–20.

DuComb, Christian. 2007. "Present-Day Kutiyattam: G. Venu's Radical and Reactionary Sanskrit Theatre." *The Drama Review: TDR* 51, no. 3: 98–118.

Dumont, Louis. 1969. "Les mariages Nayar comme faits indiens." L'Homme 1, no. 1: 11–36.

———. 1980. *Homo Hierarchicus: The Caste System and Its Implications.* Chicago: University of Chicago Press.

Eck, Diana. 1981. "The Dynamics of Indian Symbolism." In *The Other Side of God: A Polarity in World Religions,* ed. Peter L. Berger, 157–181. New York: Anchor Press/Doubleday.

———. 1998. *Darśan—Seeing the Divine Image in India* (3rd ed.). New York: Columbia University Press.

Egnor, Margaret. 1980. "On the Meaning of Śakti to Women in Tamil Nadu." In *The Powers of Tamil Women,* ed. Susan S. Wadley, 1–34. Syracuse: Maxwell School of Citizenship and Public Affairs.

Eichinger Ferro-Luz, Gabriella. 1998. "Demonology in Tamil Folktales." *Anthropos* 93: 405–415.

Emigh, John. 1996. *Masked Performance—the Play of Self and Other in Ritual and Theater.* Philadelphia: University of Pennsylvania Press.

Enros Pragna, Thakkar. 1981. "Producing Sanskrit Plays in the Tradition of Kūṭiyāṭṭam." In *Sanskrit Drama in Performance,* ed. Rachel Van M. Baumer and James R. Brandon, 275–298. Honolulu: University Press of Hawaii.

Erndl, Kathleen M. 1991. "The Mutilation of Śūrpaṇakhā." In *Many Rāmāyaṇas: The Diversity of a Narrative Tradition in South Asia,* ed. Paula Richman, 67–88. Berkeley & Los Angeles: University of California Press.

Espírito Santo, Diana. 2016a. "Recursivity and the Self-Reflexive Cosmos: Tricksters in Cuban and Brazilian Spirit Mediumship Practices." *Social Analysis* 60, no. 1: 37–55.

———. 2016b. "Clothes for Spirits: Opening and Closing the Cosmos in Brazilian Umbanda." *Hau: Journal of Ethnographic Theory* 6, no. 3: 85–106.

Evens, Terry M. S. 2008. *Anthropology as Ethics: Nondualism and the Conduct of Sacrifice.* New York: Berghahn.

Feld, Steven. 1996. "Waterfalls of Song: An Acoustemology of Place Resounding in Bosavi, Papua New Guinea." In *Senses of Place,* ed. Steven Feld and Keith H. Basso, 91–135. Santa Fe, NM: School of American Research Press.

———. 2012. *Sound and Sentiment: Birds, Weeping, Poetics and Song in Kaluli Expression* (3rd ed.). Durham, NC & London: Duke University Press.

Freeman, Rich 2016 "Śaktism, Polity and Society in Medieval Malabar." In *Goddess Traditions in Tantric Hinduism*, ed. Olesen BWernick, 141–173. New York: Routledge.

Freeman, John R. 2006. "Shifting Forms of the Wandering Yogi: The Teyyam of Bhairavan." In *Masked Ritual and Performance in South India: Dance, Healing, and Possession*, ed. David Shulman and Deborah Thiagarajan, 147–183. Ann Arbor: University of Michigan Press.

Friedman, Jonathan. 1990. "Being in the World: Globalization and Localization." *Theory, Culture & Society* 7: 311–328.

Friedson, Steven M. 1996. *Dancing Prophets: Musical Experience in Tumbuka Healing*. Chicago & London: University of Chicago Press.

———. 2009. *Remains of Ritual: Northern Gods in a Southern Land* (Chicago Studies in Ethnomusicology). Chicago: University of Chicago Press.

Foulk, T. Griffith. 2013. "Denial of Ritual in the Zen Buddhist Tradition." *Journal of Ritual Studies* (Special Issue: The Denial of Ritual and Its Return) 27, no. 1: 47–58.

Gamliel, Ophira. 2016. "The Syntax of Performance: The Mantrâṅkam as a Case Study." *Nartanam: A Quarterly Journal of Indian Dance* 16, no. 3: 166–194.

Ganser, Elisa. 2017. Theatrical and Ritual Boundaries in South Asia: An Introductory Essay. In *Theatrical and Ritual Boundaries in South India*, ed. Elisa Ganser and Ewa Dębicka-Borek. Cracow Indological Studies. 19, no. 1: vi–xxiv.

Gell, Alfred. 1998. *Art and Agency: An Anthropological Theory*. New York & Oxford: Oxford University Press.

Gentes, M. J. 1992. "Scandalizing the Goddess at Kodungallur." *Asian Folklore Studies* 51, no. 2: 295–322.

Gitomer, David L. 1991. "Such as a Face without a Nose: The Comic Body in Sanskrit Literature." *Journal of South Asian Literature* 26, no. 1/2: 77–110.

Gnoli, Raniero. 1968. *The Aesthetic Experience According to Abhinabagupta* (Chowkhamba Sanskrit Studies 62). Varanasi: The Chowkhamba Sanskrit Series Office.

Gopalakrishnan, Sudha. 2006. "The Face and the Mask: Expression and Impersonation." In *Masked Ritual and Performance in South India: Dance, Healing, and Possession*, ed. David Shulman and Deborah Thiagarajan, 135–146. Ann Arbor: University of Michigan Press.

———. 2011. Kutiyattam: *The Heritage Theater of India*. New Delhi: Niogi Books.

Gough, Kathleen. 1959. "The Nayars and the Definition of Marriage." *Journal of the Royal Anthropological Institute of Great Britain and Ireland* 89, no. 1: 23–34.

Grimes, Ronald L. 2006. "Performance." In *Theorizing Rituals: Issues, Topics, Approaches, Concepts*, ed. Jens Krienath, Jan Snoek, and Michael Strausberg, 379–394. Leiden and Boston: Brill.

Groesbeck, Rolf. 2003. "Dhim, Kam, Cappu, Pottu: Timbral Discourses and Performances Among Temple Drummers in Kerala, India." *Yearbook for Traditional Music* 35: 39–68.

Guillebaud, Christine. 2011. "Music and Politics in Kerala: Hindu Nationalists Versus Marxists." In *The Cultural Entrenchment of Hindutva. Local Mediations and Forms of Convergence*, ed. Daniela Berti, Nicolas Jaoul, and Pralay Kanungo. New Delhi: Routledge.

Halliburton, Murphy. 2002. "Rethinking Anthropological Studies of the Body: *Manas* and *Bōdham* in Kerala." *American Anthropologist* 104, no. 4: 1123–1134.

Handelman, Don. 1981. "The Ritual Clown: Attributes and Affinities." *Anthropos* 76: 321–370.

———. 1985. "Charisma, Liminality and Symbolic Type." In *Comparative Social Dynamics. Essays in Honor of S. N. Eisenstadt*, ed. Erik Cohen, Moshe Lissak and Uri Almagor, 346–359. New York: Routledge.

———. 1991. "Symbolic Types, the Body and Circus." *Semiotica* 85: 205–225.

———. 1997. "The Andhaka Outcome: Ludic Process in Indian Ritual and Myth." In *The Games of Gods and Man: Essays in Play and Performance* (Studies in Social and Ritual Morphology), ed. Klaus Peter Köpping, 100–131. Hamburg: LIT Verlag.

———. 1998a. *Models and Mirrors: Towards an Anthropology of Public Events* (2nd ed.). New York & Oxford: Berghahn.

———. 1998b. The Transformation of Symbolic Structures Through History and the Rhythms of Time. *Semiotica* 119, no. 3/4: 403–425.

———. 2004a. *Nationalism and the Israeli State: Bureaucratic Logic in Public Events*. Oxford: Routledge.

———. 2004b. "Why Ritual in Its Own Right? How So?" *Social Analysis* 48, no. 2: 1–32.

———. 2008. "Clowns in Ritual: Are Ritual Boundaries Lineal? Moebius-like?" In *Risus Sacer—Sacrum Risibile*, ed. Katja Gvozdeva and Werner Rocke, 307–325. Berlin: Peter Lang.

———. 2013. "Bruce Kapferer, Deleuzian Virtuality, and the Makings of a Ritual Masterstroke." *Religion and Society* 4, no. 1: 32–40.

———. 2014a. "Inter-gration and Intra-gration in Cosmology." In *Framing Cosmologies: The Anthropology of Worlds*, ed. Allen Abramson and Martin Holbraad, 95–115. New York: Manchester University Press.

———. 2014b. *On God, Two Goddesses, Three Studies of South Indian Cosmology*. Leiden & Boston: Brill.

Handelman, Don, and Bruce Kapferer. 1980. "Symbolic Types, Mediation and the Transformation of Ritual Context: Sinhalese Demons and Tewa Clowns." *Semiotica* 30, no. 1/2: 41–71.

Handelman, Don, and Galina Lindquist. 2011. "Religion, Politics and Globalization: The Long Past Foregrounding the Short Present: Prologue and Introduction." In *Globalization and the Politics of Religion*, ed. Galina Lindquist and Don Handelman, 1–66. New York: Berghahn.

Handelman, Don, and David Shulman. 1997. *God Inside Out: Śiva's Game of Dice*. New York: Oxford University Press.

———. 2004. *Śiva in the Forest of Pines: An Essay on Sorcery and Self-Knowledge*. New York: Oxford University Press

Hara, Kenya. 2014. *White*. Zürich: Lars Müller Publishers.

Hauser, Beatrix. 2006. "Divine Play or Subversive Comedy? Reflections on Costuming and Gender at a Hindu Festival." In *Celebrating Transgression: Method and Politics in Anthropological Studies of Cultures* (A Book in Honour of Klaus Peter Koepping), ed. Ursula Rao and John Hutnyk, 129–144. New York: Berghahn.

Hawley, John Stratton. 1979. "Krishna's Cosmic Victories." *Journal of the American Academy of Religion* 47, no. 2: 201–221.

———. 1985. *At Play with Krishna: Pilgrimage Dramas from Brindavan*. Princeton, NJ: Princeton University Press.

Hemming, Jessica 2012. "Red, White, and Black in Symbolic Thought: The Tricolour Folk Motif, Colour Naming, and Trichromatic Vision." *Folklore* 123, no. 3: 310–329.

Heywood, Paolo. 2020. "'All the Difference in the World': The Nature of Difference and Different Natures." *Philosophy of the Social Sciences*. 1–22.

Higgins, Kathleen Marie. 2007. "An Alchemy of Emotion: *Rasa* and Aesthetic Breakthroughs." *Journal of Aesthetics and Art Criticism* 65, no. 1: 43–54.

Hiltebeitel, Alf. 1976. *The Ritual of Battle: Krishna in the Mahābhārata*. London: Cornell University Press.

———. 1998. "Hair Tropes." In *Hair: Its Power and Meaning in Asian Cultures*, ed. Alf Hiltebeitel and Barbara D. Miller, 1–10. New York: State University of New York.

Holbraad, Martin, and Morten Axel Pedersen. 2017. *The Ontological Turn: An Anthropological Exposition*. New York: Cambridge University Press.

Holdrege, Barbara A. 1998. "Body Connections: Hindu Discourses of the Body and the Study of Religion." *International Journal of Hindu Studies* 2, no. 3: 341–386.

Hobsbawm, Eric, and Terence Ranger (eds.). 1992. *The Invention of Tradition.* Cambridge: Cambridge University Press.

Ilangô, Adigal Prince. 1965. *Shilappadikaram (The Ankle Bracelet).* Translated by Alain Daniélou. New York: New Directions.

Ingold Tim. 2007. *The Perception of the Environment: Essays in Livelihood, Dwelling and Skill.* London: Routledge.

Ishii, Miho. 2012. "Acting with Things: Self-poiesis, Actuality, and Contingency in the Formation of Divine Worlds." *Journal of Ethnographic Theory* 2, no. 2: 371–388.

———. 2013. "Playing with Perspectives: Spirit Possession, Mimesis, and Permeability in the *Buuta* Ritual in South India." *Journal of the Royal Anthropological Institute* 19: 795–812.

———. 2014. "Traces of Reflexive Imagination: Matriliny, Modern Law, and Spirit Worship in South India." *Asian Anthropology* 13, no. 2: 106–123.

———. 2015a. "The Ecology of Transaction Dividual Persons, Spirits, and Machinery in a Special Economic Zone in South India." *Nature Culture,* no. 3: 7–34.

———. 2015b. "Wild Sacredness and the Poiesis of Transactional Networks Relational Divinity and Spirit Possession in the "Būta" Ritual of South India." *Asian Ethnology* 74, no. 1: 87–109.

Jamison, Stephanie W. 1996. *Sacrificed Wife/Sacrificer's Wife: Women, Ritual, and Hospitability in Ancient India* (Oxford Early Christian Studies). New York: Oxford University Press.

Jefferds, Keith N. 1981. "Vidūṣaka Versus Fool: A Functional Analysis." *Journal of South Asian Literature* 16, no. 1: 61–73.

Jenett, Dianne 2005. "A Million 'Śaktis' Rising: Pongala, a Women's Festival in Kerala, India." *Journal of Feminist Studies in Religion* 21, no. 1: 35–55.

Johan, Virginie. 2011a. "Actresses on the Temple Stage? The Epic Conception of the Performance of Women's Roles in Kūṭiyāṭṭam Rāmāyaṇa Plays." In *Between Fame and Shame: Performig Women–Women Performers in India,* ed. Heidrun Brückner, Hanne M. de Bruin, and Heike Moser, 245–274 (Drama und Theater in Südasien 9). Wiesbaden: Harrassowitz Verlag.

———. 2011b. "The Flower Needs Its Roots to Continue to Grow." *Indian Folklore* 38: 20–26.

———. 2014. "Du je au jeu de l'acteur: ethnoscénologie du Kūṭiyāṭṭam, théâtre épique indien." *Thése de doctorat en Théâtre et Arts du spectacle (ethnoscénologie).* Université Paris-III Sorbonne.

———. 2017. "Dancing and Ritual on the *Kūṭiyāṭṭam* Theatre Stage." In *Theatrical and Ritual Boundaries in South India,* ed. Elisa Ganser and Ewa Dębicka-Borek. Cracow Indological Studies 19, no. 1: 59–82.

———. 2019. "Aṅgulīyāṅkam, Rāmāyaṇa-Veda of the Cākyārs." In *Two Masterpieces of Kūṭiyāṭṭam: Mantrāṅkam and Aṅgulīyāṅkam,* ed. Heike

Oberlin and David Shulman, 187–224. New Delhi: Oxford University Press.

Jones, Clifford Reis. 1984. "Notes on Comparison of Vedic Mudrās with Mudrās Used in *Kūṭiyāṭṭam* and Kathakaḷi." In *Agni—The Vedic Ritual of the Fire Altar*, ed. Frits Staal, 380–381. Berkeley, CA: Asian Humanity Press.

Jones, Clifford Reis, and V. Raghavan. 1984. *The Wondrous Crest-Jewel in Performance: Text and Translation of the Āścaryacūḍāmani of Śaktibhadra with the Production Manual from the Tradition of Kūṭiyāṭṭam, Sanskrit Drama*. Delhi & New York: Oxford University Press.

Kālidāsa. 2009. *How Úrvasi Was Won*. Translated by Velchero Narayana Rao and David Shulman. New York: New York University Press.

Kalvodová, Dana. 1965. "Clowns in the Szechuan Theatre." *Bulletin of the School of Oriental and African Studies* 28, no. 2: 356–362.

Kapferer, Bruce. 1991. *A Celebration of Demons: Exorcism and the Aesthetics of Healing in Sri Lanka*. Oxford & Washington, DC: Berg, Smithsonian Institution Press. (First published in 1983)

———. 2001. "Anthropology: The Paradox of the Secular." *Social Anthropology* 9, no. 3: 341–344.

———. 2004. "Ritual Dynamics and Virtual Practice: Beyond Representation and Meaning." *Social Analysis* 48, no. 2: 33–52.

———. 2006. "Virtuality." In *Theorizing Rituals: Issues, Topics, Approaches, Concepts*, ed. Jens Kreinath, Jan Snock, and Michael Strausberg, 671–686. Leiden & Boston: Brill.

———. 2010. "Beyond Ritual as Performance. Towards Ritual as Dynamics and Virtuality." *Paragrana* 19, no. 2: 230–249.

Kapferer, Bruce, and George Papigny. 2002. *Tovil—exorcismes thérapeutiques bouddhistes*. Paris: Editions DésIris.

Kapur, Anuradha. 2006. *Actors, Pilgrims, Kings and Gods: The Ramlila of Ramnagar*. King's Lynn: Seagull Books.

Keen, Ian. 2006. "Ancestors, Magic, and Exchange in Yolngu Doctrines: Extensions of the Person in Time and Space." *Journal of the Royal Anthropological Institute* 12, no. 3: 515–530.

Kersenboom, Saskia C. 1991. "The Traditional Repertoire of the Tiruttaṇi Temple Dancers." In *Roles and Rituals for Hindu* Women, ed. Julia Leslie, 131–148. London: Pinter Publishers.

Kidron, Carol, and Don Handelman. 2016. "The Symbolic Type Revisited: Semiotics in Practice and the Reformation of the Israeli Commemorative Context." *Symbolic Interaction* 39, no. 3: 421–445.

Kinsley, David R. 1975. *The Sword and the Flute: Kālī and Kṛṣṇa, Dark Visions of the Terrible and the Sublime in Hindu Mythology*. Berkeley, Los Angeles & London: University of California Press.

Köpping, Klaus-Peter. 1985. "Absurdity and Hidden Truth: Cunning Intelligence and Grotesque Body Images as Manifestations of the Trickster." *History of Religions* 24, no. 3: 191–214.

———. 2002. *Shuttering Frames: Transgression and Transformation in Anthropological Discourse and Practice*. Berlin: Dietrich Reimer Verlag.

Kuiper, Franciscus Bernardus Jacobus. 1979. *Varuṇa and Vidūṣaka: On the Origin of the Sanskrit Drama*. Amsterdam: North-Holland Publishing Company.

Lee, Dorothy.1950. "Linear and Nonlinear Codification of Reality." *Psychosomatic Medicine* 8, no. 2: 89–97.

Legs, Kun Mchog Dge, Dpal Ldan Bkra Shis, and Kevin Stuart. 1999. "Tibetan Tricksters." *Asian Folklore Studies* 58, no. 1: 5–30.

Lewis, Lowell J. 2008. "Toward a Unified Theory of Cultural Performance: A Reconstructive Introduction to Victor Turner." In *Victor Turner and Contemporary Cultural Performance*, ed. Graham St John, 41–58. New York: Berghahn.

Lewis, Thomas H. 1982. "Traditional and Contemporary Ritual Clowns of the Crow." *Anthropos* 77, no. 5/6: 892–895.

Lowthorp, Leah. 2013a. *Scenarios of Endangered Culture, Shifting Cosmopolitanisms: Kutiyattam and UNESCO Intangible Cultural Heritage in Kerala, India*. PhD dissertation, University of Pennsylvania, Philadelphia.

———. 2013b. "The Translation of Kutiyattam into National and World Heritage on the Festival Stage: Some Identity Implications." In *South Asian Festivals on the Move*, ed. Ute Hüsken and Axel Michaels, 193–225. Wiesbaden: Harrassowitz Verlag.

———. 2016. "Freedom in Performance: Actresses and Creative Agency in the Kutiyattam Theater Complex." *Samiyukta: A Journal of Gender & Culture* 16, no. 2: 83–108.

———. 2017. "Folklore, Politics, and the State: Kutiyattam Theatre and National/Global Heritage in India." *South Asian History and Culture* 8, no. 4: 542–559.

———. 2020. "Kutiyattam, Heritage, and the Dynamics of Culture: Claiming India's Place within a Global Paradigm Shift." *Asian Ethnology* 79, no. 1: 21–44.

Lutgendorf, Philip 1991. *The Life of a Text: Performing the Rāmcaritmānas of Tulsidas*. Berkely, Los Angeles & Oxford: University of California Press.

———. 2007. *Hanuman's Tale: The Messages of a Divine Monkey*. Oxford & New York: Oxford University Press.

Lutz, Catherine A. 1988. *Unnatural Emotions: Everyday Sentiments on a Micronesian Atoll and Their Challenge to Western Theory*. Chicago & London: University of Chicago Press.

Madhavan, Arya. 2012. "Eyescape: Aesthetics of 'Seeing' in *Kudiyattam*." *Asian Theatre Journal* 28, no. 2: 550–570.

———. 2015. "Introduction: Women in Asian Theatre: Conceptual, Political, and Aesthetic Paradigms." *Asian Theatre Journal* 32, no. 2: 345–355.

Makarius, Laura. 1972. "The Capakobam of Sonora, Mexico." *Anthropos* 67, no. 3/4: 595–596.

Margi, Madhu Chakyar. 2015. *Kuttiyatam and Kerala Temples*. Translated by L. S. Rajagopalan. Athens, GA: Pinecrest Media Group.

Marriott, McKim. 1976. "Hindu Transactions: Diversity without Dualism." In *Transaction and Meaning: Directions in the Anthropology of Exchange and Symbolic Behavior*, ed. Bruce Kapferer, 109–142. Philadelphia: Institute for the Study of Human Issues.

———. 1989. "Constructing and Indian Ethnosociology." *Contributions to Indian Sociology* 23, no. 1: 1–39.

Massumi, Brian. 2002. *Parables for the Virtual: Movement, Affect, Sensation*. Durham, NC & London: Duke University Press.

McDaniel, June. 2004. *Offering Flowers, Feeding Skulls: Popular Goddess Worship in West Bengal*. Oxford & New York: Oxford University Press.

Mehrotra, Nilika. 2004. "Gold and Gender in India: Some Observations from South Orissa." *Indian Anthropologist* 34, no. 1: 27–39.

Mencher, Joan P., and Helen Goldberg. 1967. "Kinship and Marriage Regulations among the Namboodiri Brahmans of Kerala." *Man, New Series* 2, no. 1: 87–106.

Menon, Usha 2002. "Making Śakti: Controlling (Natural) Impurity for Female (Cultural) Power." *Ethos* 30, no. 1/2: 140–157.

Merleau-Ponty, Maurice. 2002. *Phénoménologie de la perception*. Paris: Gallimard. (First published in 1945)

Mezzenzana, Francesca. 2018. "Moving Alike: Movement and Human–Nonhuman Relationships among the Runa (Ecuadorian Amazon)." *Social Anthropology* 26, no. 2: 238–252.

Michell, George. 1988. *The Hindu Temple: An Introduction to its Meaning and Form*. Chicago: University of Chicago Press.

Mitchell, William E. (ed.). 1992. *Clowning as Critical Practice: Performance Humor in the South Pacific*. (ASAO Monograph Series). Pittsburgh, PA: University of Pittsburgh Press.

Mitra, Royona. 2006. "Living a Body Myth, Performing a Body Reality: Reclaiming the Corporeality and Sexuality of the Indian Female Dancer." Postcolonial Theatres. *Feminist Review* 84: 67–83.

Moser, Heike. 2008. *Naṅṅyār-Kūttu: ein Teilaspekt des Sanskrittheaterkomplexes Kūṭiyāṭṭam; historiche Entwicklung und performative Textumsetzung* (Drama und Theater in Südasien 6). Wiesbaden: Harrassowitz.

———. 2011. "How Kūṭiyāṭṭam became Kūṭiy-āṭṭam, "Acting Together," or the Changing Role in Female Performers in the Naṅṅyār-Kūttu-

Tradition of Kerala." In *Between Fame and Shame: Performig Women–Women Performers in India*, ed. Heidrun Brückner, Hanne M. de Bruin, and Heike Moser, 169–188 (Drama und Theater in Südasien 9). Wiesbaden: Harrassowitz Verlag.

———. 2011b. *Bibliography of Kūṭiyāṭṭam*. Tübingen: Tobias-lib (Creative Commons, Print-on-Demand). http://nbn-resolving.de/urn:nbn:de:bsz:21-opus-58955

———. 2013. "Kūṭiyāṭṭam on the Move: From Temple Theatres to Festival Stages." In *South Asian Festivals on the Move*, ed. Ute Hüsken and Axel Michaels, 245–274. Wiesbaden: Harrassowitz Verlag.

———. 2014. "Jaṭāyuvadham in Kerala's Sanskrit Theatre Kūṭiyāṭṭam." In *Irreverent History: Essays for M.G.S. Narayanan*, ed. Kesavan Veluthat and Donald R. Davis, Jr., 81–92. Delhi: Primus Books.

Moser-Achuthath, Heike. 1999–2000. "*Mantrāṅkam*. The Third Act of *Pratijñāyaugandharāyaṇam* in *Kūṭiyāṭṭam*." *Bulletin d'études indiennes*. 17–18: 563–584.

Narayanan, Mundoli. 2006. "Over-Ritualization of Performance: Western Discourses on Kutiyattam." *The Drama Review: TDR* 50, no. 2: 136–153.

———. 2021. "Writing Her "Self": The Politics of Gender in Nangyarkuttu." In *Performing the Ramayana Tradition: Enactments, Interpretations, and Arguments*, ed. Paula Richman and Rustom Bharucha, 186–210. New York: Oxford University Press.

———. 2022. *Space, Time and Ways of Seeing: The Performance Culture of Kutiyattam*. London & New York: Routledge.

Neff, Deborah L. 1987. "Aesthetics and Power in Pāmbin Tuḷḷal: A Possession Ritual of Rural Kerala." *Ethnology* 26, no. 1: 63–71.

Ngai, Sianne. 2005. *Ugly Feelings*. Cambridge, MA: Harvard University Press.

Noble, William A. 1981. "The Architecture and Organization of Kerala Style Hindu Temples." *Anthropos* 76, no. 1/2: 1–24.

Oberlin, Heike, and David Shulman (eds.). 2019. *Two Masterpieces of Kūṭiyāṭṭam: Mantrāṅkam and Aṅgulīyāṅkam*. Oxford & New Delhi: Oxford University Press.

Obeyesekere, Gananath. 1980. *Women, Androgynes, and Other Mythical Beasts*. Chicago & London: University of Chicago Press.

———. 1981. *Medusa's Hair: An Essay on Personal Symbols and Religious Experience*. Chicago & London: University of Chicago Press.

O'Flaherty, Doniger Wendy. 1984. *Dreams, Illusions and Other Realities*. Chicago & London: University of Chicago Press.

Osella, Filippo, and Caroline Osella. 1996. "Articulation of Physical and Social Bodies in Kerala." *Contributions to Indian Sociology* 30: 37–68.

———. 1999. "Seepage of Divinised Power through Social, Spiritual, and Bodily Boundaries: Some Aspects of Divination in Kerala." In *La*

*Possession en Asie du Sud: Parole, corps, territoire*, ed. Jackie Assayag and Gille Tarabout, 183–210 (Collection Puruṣārtha 21). Paris: Éditions de l'École des Hautes Études en Sciences Sociales.

Pacciolla, Paolo. 2021. "The Brimming Vessel: An Analysis of the Ritual Repertoire of the *Miḻāvu* from a Tantric Perspective." *Analytical Approaches to World Music* 9, no. 1.

———. 2022. Like a Single Body—the Beauty in the Harmonic and Organic Actions of Actors and Drummers in *Kūtiyāṭṭaṃ*. March 9, 2022. https://paolopacciolla.com/2022/03/09/like-a-single-body

Palmer, Gary B., and William R. Jankowiak. 1996. "Performance and Imagination: Toward an Anthropology of the Spectacular and the Mundane." *Cultural Anthropology* 11, no. 2: 225–258.

Paniker, Nirmala. 1992. "Nangiar Koothu: The Classical Dance—Theater of the Nangiār-s. Irinjalakuda: Natana Kairali" (Documentation of Kutiyattam Series, 2).

Parpola, Marjatta. 2000. "Kerala Brahmins in Transition: A Study of a Nampūtiri Family" (Studia Orientalia 91). Helsinki: Finnish Oriental Society.

Parr, Adrian. 2005. "Repetition." In *The Deleuze Dictionary*, ed. Adrian Parr, 223–224. Edinburgh: Edinburgh University Press.

Pasty, Marianne. 2012. Un théâtre pour le plaisir de la déesse: culte, dévotion et société au Kerala (Inde du Sud). *Théâtres d'Asie à l'œuvre. Circulation, expression, politique*. Dir. Hélène Bouvier et Gérard Toffin, Ecole Française d'Extrême Orient (Coll. Etudes thématiques), 59–81.

Pasty-Abdul Wahid, Marianne. 2020. "Bloodthirsty, or Not, That Is the Question: An Ethnography-Based Discussion of Bhadrakāḷi's Use of Violence in Popular Worship, Ritual Performing Arts and Narratives in Central Kerala (South India)." *Religion* 11: 170. https://doi.org/10.3390/rel11040170

Paulose, Karakkattil Gheevargese. 1993. *Natāṇkuśa: A Critique on Dramaturgy*. Tripunithura: Government Sanskrit College Committee (Ravivarma Samskṛta Granthāvali 26).

Pickering, Andrew 2017. "The Ontological Turn: Taking Different Worlds Seriously." *Social Analysis* 61, no. 2: 134–150.

Pitkow, Marlene B. 2001. Putana's Salvation in *Kathakaḷi*: Embodying the Sacred Journey. *Asian Theater Journal* 18, no. 2: 238–248.

Rajagopalan, L.S. 1968. "Music in Kootiyattam." *Sangeet Natak Akademi Journal* 10: 12–35.

———. 1974a. "Eloquent Eyes: Netra-Abinaya in Koodiyattam. With Special Reference in Abhinaya with the Eyes." *The Journal of the Music Academy* 45, no. 1–4: 93–108.

———. 1974b. "The Mizhavu." *The Journal of the Music Academy* 14, no. 1–4: 109–116.

ç1987. "Consecration of the Kūttampalam Temple Theatres of Kerala." Special Silver Jubilee Volume. *The Samskrita Ranga Annual* (Madras) 8: 22–40

Rajendran, Chettarthodi. 2012. "Changing Paradigms in Performance: Kūṭiyāṭṭam in Historical Perspective." *Sanskrit Vimarsah* 6: 254–263.

Ramberg, Lucinda. 2009. "Magical Hair as Dirt: Ecstatic Bodies and Postcolonial Reform in South India." *Culture, Medicine, and Psychiatry* 33: 501–522.

———. 2013. "Troubling Kinship: Sacred Marriage and Gender Configuration in South India." *American Ethnologist* 40, no. 4: 661–675.

Ramanujan, Attipate K. 1989. "Is There an Indian Way of Thinking? An Informal Essay." *Contribution to Indian Sociology* 23, no. 1: 41–58.

Rāmaswamy, Vijaya. 2009. "Tragic Widows or Cunning Witches? Reflections on Representations of Women in Tamil Myths and Legends." *Economic and Political Weekly* 44, no. 12: 57–61, 64–67.

Richman, Paula (ed.). 1991. *Many Rāmāyaṇas: The Diversity of a Narrative Tradition in South Asia*. Berkeley: University of California Press.

Richmond, Farley P. 1971. "Some Religious Aspects of Indian Traditional Theater." *The Drama Review: TDR* 15, no. 2: 122–131.

———. 1989. "The Bhāsa Festival, Trivandrum, India." *Asian Theatre Journal* 6, no. 1: 68–76.

———. 1990a. "Introduction to Kuttiyattam." In *Indian Theater, Traditions of Performance*, ed. Richmond. Farley P., Darius C. Swann, and Phillip B. Zarrilli, 87–117. Honolulu: University of Hawai'i Press.

———. 1990b. "*Kūṭiyāṭṭam*." In *Indian Theater, Traditions of Performance*, ed. Farley P. Richmond, Darius L. Swann, and Phillip B. Zarrilli. Honolulu: University of Hawai'i Press.

Richmond, Farley, and Yasmin Richmond. 1985. "The Multiple Dimensions of Time and Space in Kūṭiyāṭṭam, the Sanskrit Theatre of Kerala." *Asian Theater Journal* 2, no. 1: 50–60.

Robb, David (ed.) 2007. *Clowns, Fools and Picaros: Popular Forms in Theater, Fiction and Film*. Amsterdam: Editions Rodopi.

Roffe, Jonathan. 2005. "Multiplicity." In *The Deleuze Dictionary*, ed. Adrian Parr, 176–177. Edinburgh: Edinburgh University Press.

Saindon, Marcelle. 1995. "Le *Pitṛkalpa* du *Harivaṃśa* et le concept de Pitṛ." *Journal Asiatique*. 283, no. 1: 91–120.

———. 1997. "La crémation hindoue: perfectionnement rituel et cuisson sacrificielle du cadavre en vue de l'ultime offrande." *Sciences Religieuses* 26, no. 1: 57–74.

Satsuka, Shiho. 2018. "Sensing Multispecies Entanglements: Koto as an 'Ontology' of Living." *Social Analysis* 62, no. 4: 78–101.

Saunders, Barbara. 2000. "Revisiting *Basic Color Terms*." *Journal of the Royal Anthropological Institute* 6, no. 1: 81–99.

Sauvagnargues, Anne. 2019. Deleuze—l'empirisme transcendental. Paris: PUF, Philosophie D'aujourd'hui.

Sax, William S. 1990. "The Ramnagar Ramlila: Text, Performance, Pilgrimage." *History of Religions* 30, no. 2: 129–153.

Schechner, Richard. 2017. "Encountering the Ramlila of Ramnagar: From Fieldnotes in 1978 and 2013." *Performance Matters* 3, no. 1: 147–156.

Schechner, Richard, and Linda Hess. 1977. "The Ramlila of Ramnagar." *The Drama Review: TDR* 21, no. 3: 51–82.

Schieffelin, Edward L. 1998. "Problematizing Performance." In *Ritual, Performance, Media*, ed. Felicia Hughes-Freeland, 194–207 (ASA Monograph 35). London & New York: Routledge.

Scott, Michael W. 2015. "Cosmogony Today: Counter-Cosmogony, Perspectivism, and the Return of Anti-Biblical Polemic." *Religion and Society: Advances in Research* 6: 44–61.

Seamone, Donna Lynne. 2013. "Pentecostalism: Rejecting Ritual Formalism and Ritualizing Every Encounter." *Journal of Ritual Studies* 27, no. 1: 73–84.

Seizer, Susan. 2005. *Stigmas of the Tamil Stage: An Ethnography of Special Drama Artists in South India*. Durham, NC & London: Duke University Press.

Shapiro, Matan. 2015. "Curving the Social, or, Why Antagonistic Rituals in Brazil Are Variations on a Theme." *Journal of the Royal Anthropological Institute* 22: 47–66.

Shāstrī, Prabhu Dutt. 1911. *The Doctrine of Māyā in the Philosophy of the Vedānta*. London: Luzac and Co.

Sheets-Johnstone, Maxine. 1999. *The Primacy of Movement* (2nd ed.). Advances in Consciousness Research. Amsterdam & Philadelphia: John Benjamins Publishing Company.

———. 2013. "Movement as a Way of Knowing." *Scholarpedia* 8, no. 6: 30375.

———. 2017. "Moving in Concert" *Choros: International Dance Journal* 6: 1–19.

Shulman, David D. 1987. *The King and the Clown in South Indian Myth and Poetry*. Princeton, NJ: Princeton University Press.

———. 1991. "Fire and Flood: The Testing of Sītā in Kampaṉ's *Irāmāvatāram*." In *Many Rāmayanas: The Diversity of a Narrative Tradition in South Asia*, ed. Paula Richman, 89–112 Berkeley & Oxford: University of California Press.

———. 2001. "First Grammarian, First Poet. A South Indian Vision of Cultural Origins." *Indian Economic and Social History Review*, 38 no. 4: 352–373.

———.2005. "Axial Grammar." In *Axial Civilization and World History: Jerusalem Studies in Religion and Culture*, Vol. 4, ed. Arnason Johann P., Shmuel N. Eisenstadt, and Björn Wittrock, 369–395. Lieden: Brill.

———. 2012a. "Creating and Destroying the Universe in Twenty-Nine Nights." *The New York Review*, November 24, 2012.

———. 2012b. *More than Real: A History of the Imagination in South India*. Cambridge, MA: Harvard University Press.

———. 2016a. "Deep Seeing: On the Poetics of Kūṭiyāṭṭam." In *The Bloomsbury Research Handbook of Indian Aesthetics*, ed. Arindam Chakrabarti, 221–248. London: Bloomsbury.

———. 2016b. "Second Budding: The Musical Self. Anupallavi." In *Tamil: A Biography*, ed. David Shulman, 107–149. Cambridge, MA & London: Belknap Press of Harvard University Press.

———. 2022. *The Rite of Seeing: Essays on Kūṭiyāṭṭam*. Delhi: Primus.

Shweder, Richard A. 1987. "How to Look at Medusa Without Turning to Stone." *Contributions to Indian Sociology* 21, no. 1: 37–55.

Siegel, Lee. 1987. *Laughing Matters: Comic Tradition in India*. Chicago & London: University of Chicago Press.

Singer, Milton. (ed.) 1966. *Krishna: Myths, Rites, and Attitudes*. Chicago: University of Chicago Press.

Skora, Martin Kerry. 2007. "The Pulsating Heart and Its Divine Sense Energies: Body and Touch in Abhinavagupta's Trika Śaivism." *Numen* 54, no. 4: 420–458.

———. 2009. "Hermeneutics of Touch: Uncovering Abhinavagupta's Tactile Terrain." *Method and Theory in the Study of Religion* 21: 87–106.

Soneji, Davesh. 2004. Living History, Performing Memory: *Devadāsī* Women in Telugu-Speaking South India. *Dance Research Journal* 36, no. 2: 30–49.

———. 2012. *Unfinished Gestures—Devadāsīs, Memory, and Modernity in South India*. Chicago: University of Chicago Press.

Sreejith, P. K., and V. Sreekanth. 2014. "The Oldest Known Kutiyattam Photos." *Nartanam: A Quarterly Journal of Indian Dance* 14, no. 4: 27.

Staal, Frits. 1976. "The Nampūdiri Agnicayana of April 1975." *Journal of the American Oriental Society* 96, no. 1: 113.

———. 1979a. "Comment: Altar of Fire." *American Anthropologist* (N.S.) 81, no. 2: 346–347.

———. 1979b. "The Meaninglessness of Ritual." *Numen* 26, no. 1: 2–22.

———. 1983. *Agni: The Vedic Ritual of the Altar of Fire*. Berkeley, CA: Asian Humanities Press.

———. 1986. "The Sound of Religion." *Numen* 21, no. 1: 33–64.

———. 2008. *Discovering the Vedas: Origins, Mantras, Rituals, Insights*. New Delhi: Penguin Books.

Stagoll, Cliff 2005. "Becoming." In *The Deleuze Dictionary*, ed. Adrian Parr, 21–22. Edinburgh: Edinburgh University Press.

Sullivan, Bruce M. 1995. "The Religious Significance of Kūṭiyāṭṭam Drama." In Narayanan P. Unni and Bruce M. Sullivan. *Tapatī-Samvaranam and the Kūṭiyāṭṭam Drama Tradition*. 33–53. Delhi: Nag Publishers.

———. 1997. "Temple Rites and Temple Servants: Religion's Role in the Survival of Kerala's Kūṭiyāṭṭam Drama Tradition." *International Journal of Hindu Studies* 1, no. 1: 97–115.

———. 2009. "How Does One Study a 'Masterpiece of the Oral and Intangible Heritage of Humanity'? Ethnographic Reflections on Kerala's *Kūṭiyāṭṭam*." *Method & Theory in the Study of Religion* 21: 78–86.

———. 2010. "Kerala's Mahabharata on Stage: Texts and Performative Practices in Kūṭiyāṭṭam Drama." *The Journal of Hindu Studies* 3, no. 1: 1–19.

———. 2011. "Experiencing Sanskrit Dramas in Kerala: Epic Performances and Performers." In *Studying Hinduism in Practice,* ed. Hillary P. Rodrigues, 158–169. Milton Park & New York: Routledge.

Tambiah, Stanley J. 1996. "A Performative Approach to Ritual." In *Reading in Ritual Studies,* ed. Ronald L. Grimes, 459–511. Upper Saddle River, NJ: Prentice-Hall.

Tapper, Bruce E. 1979. "Widows and Goddesses: Female Roles in Deity Symbolism in a South Indian Village." *Contributions to Indian Sociology* (NS) 13, no. 1: 1–13.

Tarabout, Gilles. 1997. "Maîtres et serviteurs. Commander à des dieux au Kérala (Inde du Sud)." In *Religion et pratiques de puissance,* ed. Albert de Surgy, 253–284. Paris: L'Harmattan.

———. 1998 "Des gags dans le culte: Remarques sur la buffonnerie ritualle au Kérala." In *Théâtre Indian: Notes sur théâtre et possession, ou petite collection d'historiettes,* ed. Lyne Bansat-Boudon, 269–299 Paris: EHESS.

———. 1999. "Prologue: Approches anthropologiques de la possession en Asie du Sud." In *La Possession en Asie du Sud Parole, Corp, Territoire,* ed. Jackie Assayag and Gilles Tarabout, 9–30 Paris: EHESS.

———. 2000. " 'Passions' in the Discourses of Witchcraft in Kerala." *Journal of Indian Philosophy* 28, no. 5/6: 651–664.

———. 2001. "Ancêtres et revenants. La construction sociale de la malemort en Inde." In *De la malemort en quelques pays d'Asie,* ed. Brigitte Baptandier, 165–199. Paris: Karthala.

———. 2003. "Résonances et métaphores corporelles dans l'astrologie appliquée aux temples (Kerala)." In *Images du Corps dans le Monde Hindou,* ed. Véronique Bouillier and Gilles Tarabout, 135–163. Paris: Éditions CNRS.

———. 2004. "Theology as History: Divine Images, Imagination, and Rituals in India." In *Images in Asian Religions: Text and Contexts,* ed. Phyllis Granoff and Koichi Shinohara, 56–84. Vancouver: UBC Press.

———. 2011. "Visualizing the Gods." *Maarg, A Magazine of the Arts* 63, no. 2: 16–25.

Taussig, Michael. 2006. "What Color Is the Sacred?" *Critical Inquiry* 33, no. 1: 28–51.

Thorpe, Ashley. 2005. "Only Joking? The Relationship between the Clown and Percussion in *Jingju*." *Asian Theatre Journal* 22, no. 2: 269–292.

Timalsina, Sthaneshwar. 2009. "Ritual, Reality, and Meaning. The Vedic Ritual of Cremating a Surrogate Body." *Zeitschrift der Deutschen Morgenländischen Gesellschaft* 159, no. 1: 45–69.

Timm, Jeffrey 1991. "The Celebration of Emotion: Vallaba's Ontology of Affective Experience." *Philosophy East and West* 41, no. 1: 59–75.

Turner, Victor. 1967. *The Forest of Symbols: Aspects of Ndembu Ritual*. Ithaca, NY & London: Cornell University Press.

Unni, Narayanan P. 1990. "Nāgānanda on the Kerala Stage." *Sri Ravivarma Samskrita Granthavali Journal* 15, no. 2: 1–24.

Unni, Narayanan P., and Bruce M. Sullivan. 2001. "The Wedding of Arjuna and Suhadra: The Kutiyattam Drama Subhadra Dhananjaya." Review by Bozena Sliwczynska. *Asian Theater Journal* 20, no. 1: 102–104.

Van der Veer, Peter. 2014. "The Spiritual Body." In *The Modern Spirit of Asia: The Spiritual and the Secular in China and India*, ed. Peter van der Veer, 168–249. Princeton, NJ: Princeton University Press.

Varadpande, Manohar Laxman. 1987. *History of Indian Theater (Loka Ranga Panorama of Indian Folk Theater)* (2 Vols.). New Delhi: Abhinav Publications.

Venkatesan, Soumhya. 2015. "Auto-Relations: Doing Cosmology and Transforming the Self the Saiva Way." In *Framing Cosmologies: The Anthropology of Worlds*, ed. Allen Abramson and Martin Holbraad, 77–94. Manchester: Manchester University Press.

———. 2020. "Object, Subject, Thing: Tamil Hindu Priests' Material Practices and Practical Theories of Animation and Accommodation." *American Ethnologist* 47, no. 4: 447–460.

Venu, Gopalan. 2002. *Into the World of Kutiyattam with the Legendary Ammannur Madhava Chakyar. Memoirs*. Kōṭṭayam: Kaṟanṭ Buks.

Viveiros de Castro, Eduardo. 1998. "Cosmological Deixis and Amerindian Perspectivism." *Journal of the Royal Anthropological Institute* 4, no. 3: 469–488.

———. 2012. "Cosmological Perspectivism in Amazonia and Elsewhere." (Four Lectures Given in the Department of Social Anthropology, University of Cambridge, February–March 1998). *HAU Master Class Series* 1: 45–168.

Vizenor, Gerald. 1990. "Trickster Discourse." *American Indian Quarterly* 14, no. 3: 277–287.

Wadley, Susan Snow. 1975. *Śakti: Power in the Conceptual Structure of Karimpur Religion*. (Series in Social, Cultural and Linguistic Anthropology 2). Chicago: University of Chicago Studies in Anthropology.

Wagner, Roy 1991. "The Fractal Person." In *Big Men and Great Men: Personifications of Power in Melanesia*, ed. Maurice Godelier and Marilyn Strathern, 159–173. New York: Cambridge University Press.

———. 2019. "The Energy of Liminality." In *The Intellectual Legacy of Victor and Edith Turner*, ed. Frank A. Salomone and Marjories M. Snipes, 85–88. Lanham, MD: Lexington Books.

Wessels, Michael. 2008. "Foraging, Talking, and Tricksters." *Journal of Folklore Research* 45, no. 3: 299–327.

Whitaker, Jarrod L. 2002. "How the Gods Kill: The *Nārāyaṇa Astra* Episode, the Death of Rāvaṇa, and the Principles of *Tejas* in the Indian Epics." *Journal of Indian Philosophy* 30, no. 4: 403–430.

Wierzbicka, Anna. 2008. "Why There Are No 'Colour Universals' in Language and Thought." *Journal of the Royal Anthropological Institute* 14, no. 2: 407–425.

Wilkinson-Weber, Clare M. 2012. "An Anthropologist among the Actors." *Ethnography* 13, no. 2: 144–161.

Xin, Wei Sha. 2012. "Topology and Morphogenesis." *Theory, Culture & Society* 28, no. 4/5: 220–246.

Yalom, Marilyn. 1998. *A History of the Breast*. New York: Random Books.

Zarrilli, Phillip B. 1998. *When the Body Becomes All Eyes: Paradigms, Discourses and Practices of Power in Kalarippayattu, a South Indian Martial Art*. New Delhi: Oxford University Press.

———. 2000. "Embodying the Lion's 'Fury': Ambivalent Animals, Activation and Representation." *Performance Research* 5, no. 2: 41–54.

# Index

www.ingramcontent.com/pod-product-compliance
Lightning Source LLC
LaVergne TN
LVHW040158080826
844660LV00001B/19

* 9 7 8 1 4 3 8 4 9 6 9 2 4 *